Salant, CBS, and the Battle for the Soul of Broadcast Journalism

The Memoirs of Richard S. Salant

Foreword by Mike Wallace

Edited by
Susan and Bill Buzenberg

Westview Press
A Member of the Perseus Books Group

Copyright © 1999 Susan and Bill Buzenberg

Published in 1999 in the United States of America by Westview Press, 5500 Central Avenue, Boulder, Colorado 80301-2877, and in the United Kingdom by Westview Press, 12 Hid's Copse Road, Cumnor Hill, Oxford OX2 9JJ

Library of Congress Cataloging-in-Publication Data
Salant, Richard S., d. 1993.
  Salant, CBS, and the battle for the soul of broadcast journalism :
the memoirs of Richard S. Salant / foreword by Mike Wallace ; edited
by Susan and Bill Buzenberg.
    p. cm.
  Includes index.
  ISBN 0-8133-9091-5
  1. Salant, Richard S., d. 1993.   2. Columbia Broadcasting System,
Inc.—History.   3. Television broadcasting of news—United States.
4. Broadcasters—United States—Biography.   5. Businesspeople—
United States—Biography.   6. Executives—United States—Biography.
I. Buzenberg, Susan.   II. Buzenberg, Bill.   III. Title.
HE8689.8.S3   1999
070.1'95'092—dc21   98-23296
                                                                              CIP

Design by Heather Hutchison

The paper used in this publication meets the requirements of the American National Standard for Permanence of Paper for Printed Library Materials Z39.48-1984.

10   9   8   7   6   5   4   3   2   1

Dedicated to the memory of Richard S. Salant

*To his CBS News colleagues
and to Frank Stanton*

*Also, to Frances
And Priscilla, who kept her promise to her dad*

Dick Salant, undated photograph, about 1980.

Contents

Photos and Illustrations

Photos

Second Photo Section

Foreword

Mike Wallace

OVER A SERIES OF SUMMERS during the late 1980s, I received a number of $100 checks from Dick Salant.

"You'll never finish that damn book," I bet him, "never." "You'll write and write and refuse to edit it; $100 says so." So each July when he and Frances arrived in Vineyard Haven for their annual respite, I got my hundred bucks over dinner the first night they were in residence; it became a sheepish ritual for Dick. Now, happily, Bill and Susan Buzenberg have done the editing for him.

Dick saved my professional life back in 1963 when he took me on—ignoring the wisdom of some of his confreres—as a CBS News correspondent. I'd already been at CBS from 1951 to 1955 doing a variety of chores, including both news and entertainment, at a time when such was permissible. But then, impetuously, in 1955 I departed the CBS premises in search of greener fields, including a stint on Broadway, some television commercials, and a local newscast and interview series. But when I turned serious about getting back to a network news operation, I appealed for a job not just to Dick but also to news chiefs Bill McAndrew at NBC and Jim Hagerty at ABC, who looked down their noses at this soiled intruder who'd abandoned the Grail for Mammon.

Only the unlikely Salant—the lawyer, the nonjournalist, the purist, who had himself overcome the initial skepticism of colleagues like Cronkite and Sevareid and Collingwood—only Salant was willing to give this prodigal a second chance. And of course I came cheap because I was so anxious to get back at work at the universally esteemed CBS News, which appealed to Dick for he was a tightwad. Not with his own money, but with CBS's.

Case in point, as far as I was concerned: Only after *60 Minutes* had achieved a certain credibility and commercial success did I feel secure enough to ask him for a substantial raise. Tentatively, I knocked on his office door to raise the subject with him; it must have been in the late 1970s. This was after *60 Minutes* had been on the air for about a decade, and we were comfortably ensconced in the top twenty-five broadcast series, and very profitable.

"Do you think you deserve as much as Cronkite?" he asked me. "Well, no, of course not." "As much as Sevareid?" "Well, hardly."

I'd begun to feel embarrassed by my own effrontery at even hinting at the notion that my contributions were in the same approximate league as these two giants. In any case, he turned me down flat, and years later, after he'd retired from CBS and we were reminiscing, he chuckled retrospectively at his niggardliness.

Any journalist, print or broadcast, will find gems to ponder in these pages. Some readers may find cloying and hyperbolic the unrelieved encomia you're about to bathe in. Well, hold your skepticism; every word you'll read, from his devoted colleagues and even from his few adversaries, every word of respect and admiration is genuine. He was a strong, loyal, devoted, introspective, and utterly decent man.

He saw the best in us—and we were determined to honor what he saw in each of us.

Editors'
Acknowledgments

Richard Salant's story has had a long, somewhat complicated gestation. Salant wrote the material for this book after his retirement, between 1984 and 1990, at his home in New Canaan, Connecticut. He spent endless hours on a new computer given to him by his children. They thought it would be good retirement therapy for him to write, but he often stomped out of his book-lined study in frustration. "I can't do it," he complained many times.[1] Eventually, however, Salant "hunted and pecked the world's longest unfinished book on news."[2]

Salant set the work aside in 1990, after writing nearly 3,000 pages and filling seven thick black binders. He referred to it as his "opus"—it weighed about forty pounds—but he was discouraged by publishers' lack of interest. He circulated the manuscript among several friends and former CBS colleagues, as well as others in publishing. Although they tried to be encouraging, it was clear a great deal of work needed to be done.

Salant was told the manuscript in its raw form was simply too unwieldy to ever be published. In the words of his former deputy, Blair Clark, Salant "had an interesting story to tell if the slim person inside the obesity could be extracted."[3] Clark thought Salant had "extruded (not written)" perhaps two separate books: one a journalism textbook, the other "a memoir of his experiences as head of what was the best news organization in broadcasting. Salant is unquestionably the ablest and most intellectually interesting of the people who have managed electronic journalism, and he is widely so regarded." But Clark worried that Salant's "niceness made him leave out all the etching acid."[4]

---

[1]Frances Salant said her husband had this stormy reaction many times during the years he spent writing.

[2]Stepson Peter Goldmark Jr. made these remarks at the February 22, 1993, memorial service for Salant.

[3]Blair Clark letter to publisher Michael Bessie, June 20, 1991.

[4]Blair Clark letter to publisher Michael Bessie, July 22, 1991.

xiv • EDITORS' ACKNOWLEDGMENTS

By the early 1990s, Salant had no desire to wade back into the project to add drama or reduce what he had written to a publishable size. However, he continued off and on to edit it, making changes, scribbling notes in the margins, crossing out whole passages. In March 1992, he sent the entire manuscript in black binders to his children, along with a letter. His note was typically self-deprecating:

> Some of you . . . have begged for a copy of my book. You're gluttons for punishment, but here it is—or rather, here *they* are—in all [its] naked glory. It's so bad that I'm not bothering further with it. Somewhere buried deep in there is a publishable book, but I haven't the appetite or the energy to find it. . . . It is part textbook about what broadcast journalism is all about, part narrative autobiography. The two don't mix. It's also badly organized, badly written . . . Some of the sentences go on forever—blame that on my first use of the wonderful computer you all gave me—it made me depend on just letting loose, with corrections planned for later. But I've never done them. So scan, skip, and sleep . . . you asked for it. Suffer or enjoy—take your pick.

● ● ●

Our involvement with this project got its start in 1994. That July, we received a letter from Peter Herford, a former CBS producer who had worked with Dick Salant. At that time, Peter was a professor of journalism at Columbia University. He wrote to ask if we knew anyone who would be interested in editing Salant's memoirs. "In typical Salant fashion, Dick produced three volumes of gold ore," Herford explained. "Now it's up to someone to extract the real stuff, a lot easier than alchemy, but a challenge nonetheless." Herford thought there might even be three books hidden in what Salant had written.

When my wife, Susan, an editor, and I saw Herford's letter, we knew we were interested in the project and jumped at the chance. As vice

---

[5]As strange as it may seem for a man who helped create the standards for television news, Salant also loved radio. He also deplored the state of most commercial radio network news and, by contrast, admired NPR. "I believe NPR news is about all that's left of serious, responsible radio network news," he said at Columbia University in 1990, all of which made it even more sad when he believed he had to resign from the NPR board.

In keeping with his well-developed sense of how principles might be eroded in practice, it was Salant's concern that designated grant money could allow funders to "buy" programming on public radio. "I am deeply disturbed by the fact that NPR continues to accept funds from private entities who are permitted to earmark their grants for the coverage of particular subjects or geographical areas." According to Salant, this practice "involves an unacceptable sharing with outsiders—however benign—the responsibility president of news for National Public Radio, I had met Richard Salant, but only once. That was in the autumn of 1989, when Salant was a member—soon to resign in protest—of NPR's Board of Directors.[5] Susan and I told Herford we would indeed be interested in taking on the project as an editorial team. We thought it might take us a year to complete, with Susan working on it full-time, while I worked part-time, adding it to my duties at NPR.

Herford put us in touch with the Salant family, and we met in New York City with Salant's wife, Frances, his daughter Priscilla, and Frances's son Peter Goldmark Jr. In time, it became clear that along with Frances, the driving force behind our involvement in this book was to be Priscilla Salant.

Priscilla had promised her father that one day his work would be published, and she was determined to make that happen. Priscilla and Frances have been a constant source of encouragement and support. We deeply appreciate all of their help and, especially, the editorial freedom given by the family.

We began working on the manuscript in early 1995. During that year, Susan and I were Salant visiting professors at Washington State University. The visiting professorships brought us into contact with the then WSU dean of the College of Liberal Arts, John Pierce, who provided us with more encouragement and sound advice. We had the additional support of many of the faculty at the Edward R. Murrow School of Communications at Washington State. Thanks also to Richard Schaefer, journalism professor at the University of New Mexico.

Besides Peter Herford and his colleague at Columbia University, Jim Carey, we have benefited greatly from a number of key people who were formerly with CBS, especially Dr. Frank Stanton and Mike Wal-

---

for independent news judgment." He urged NPR to forgo any and all grants that were designated for certain areas of news coverage, such as the German Marshall Fund for the coverage of Western Europe.

Salant took this issue before the full NPR board. Senior management fought against him, unwilling and indeed financially unable to forgo substantial amounts of designated funding. The NPR board ultimately voted with senior management against Salant, and he promptly resigned from the board on April 2, 1990. "I regret deeply that I find that my resignation would best serve the interests of NPR. . . . I have managed to sour an atmosphere which is unhealthy for NPR, and can be cured only by my resignation."

Salant may have been initially bitter over his rebuke by NPR board members, but he did not stay that way. In early 1993, after NPR News was recognized by a DuPont-Columbia University Award, Salant wrote to then NPR president Douglas Bennet. "Once a decade, award givers get it exactly right, and do themselves, as well as the recipient honor. DuPont-Columbia's gold baton did just that this year. You and your news associates deserve the baton. Congratulations to all of them. As ever, Dick Salant." He died of a heart attack three weeks later.

lace, along with Daniel Schorr, Blair Clark, Marvin Kalb, Ernest Leiser, Gordon Manning, Ed Fouhy, Joe Dembo, and the former general manager of the CBS affiliate in Charlotte, North Carolina, Charles Crutchfield. Producer Jay Kernis, now at *60 Minutes*, took us on a wonderful tour of CBS News.

During the more than three years we spent on this project, we had considerable help from many others. We gratefully acknowledge the support we've received from Westview Press staff, including senior editor Catherine Murphy in San Francisco, who believed in this project from the beginning, and senior editor Leo A. W. Wiegman in New York. Linda Killian helped lead us to Westview, where project editor Lisa Wigutoff and copy editor Michele Wynn helped us complete the project.

We had additional publishing advice from Peter Osnos, Gail Ross, Susan King, Kathleen Hall Jamieson, Keith Peterson, and Kate Torey. While at NPR, I received advice and support from Bruce Drake, John Dinges, Tom Gjelten, and Noah Adams. Although Noah was brutally frank about the difficulties with any book project, his challenge nevertheless encouraged us. Rick Jarrett and Love Henderson also helped us.

We also want to thank Ken Auletta for his assistance and Peter Boyer for lending us the tapes of his interview with Salant. We also had help at various stages in this project from director David Bryant and his staff at the New Canaan Library, where Salant's papers are kept in the Richard Salant Room.

While working on this project in the autumn of 1997, I was a fellow at the Institute of Politics at Harvard's Kennedy School of Government. Susan and I both want to thank the IOP's director at the time, Phil Sharp, and notably fellowship director Theresa Donovan, and the IOP staff. Seth Halverson was a constant help with our logistics and shipping heavy cartons of material.

At Harvard, as throughout my management career at NPR, I received continual philosophical and journalistic support from Bill Kovach, curator of the Nieman Foundation. In my new position as senior director of news and information for Minnesota Public Radio, I wish to thank Bill Kling and Dennis Hamilton for their support during the final stages of publishing the book.

• • •

We believe strongly, along with Frances and Priscilla Salant, Frank Stanton, Mike Wallace, and others, that this book deserves to be published; its message needs to be heard. Although we cannot say this is the precise book Richard Salant would have wanted to publish, we are confident in the end that this is a faithful version of the best of what he wrote, sifted from thousands of pages of his original manuscript and several thousand additional pages of personal papers, letters, memos, and speeches.

We are pleased to have been able to play a role in bringing to a wider public the life, lessons, and thoughts of this exceptional leader in broadcast journalism.

Bill and Susan Buzenberg

Salant, CBS, and the
Battle for the Soul
of Broadcast Journalism

Editors' Introduction

This is about a man we admire. "Love" is not too strong a word. But most of this is about what he did, not how we feel about him. What he did was take over a little band of journalists—ourselves—and make us into a great news organization starting eighteen years ago in some dusty rooms above Grand Central Station.

—**Charles Kuralt, "The Salant Years," 1979**[1]

MOST AMERICANS RECOGNIZE the names of Mike Wallace, Walter Cronkite, and Eric Sevareid but are unlikely to have ever heard of their behind-the-scenes boss, Richard Salant, president of CBS News for nearly two tumultuous decades in the 1960s and 1970s.

Dick Salant became one of the longest-serving and most highly respected leaders in television news. But he did not even appear to be a suitable choice to head the News Division at his debut in February 1961. To start with, Salant was not a journalist. Walter Cronkite admitted he was "shocked" and "alarmed" when word came down from the CBS executive suites that the Harvard-trained corporate lawyer had been named president of CBS News. "We were naturally terribly worried," Cronkite remembered. Salant was "a nonprofessional, a man who as far as we knew never had set foot in a newsroom."[2]

Within hours of the announcement, Eric Sevareid wanted to talk to the man who had picked Salant, Dr. Frank Stanton. Highly esteemed by his CBS colleagues, Stanton was CBS president and chief operating

---

[1]From "The Salant Years," a documentary written and narrated by Charles Kuralt and produced by Bernard Birnbaum, on the occasion of Salant's retirement from CBS in April 1979. CBS broadcast part of the documentary on the *CBS Evening News* when Salant died on February 16, 1993.

[2]Cronkite address at the New Canaan (CT) Library, November 24, 1996.

officer, the man who would guide CBS for thirty years. Salant was Stanton's protégé and close friend; the two had worked side by side since 1952 in CBS's corporate offices, where Salant had been a vice president and special assistant to Stanton.

When they met with Stanton over lunch, Sevareid, Cronkite, and Charles Collingwood all bluntly told him they did not want a lawyer to oversee CBS News. Cronkite believed the imposition of a lawyer meant only one thing: Every word in the news would be looked at and censored beforehand. "I couldn't see any other function that a lawyer would be serving in the CBS newsroom. We were all depressed."[3]

Since its earliest days, CBS News had always been under the command of professional journalists, starting with Ed Klauber, who came from the *New York Times* in 1930, just two years after William Paley took charge of the infant network. Klauber was joined by Paul White from United Press; "together they became the founding fathers of broadcast journalism."[4] And that tradition extended to Edward R. Murrow, who, though not a journalist at first, learned at the feet of Klauber about journalistic standards and ethics.

"With this appointment of Richard Salant, it seemed to most of us, went the vaunted and jealously guarded independence that had made CBS News the distinguished news organization it was," Cronkite said. "As I recall, we even talked about a walkout to protest this serious break with tradition and obviously the serious implications."

But Stanton counseled patience to his senior correspondents. "I spoke to Dick's unusual qualifications. . . . He understood radio and television's potentials. He understood current affairs at home and abroad. He knew history. [He was] a man of outstanding intellect, quick of mind and courage."

Even more, Stanton said it was Salant who would give policy and substance to CBS News. "This remarkable man was intolerant of anything or anybody who stood in the way of truth. His North Star was the First Amendment. He could not abide double-talk in any form or in any medium. He absolutely abhorred glitz and gloss."

Given all that, Stanton said, it was not long after the meeting that the on-air trio—Sevareid, Cronkite, and Collingwood—"sought me out to pay tribute to Dick's leadership."[5]

---

[3]Cronkite speaking at Salant's memorial service at the Museum of Television and Radio in New York City, February 22, 1993.

[4]Gary Paul Gates, *Airtime: The Inside Story of CBS News* (New York: Harper and Row), 1978, pp. 98–99.

[5]Stanton's remarks were made at the memorial service for Salant in New York City on February 22, 1993.

In the early 1960s, at the time Salant took over his new post, CBS News had lost its way, falling into second place in what was then a de facto two-network race between CBS and NBC. Until 1957, CBS and Bill Paley had been accustomed to being number one. "CBS News had been the pioneer [first in radio and later in television journalism], the dominant network news organization, and recognized as such by the public and critics, and by journalistic peers," Salant wrote. "But as happens to almost all enterprises after a long period of dominance, complacency sets in, and a restless public seizes on something new, when something new is offered." That something new was NBC, with its remarkable coanchors Chet Huntley and David Brinkley.

It took Salant six years, until 1967, to put the *CBS Evening News* back on top—where it stayed for the next twenty years. But before that triumph, Salant faced two years in management limbo, working once again as an assistant to Stanton. In March 1964, Salant was ejected from his spot as president of News, replaced by Fred Friendly, in what some called "Friendly's Coup." Backed by an impatient Bill Paley, Friendly attempted to get CBS News back into first place. In Paley's eyes, being in second place was "a denial of the network's birthright."[6]

But just two years later, in January 1966, after a battle over airtime coupled with a change in the corporate pecking order, Friendly resigned, and Salant was named News president once again. Many on the CBS News staff were relieved to see a return to Salant's less hands-on management style. Salant had been given a second chance and was fiercely determined to succeed this time around. The young "brush-cut dynamo," as Cronkite described him in those early days, would lead CBS News for the next thirteen years.

•   •   •

One of Salant's first and most important innovations as president was doubling the length of the *Evening News*. Since 1948, when nightly television news began, CBS and the other networks had produced evening newscasts lasting just fifteen minutes. Salant replaced anchor Douglas Edwards with Walter Cronkite and, in 1963, working on a plan put together by Ernie Leiser, launched the nation's first thirty-minute evening news broadcast.

"Good evening, everybody, coast to coast, Douglas Edwards reporting" was replaced with "Direct from our newsroom in New York, this is the *CBS Evening News with Walter Cronkite* and . . . Nelson Benton in

---

[6]Gates, *Airtime*, p. 98.

Tuskegee, Alabama . . . Dan Rather in Plaquemine, Louisiana . . . Bernard Kalb in Saigon."

Salant's move was quickly copied by NBC and later by ABC. The expanded broadcasts came just in time to cover in more depth and detail some of the biggest stories of a news-filled decade. It was also a time when more Americans began to depend on television for most of their news.

For years afterward, Salant fought to get approval for an hour-long *CBS Evening News*. And long before the Cable News Network started, he and Stanton had plans to create a twenty-four-hour CBS News channel. All his expansion plans, however, were defeated by the unwillingness of CBS affiliates to give up the necessary airtime to the network.

Besides expanding the flagship CBS News broadcast and making it the nation's most watched news program, Salant is given credit for a number of major programs launched during his era. At the top of the list, although Salant originally rejected the idea, is television's first newsmagazine—*60 Minutes*—which went on the air in the fall of 1968. Many attempts were made to clone *60 Minutes*, yet under producer Don Hewitt, it became, and thirty years later still remains, one of the highest rated, and highest earning, news programs in the history of television.

Salant also began the *CBS Morning News* as a hard news program. He began planning for the launch of *Sunday Morning*, featuring host Charles Kuralt.[7] Salant also started the *CBS Evening News* on weekends, *Magazine, In the News* (for children), *Inside CBS News, 30 Minutes, Your Turn: Letters to CBS News, Who's Who,* and *Calendar.*

• • •

Salant's career at CBS spanned some of the most important events in the life of the nation: the civil rights movement, Watergate, the Vietnam War, and the assassination of President John F. Kennedy.

In 1963, Kennedy was interviewed by Walter Cronkite during the first *CBS Evening News* half-hour broadcast:

CRONKITE: Mr. President, the only hot war we've got running at the moment is, of course, the one in Vietnam. And we've got our difficulties there, quite obviously.

---

[7]*Sunday Morning* was launched in 1979 by Salant's successor, Bill Leonard. The original host, Charles Kuralt, died on July 4, 1997, at the age of sixty-two.

PRESIDENT KENNEDY: I don't think that unless a greater effort is made by the government [of South Vietnam] to win popular support that the war can be won out there. In the final analysis, it's their war. They're the ones who have to win it or lose it. We can help them, we can give them equipment, we can send our men out there as advisers, but they have to win it—the people of Vietnam against the Communists.

Two months after that interview, Cronkite was on the air in his shirtsleeves announcing in one of the first news bulletins at 1:40 P.M. on Friday, November 22, 1963, that President Kennedy had been shot in Dallas. CBS News covered the assassination for the next four days without interruption and without commercials, although there were solemn musical interludes.

"Afterwards, we knew that television would always be the place people would turn to in moments of national absorption," Kuralt said.[8]

Television coverage of the Vietnam War, particularly on CBS News, became a matter of extreme controversy. Such thorough, vivid, and skeptical war coverage streaming into the living rooms of the nation was not always appreciated. A number of managers of CBS-affiliated stations, along with some of their viewers, did not want to see critical reporting on the war, and there was a strong undercurrent of blame that CBS was being unpatriotic. In a theme that would repeat itself whenever pressure was applied, Salant resisted protests by angry CBS stations and defended the coverage and his team of reporters in Vietnam, even though he, too, was privately concerned about that coverage.[9] When CBS producer Ed Fouhy asked Salant what his budget for the Saigon Bureau would be, he was told to "spend whatever it takes." In effect, Salant was saying, "Don't worry about money, or affiliates, or advertisers," Fouhy said. "He would handle all that; the journalists just had to worry about doing the right thing."[10]

CBS journalists knew that Salant could take the heat in what was an exceptionally hot seat. Beneath Salant's protective shield, the

---

[8]Kuralt, "The Salant Years."

[9]Salant defended the network's Vietnam coverage publicly, but privately he was concerned: "I have the troubled feeling that even though we all say that this is the best reported war in history and that it is the first television war, television making it more meaningful to more Americans than ever before in history, the fact is—and I would never admit it outside—that I feel it is not a well-reported war." From a Salant memo, October 13, 1966, quoted by Richard Schaefer, "Richard S. Salant and the CBS Television News Guidelines," April 8, 1995, Texas A&M University.

[10]Interview with the editors, November 1997.

News Division was able to make its own independent news judgments, largely without management or government interference. Cronkite said what he remembered most of all about Salant was his defense of the News Division when times were really tough, particularly in the Vietnam War years and later during Watergate. According to Cronkite, "He stood up all the way." There was "iron in his spine," Kuralt said.

Throughout the Salant years, even while Vietnam was polarizing the nation, CBS News produced dozens of major documentaries. One in particular, in the spring of 1971, generated enormous political criticism. "The Selling of the Pentagon" examined the military's manipulation of public opinion and the news media, focusing on how the Pentagon spent millions of dollars to enhance the image of the military and its weapons. The program grew from an idea Salant had suggested to his producers.

Vice President Spiro Agnew denounced "The Selling of the Pentagon" as a "clever propaganda attempt to discredit the Defense establishment." The chairman of the House Armed Services Committee said the broadcast was "one of the most un-American things I've ever seen on a screen."

A congressional investigation looked into charges that CBS News was guilty of distortions in editing the program. A House committee cited Frank Stanton for contempt for refusing to turn over to Congress CBS's outtakes (material not used in the documentary). Stanton could have been jailed, but the full House refused to vote the contempt citation. During this period of confrontation, it was Salant who concealed the outtakes. He carried around reels of film and other material from "The Selling of the Pentagon" hidden in the trunk of his car to protect them from congressional subpoena.

The House's refusal to find Stanton in contempt "was a victory for CBS," according to Kuralt, and one of Stanton's finest hours. "It was also a victory for the First Amendment and the First Amendment's bravest advocate in broadcasting—Dick Salant."[11]

Perhaps the heaviest pressure against CBS News came during the Nixon administration's assault on the networks. There were many angry White House telephone calls to William Paley and Frank Stanton and a few calls and visits to Salant. But "no reporter was replaced, no one was censored," Kuralt said.

White House pressure did affect CBS's coverage on at least one occasion. In his memoirs, Salant acknowledges cutting out "about three minutes" from a Daniel Schorr piece during the second of two special

---

[11]Kuralt, "The Salant Years."

Watergate reports. These reports aired on the *Evening News* shortly before the 1972 presidential election. Salant said his actions may have been influenced by Paley, who had called Salant to a meeting to complain about the coverage. Paley, in turn, was being pressured by Charles Colson in the White House. To cut an important report under such circumstances was a mistake on Salant's part, and he was properly troubled by the incident.[12]

• • •

Compiling and publishing a policy manual of television news standards was one of Salant's most important legacies; it was the first such compilation ever produced—and enforced—by a network.[13] The standards instructed journalists to be wary of conflicts of interest and prohibited editorializing. The guidelines also banned staging and other deceptive techniques borrowed from the entertainment side of television. In an era of evolving television news practices, Salant was, in effect, defining standards not only for CBS News but for all of broadcast journalism.

Journalists at CBS News knew Salant wanted their work to reflect the best professional ethics and policies, but having written rules to work from was both a blessing and a burden.

"It might sound, from what you've heard, that all of us who worked for Dick in those days were enthusiastic about those rigid standards he maintained. But the fact is," Andy Rooney said, "that they were of-

---

[12]Salant is quoted as saying that when he worked with evening news producers to cut the second Watergate report, "They knew I had been on the carpet with Paley. They knew I was troubled when I said, 'I hope I feel this way because I am fair and honest.'" The segment ran only seven minutes instead of the planned fourteen, meaning more than three minutes had been cut. In the view of some, the piece had become a superficial summary minus the detail that could have given it muscle. Sally Bedell Smith, *In All His Glory: The Life of William S. Paley* (New York: Simon and Schuster, 1990), pp. 476–478, as quoted in Corydon B. Dunham, *Fighting for the First Amendment: Stanton of CBS vs. Congress and the Nixon White House* (Westport, CT: Praeger, 1997), p. 186.

[13]The book of news policies is called "CBS News Standards," compiled by David Klinger, administrative vice president for CBS News, and originally issued April 14, 1976, with a preface from Salant. Actually, it is a loose-leaf notebook allowing new guidelines to be added as needed. Professor Richard Schaefer makes the point that Salant used these standards for internal and external purposes "as part of a complex strategy for defending, legitimizing, and upgrading the network's journalistic products. The guidelines that Salant embraced endorsed an 'objective' form of journalism, similar to that embraced by print journalists of earlier decades." Salant also said the guidelines were important for the public, including Congress and critics, to "measure our performance against our stated policies." Two papers by Professor Richard Schaefer address this subject: "Richard S. Salant and the CBS Television News Guidelines," April 8, 1995, Texas A&M University, and "The Development of the CBS News Guidelines During the Salant Years," *Journal of Broadcasting and Electronic Media* (Winter 1998), pp. 1–20.

ten dismaying to those of us trying to produce broadcasts. I want to put this as delicately as I know how, but, to tell you the truth, he could be a pain in the ass."[14]

Cronkite also admitted that Salant "drove us nuts at times. He picked an awful lot of nits." Salant's deputies, Bill Leonard and Gordon Manning, saw the standards as onerous. Manning said the written guidelines were impractical and claimed they were generally ignored by working journalists. Bill Leonard acknowledged that detailed standards were as routinely "honored with a wink as with an observance," but he said most violations were minor.[15]

Salant described his management style as "loose reins." He was not an "empty-suit" executive, yet neither was he a hands-on producer-manager like Fred Friendly. Bill Leonard, who followed Salant as president of CBS News, said in his own memoirs that one way Salant "tried to keep in touch with the troops was simply to wander coatless, often with a shirttail hanging out, through the dingy hallways of the old Sheffield milk plant that housed us at CBS News, poking his nose in this or that office, chatting cheerily."[16] To Salant, the newsroom was a little like a college dormitory, with people wandering around, dropping in, and holding bull sessions.

Marvin Kalb remembers Salant as a terrific boss; his journalistic ethics were impeccable. But, Kalb said, Salant could also be impatient, stubborn, and "absolutely sure he was right." Kalb said Salant was not what you called "a nice guy—he was too honest to be a nice guy." He was blunt, candid to a fault. "But if you got in trouble [and the pressure was on], he was just the fellow you wanted in charge; he stood behind you."[17]

Leonard wrote that Salant had "a high sense of what's right, fair, and just, a sense that sometimes ran afoul of fast-paced programming." He said Salant was almost completely innocent of the technology that drove television. He did not care much for pictures on the screen. According to Leonard, "Content is what concerned him—what we did or did not do; how well we did it; how fairly. He had no interest in the quick or the slick. And he was, let's face it, a junkie, a news junkie, above and beyond the call of duty."

Frances Salant recalled that her husband left home for the office promptly each morning at 7:30 A.M., when CBS sent a car with a driver to pick him up. He did not return until after 7:30 P.M. Salant of-

---

[14]Quoted from Rooney's remarks at Salant's memorial service, February 22, 1963.

[15]Schaefer, "The Development of CBS News Guidelines During the Salant Years," p. 13.

[16]Bill Leonard, *In the Storm of the Eye: A Lifetime at CBS* (New York: G P Putnam's Sons, 1987), p. 162.

[17]Interview with the editors, September 1997.

ten watched the *CBS Evening News* in his limousine on the way home, while he recorded ABC and NBC News to watch later in the evening. "He liked his family and friends," Frances said. "But if anything came up in the news, he dropped everything like a shot and was on it in an instant."

Salant was known as a relentless memo writer. According to Leonard:

> He would leave the office in time to get home to watch, record, and play back all the network news broadcasts. [Salant had three televisions lined up in his home for just this purpose.] He would beat Manning and me into the office in the morning by at least an hour; and then, as often as not, there would be on our desks a memorandum of infinite length, chock full of suggestions, ideas, observations, complaints, admonitions, and/or praise. I remember one time when a Salant memo hit his desk, Gordon Manning turned to me, rolled his eyes, and sighed "My God, he's writing them faster than I can read them."[18]

Even Frank Stanton marveled at Salant's memo-writing ability, "in terse handwritten notes you could barely read, or in the lengthiest memoranda I ever received. To this day, I could never figure out how he could formulate his thoughts and get them on paper as quickly as he did."[19]

The memos, standards, and loose-reins management style were all part of Salant's approach, keeping the newsroom aware that he was listening and watching, that he cared deeply about everything CBS News did. It was principled news management, not something television viewers saw directly, but it nourished the news organization and helped produce an extraordinary period of quality news coverage. The credibility of CBS News during the Salant years was unsurpassed. Even if he was aloof from the day-to-day workings of television production, the News Division felt Salant's presence; his values permeated the place.

Salant protected the News Division and fought for it against all intruders, assuming what he often described as the guise of a porcupine, firing off quills whenever he sensed a threat. In terms of staff and budget, he almost always won his battles. With Stanton's backing, Salant presided over a period of enormous News Division growth. In 1961,

---

[18]In another version of this story, Gordon Manning remembers Bill Leonard sitting in the office one day, looking hassled. Leonard, who was left-handed, was busy having to initial a number of Salant memos, writing "WAL" and the date. Manning says it was Leonard who said, "My God, he's writing them faster than I can initial them." According to Leonard's memoirs, Salant "could be orally articulate when aroused, but he was happiest writing his memos. Woe to the man or woman, inside or outside the company, who tried to tangle with him on paper." Leonard, *In the Storm of the Eye*, p. 141.

[19]Quoted at Salant's memorial service, February 22, 1993.

when Salant started, CBS News had an annual budget of $20 million and about 450 news staff members. At the end of Salant's CBS career in 1979, the figures were closer to $90 million and about 1,000 staff members.[20]

From awkward adolescence in 1961, TV journalism was growing up, and Salant could take credit for its development.[21] And as his long tenure at CBS News came to its end, the news staff would sometimes say nice things about him behind his back, as Andy Rooney put it. He was "the patron saint of broadcast journalism," Rooney said. Walter Cronkite placed him in the pantheon of journalists: "He belongs up there on a pedestal alongside Ed Murrow and Eric Sevareid and Walter Lippman." To Dan Rather, Salant "built his organization's reputation into that of the world's standard for broadcast news and made his own reputation for news management into one against which all others are still judged."[22]

In his analysis of the Salant years, Ed Fouhy says that on three critical issues—Watergate, Vietnam, and civil rights—the country eventually arrived at a fair consensus, in large part because of the credibility of Salant's CBS News broadcasts.

"The country had a common data base in the 1960s and 1970s," Fouhy said, "and it was forged by the *CBS Evening News*. Everything important could be set before the public every day, with honesty and objectivity." What went out on CBS News each night, he explained, helped a majority of people to understand and eventually accept that Vietnam was a stalemate; that civil rights for black people was the right thing to do; and that the Watergate break-in and cover-up were wrong. Fouhy believes the nation got through this period of upheaval and travail in part because of the mostly fair, accurate, and independent information—the credibility—supplied by CBS News under Salant.[23]

Charles Kuralt made a similar point.

Things were happening that had never happened before, and the ship of state was sailing through some very heavy weather. If ever network news needed a calm and judicious helmsman, it was then. As it happened, CBS

---

[20]Gates, *Airtime*, p. 400.
[21]Ibid.
[22]Rooney, Cronkite, and Rather's comments were made at Salant's memorial service, February 22, 1993.
[23]Interview with the editors, November 1997.

News had one. And some of us have thought, "Dick Salant helped the country through the storm."

Dick Salant always claimed he was not a journalist. That his job was to protect and encourage those of us who are. But he is a journalist. Those of us who have worked under him never hope to meet a better one. He thought a lot about standards and practices. . . . He protected those standards from opponents outside CBS and from those inside who wanted to bend them to popular taste to win bigger audiences. And he won both ways. As he stands down, CBS News is first in honor *and* in audience.[24]

• • •

After sixteen years as CBS News Division president, mandatory retirement forced Salant to step down from his cherished post in April 1979. After a further four years at NBC as vice chairman and a year as president of the National News Council, he finally retired.

Television news was changing by then, not always for the better. From today's vantage point, the network news industry during the Salant era was different in style and substance, in standards and ownership.

Twenty years ago, Salant's *CBS Evening News with Walter Cronkite* was almost all serious news—hard news—with few soft features. The stories themselves were minutes longer, more straightforward, less glib.

The history and the analytical context of a story were considered as a necessary part of a literate package. Sound bites were often one minute each, which allowed enough time for a complete thought to be expressed. (Today's sound bites are about ten seconds in length.)

There were far fewer quick-cut pictures and graphics flashing past. Salant believed that a few well-chosen, well-written, thoughtful words were worth more than mere pictures. It was for that reason that he added Eric Sevareid's news analysis to the *Evening News* four times a week, devoting about 10 percent of the available broadcast time to a "talking head."

Salant also sought to draw the sharpest possible line between news broadcasts and entertainment programs. Consequently, there was no music or sound effects in his news broadcasts—no opening fanfare, no music at the breaks, no music at the conclusion. Music and sound effects, according to Salant, represented entertainment values.

For Salant, according to Bill Leonard, "the term 'show business' was like syphilis: He didn't want to catch it. Even a story that smacked of

---

[24]From Kuralt's "The Salant Years."

'human interest' was hardly worth our precious airtime." Leonard wrote that Salant was almost afraid that by seeking to attract a bigger audience, he might dilute the purity of his news product.[25]

Salant's approach is considered old-fashioned today. But network news was serious business for him. And what CBS News produced back then seemed to have more substance and contain less entertaining trivia than today. Salant summed up one of the major differences between then and now when he criticized the networks' tendency today to aim at the senses, the emotions, the feelings, rather than aiming for the mind.

At the end of his life, although Salant was nostalgic at times for the way things used to be, he recognized he was "Mr. Yesterday." He was also aware that news coverage even in the Golden Age he presided over at CBS was never perfect. He liked to quote Will Rogers: "Thing's aren't like they used to be and they probably never were."

• • •

In 1960, Edward R. Murrow suggested that the death knell for broadcast news would occur the moment broadcasting corporations discovered that news could be made profitable. That became a reality by the mid-1980s, when new corporate owners began to buy and run the networks with an eye on their profitability, not on their potential for public service journalism. CBS was taken over by the cost-cutting investor Lawrence Tisch in 1986, who downsized CBS News and CBS. The company was finally purchased by Westinghouse in 1997.

In Salant's day, news broadcasting had been mostly about public service, not merely profits. And where once the News Division had been the crown jewel, protected by Paley and Stanton, under Tisch, CBS News saw the loss of more than 350 staff members. The number of domestic and overseas bureaus dwindled. Some former CBS News employees began to look back in sadness at "a stunted network. The standards are worn at the edges, and the jewels are missing from the crown."[26]

Making news more profitable means making it more popular and appealing. Salant knew, and it has become true, that as the line between news and entertainment is blurred and standards are eroded, broadcast journalism loses its credibility. And credibility, Salant believed strongly, was the most precious thing a news organization has—its single most important asset.

---

[25]Leonard, *In the Storm of the Eye*, p. 142.

[26]From "The Communicator," a December 1990 article by Emerson Stone, a thirty-five-year employee of CBS News, writing on the death of William Paley in October 1990.

The Salant era "was a very rich period in terms of the things television news did," Frank Stanton said in a 1995 interview, reflecting on Salant's leadership. "I think if this [Salant's] book had come out immediately after Dick left, there would have been less interest in it than there is today."

Stanton said journalists are looking for the values CBS News represented back then. "Quite frankly, I don't see [these values] today. I think a lot of people in the news business are interested in how the hell we operated and developed the policies we did. And Dick's life is central to that whole question."[27]

• • •

Salant's voice throughout his memoirs speaks the language of journalism, not marketing or entertainment. His accomplishments still matter today because public service values—the very soul of broadcast journalism—are what democracy needs to survive and thrive. Values matter in the news business. But when news is being managed for the last nickel, what media manager or owner today is publicly articulating the themes of high standards and high ideals?[28]

Richard Salant's life in broadcast journalism has come to symbolize the profession's highest standards and ideals, which he articulated eloquently. Someday, in a less profit-and-ratings-driven era, his enlightened blueprint for broadcast journalism will again point the way for others who know that the First Amendment is not just a license to make money but that it comes with enormous responsibility to serve the public.

---

[27]Interview with the editors, February 1995.

[28]The question comes from Joan Konner, of Columbia University's Graduate School of Journalism, in her address "Is Journalism Losing Its Professional Standards?" July 13, 1995, Hamburg, Germany, as quoted by Dunham, *Fighting for the First Amendment*, p. 196.

Part One
Signing On: The Early Years

CBS Memorandum
To: Senior Vice President, Hard News
From: Richard Salant
Re: Music and Sound Effects
Date: January 19, 1978

The animation is OK with me, but I am afraid that whoever made those noises has been looking at *Close Encounters of the Third Kind* too often. We are dealing with reality and the noises are unreal. They are jarring, unpleasant, and irrelevant. All those creeping sound effects on our news broadcasts should be uncrept.

CBS Memorandum
To: Senior Vice President, Hard News
From: Richard Salant
Re: Truth
Date: June 16, 1978

This is a small niggling thing—but last evening's special reminds me that we must be very careful to avoid having our anchorperson (as we had Walter [Cronkite] say on two separate occasions last evening) that we would be back "in a minute" as a lead-in to two minutes of commercials.

1
Leaving the Law

When I told my parents that I was going into the broadcast business, my mother, who thought broadcasting was not a respectable way to earn a living, reacted as though I had told her that I was about to start a career playing piano in a brothel. I assured her that she was wrong. But in my most pessimistic moments [during the period when all three networks aired docudramas about Amy Fisher, a teenager who shot her lover's wife], I wondered whether Mother wasn't closer to the truth than I had ever dreamed.

—Final speech, Senior Men's Club,
Fairfield, Connecticut, February 16, 1993

IN 1952, I TOLD MY FATHER that I was leaving the law and going to work for Frank Stanton and CBS. He was disappointed.

My father, Louis Salant, was a dedicated and successful lawyer—a trial lawyer, a lawyer's lawyer. From the time of my birth, it had always been assumed that I would be a lawyer, too. There never had been any question or discussion about it.

When I told Dad, he argued that I would waste my fine education: private school in New York City; Exeter; Harvard College; Harvard Law School. And, after all that, what about my experience with the government and then my work with an outstanding private law firm, of which I had become a partner?

"Son," Dad said, "you know I believe that being a lawyer is the finest of all ways to earn a living—it is earning your income by the exercise of your mind. But I have always thought that there are three classes of lawyers. First, and the most respectable, are practicing lawyers; then second, and less respectable, are disbarred lawyers; but third, and the least respectable, are ex-lawyers."

•　•　•

Later, after I became president of CBS News, when the young and ambitious came into my office asking for advice, usually they didn't want advice at all—they wanted a job. And the most keen didn't want just any job, they wanted my job. Surely, they insisted, I had followed a career path—a path clearly marked like a fine map which would show them precisely how to get from the starting point of my career to the chair behind my desk.

In fact, when my career began, I hadn't even heard of a career path. After graduating from law school in 1938, I went to work in Washington for the federal government. But the first step to my ultimate destination at CBS did not occur until 1946 when I was released from the navy as World War II ended and I became an associate in the firm of Rosenman Goldmark Colin and Kaye.

Rosenman's firm was large, with a varied practice, and perhaps its most important, and certainly best-known, client was the Columbia Broadcasting System. Ralph Colin, one of the firm's senior partners, had been Bill Paley's lawyer when Paley bought a small, foundering radio network in 1928. Colin had handled the legal aspects of the purchase and organization of the new company, which became CBS.

In 1946, at the time I went to the Rosenman firm, only a few television sets were in American homes and all television broadcasting was in black and white. But Dr. Peter C. Goldmark, the head of CBS laboratories, was already completing work on the development of a color television system. Before any broadcaster could broadcast in color, standards had to be tested and approved by the FCC [Federal Communications Commission]. CBS applied for approval of its system, but was challenged by RCA [Radio Corporation of America], NBC's parent organization.

Bill Paley and General David Sarnoff, the founder and chairman of RCA, were intensely competitive and very proud men. Sarnoff had already been badly stung by Goldmark's, and CBS's, successful development of the 33 rpm long-playing record, which had revolutionized the record industry. (Sarnoff had tried to counter with the 45 rpm record, but it never was as successful.)

To avoid another defeat—this time in the color television field—Sarnoff drove his laboratories to come up with a compatible color system which could head off the CBS system. Since CBS had been working on its system for several years, RCA had to catch up. The FCC hearings were drawn out and for the most part deadly serious, and the duel between the competing systems finally ended in the Supreme Court. With Sam Rosenman, I participated in the hearings before the FCC and on the briefs in the Court.

I also worked with Rosenman on a number of other cases for CBS, which threw me into working with top CBS executives, including Dr. Frank Stanton, the president of CBS. I soon developed great respect and affection for Stanton. So in 1952 when Frank asked me to come over to CBS as vice president, general executive, and his assistant, despite my father's reservations, I accepted, for a number of reasons.

First, I was pleased by the prospect of working with and learning from Frank. I had discovered from the time I went to work after law school that however attractive a job might be on paper, the joy of working depended on one's boss. To me, Frank Stanton was the finest of all the great and brilliant people I had worked with. I wanted to work for him.

Second, I was not enchanted with private law practice. Too often, it seemed to me, an exhausting amount of time and energy was spent on little of consequence to anybody except clients and their antagonists. I had been spoiled by the exciting years of working for the government, where the cases and issues we dealt with were important. Broadcasting, in contrast to the private practice of law in New York City, was the one field of private business which had some of the public importance that working for the federal government had. The decisions of a broadcaster had huge reach; they could make a difference to many people. If a broadcaster's decisions were good ones—right ones by my standards—they could add to the sum total of human happiness, satisfaction, or knowledge.

And the third reason I was willing to leave the law and work for CBS was that sometimes I found it difficult to remember that I was just a lawyer—the client was the policymaker. I hated having to sharply cut short my participation in matters with which I had become deeply, and sometimes passionately, involved. My frustration with the law, and my belated recognition of the line between lawyering and decisionmaking was compounded by the ultimate outcome of the color television system controversy. After pouring so much time, energy, and emotion into the CBS color television system, I was saddened to watch from the sidelines as it died and was abandoned, replaced by the RCA system we fought against so hard.

What happened is that as the case dragged on through the FCC, through the circuit court of appeals, and through the Supreme Court, the public kept buying greater and greater numbers of black-and-white television sets. Since those receivers could not receive the CBS color signals, even in black and white, the problem of incompatibility became overwhelming.

The coup de grâce came during the Korean War, when the Defense Department issued an order which reserved a special kind of copper for military use only; this was the same copper necessary for the manufacture of receivers using the CBS color system. At this point, CBS gave up and abandoned its color system. I was not involved in the decision—it was a policy decision, not a legal matter. But it was hard for me to watch two years of work go down the drain without any opportunity to put in my two cents.

The color case crystallized my realization that lawyers are not usually at the takeoffs or the landings. If I remained a lawyer, I would have to devote my blood, sweat, tears, heart, and soul to defending whatever the pilots decided. I wanted to get in the cockpit—I wanted to be closer to the decisionmaking process and not have to devote my life trying to vindicate other people's decisions.

So these three factors—working for Frank Stanton, working in a field which seemed to me to have some potential for a satisfying life because the work might make a difference to many people, and the frustration of being excluded from the decisionmaking process—led me to accept Frank Stanton's offer. I left the law and went to work for Frank Stanton and CBS—as an ex-lawyer.[1]

My father had been so satisfied with his life as a lawyer, I had neither the courage nor the heart to tell him how disappointed I had been in the private practice of law. Dad's disappointment in me was compounded by his conviction that there was something rather raffish about broadcasting—that it was not serious, not quite nice—like show business or streetwalking.

Ultimately, my parents became reconciled to my defection. I doubt, though, that when talking to his friends, my dad ever referred to me as "My son, the broadcaster."

---

[1]*Editors' note:* At Salant's memorial service, Frank Stanton described the scene when he had asked Salant to join CBS as his assistant in 1952: "Without a moment's hesitation, he put out his hand enthusiastically. There was no negotiation, there was no talk of money, there was no talk of title." In the Fiftieth Anniversary Report for Harvard's class of 1935, Salant wrote that his career shift from law to journalism "was the best move I ever made."

2
Paley: The Road to Responsibility

*Bill Paley invented network news. It was his pride and—usu-
ally—his joy. Frank Stanton nurtured the invention. They
loved broadcast news; the News Division was the spoiled one.
It was the first among equals, even listed first and out of alpha-
betical order in the CBS Annual Report. They said that news
was the company's crown jewel and that's the way they acted.
. . . Today's proprietors don't carry with them that very special
emotional investment which the pioneer broadcasters and
journalists brought to their trade.*

—**Benton Lecture, University of Chicago, March 3, 1988**

CBS WAS THE CHILD OF A BROADCASTER. It was created by
William Paley, a man who fell in love with broadcasting and, as it
turned out, had an extraordinary flair for it.

In 1927, a couple of entrepreneurs who wanted to compete with
David Sarnoff's radio giant RCA-NBC created a fledgling radio network called United Independent Broadcasters—a struggling group of
sixteen stations. At the time, Bill Paley was an enterprising young
man in his twenties who was in charge of advertising for his father's
successful La Palina cigar company. Paley—in a bold and radical step
which older heads in the business thought was exceedingly foolish—
decided to advertise La Palina cigars on a radio musical program. His
idea was a great success.

Paley became fascinated by the business of radio—the programming, the selling, the buying. With about half a million dollars given
to him by his father, he bought an interest in the upstart competitor to

NBC. Before long, Paley had acquired the remaining interests in the company, and in 1928, the Columbia Broadcasting System was born.

Although NBC and CBS were in the same line of business, they were very different in character. Even in later years, the difference in the circumstances and reasons for their inception accounted for inherent differences in the character and philosophy of the two organizations, and in their way of doing business.

NBC's David Sarnoff earned prominence as a young telegraph operator for the Marconi Wireless Company. In 1912, Sarnoff sent the first telegraph dispatches of the news of the sinking of the *Titanic*. But more important, he later conceived the idea of radio—of utilizing wireless communication for transmission to the public—and he created the Radio Corporation of America (RCA) to carry out his idea.

RCA's core business was making radio transmitters, radio studio equipment, and, most of all, radio receivers. However, Sarnoff soon realized that there was no future in inventing and manufacturing all of this equipment unless there was something—programming—that the public wanted to hear on their radios. And so RCA had to get into the business of radio programming. It was to fill that need that Sarnoff and RCA created the National Broadcasting Company.

General Sarnoff never was as interested in the programs, or software, as he was in selling the hardware—the transmitting and receiving equipment. Many years later, Sarnoff compared his networks and stations to pipelines:[1] He supplied the pipelines so that other people could fill them with programs. To him, NBC was just a necessary means to motivate the public to buy radios—as indeed they quickly did by the tens of millions—and later, televisions.

NBC was a postscript. Its creator created it not because he wanted to, or because he loved it, but because he felt he had to. Sarnoff's great business genius and energies were reserved for other parts of his company. Paley's great business genius and energies, at least during the formative years of CBS, and for a considerable period thereafter, were devoted to programming and broadcasting.

• • •

Bill Paley was not only the founder of the CBS network, he also was truly the father of CBS News. In the earliest days of broadcasting, there was no broadcast news. But from the outset, it was Paley, alone among the pioneers in that strange new business called broadcasting,

---

[1] Until 1943 when the government intervened, RCA had two radio networks—the Red and the Blue. RCA was required to discard the Blue network, which became ABC.

who recognized the importance of news, not as a peripheral activity but as an essential part of broadcasting. Soon after he created CBS, Paley moved to establish CBS's own news capability.

Typically, because Bill Paley never did anything halfway, when he created broadcast news, with his usual determination to be first and best, he moved decisively and wisely. He turned to professional, hard-nosed news people to create the CBS News Department. Ed Klauber, a *New York Times* editor, was the first head of CBS News.

With the support of Paley, Klauber set the professional standards which have governed CBS News ever since: the principle of fairness and objectivity; emphasis on factual reporting and analysis and avoidance of editorializing; autonomy and independence of the news operations, including separation from advertising and advertiser influence; and the News Department's direct access to senior management, which at CBS was Bill Paley.

When Hitler invaded Czechoslovakia in 1939, CBS had a bright young man named Edward R. Murrow, who was wandering around Europe arranging CBS Radio Network broadcasts of talks and cultural events from the Continent—including, so go the reminiscences, such exotica as a concert of instruments and songbirds from Vienna.

Murrow did not have the journalistic experience to become the first, and greatest, broadcast journalist. He needed none: He was a natural. Paley and Klauber, at the time of the Anschluss, assigned Murrow not only to begin radio broadcasting to report what was happening but also to put together a team of reporters to help. This Ed did, and that remarkable corps of brilliant young reporters known as "Murrow's boys" came into being.

They should have also been known as Bill Paley's and Ed Klauber's boys, for Paley and Klauber had the wisdom and insight not only to recognize Ed Murrow's extraordinary talents but to give him a free hand, and the means, to create that CBS News team. Murrow recruited Eric Sevareid, William L. Shirer, Charles Collingwood, Howard K. Smith, Richard C. Hottelet, and the rest of the distinguished crew.[2] Together they created a new form of journalism—broadcast journalism—oral reporting of the sights and sounds of history as it was being made.

---

[2]*Editors' note:* There are generally considered to be eleven "Murrow boys," including one woman, Mary Marvin Breckinridge. The others were Cecil Brown, Winston Burdett, Charles Collingwood, William Downs, Thomas Grandin, Richard C. Hottelet, Larry LeSueur, Eric Sevareid, William L. Shirer, and Howard K. Smith. From Stanley Cloud and Lynne Olson, *The Murrow Boys, Pioneers on the Front Lines of Broadcast Journalism* (Boston: Houghton Mifflin, 1996).

Thanks to the philosophy of Paley and Stanton, and to the professional leadership of Klauber, and after he retired to Paul White, and to Murrow's brilliant reporting and eye for journalistic talent, broadcast journalism at CBS never went through the long pain of childhood and adolescence. More quickly than any form of journalism in history, broadcast journalism, as Frank Stanton used to say it, "put on long pants."

The principle of the special relationship of news to senior management—a recognition of the importance and sanctity of broadcast news—was laid out by Paley in a landmark 1954 speech, "The Road to Responsibility." I worked with Paley in preparing this speech. It was the first time I had ever worked closely with him—I was still a corporate officer with no idea that someday I would get into news myself—and it marked the most continuous working contact with him in all of my CBS career. And since he was probing about speeches prepared for him, it served as my initial intensive schooling in the admirable CBS philosophy on the role of news in the broadcasting business, the obligation of CBS senior management to give news priority in management support, and CBS's obligation to establish and maintain high professional standards.[3]

Paley called for "scrupulous and conscientious judgment by broadcasters as the best assurance of overall fairness and balance in news and public affairs broadcasting." He emphasized "the inseparability of freedom from a high sense of responsibility."

In the early days, Bill Paley maintained an almost daily relationship to CBS's network news operations. But eventually he became less personally involved in the activities of CBS News. With huge growth and success, the Columbia Broadcasting System itself became a conglomerate. It branched out into a variety of nonbroadcasting businesses, and it changed its name officially to CBS so as to reflect the fact that it was no longer so predominantly a broadcasting business. Because of the distractions of his many other interests and the incredible growth and diversification of CBS, CBS lost some of its characteristics of a family. It necessarily became a less personal enterprise for Bill Paley and more of a corporate hierarchy.

In 1946, when Frank Stanton became the president and chief operating officer of CBS, a new layer of management was created between

---

[3]After we finished, Paley sent me this letter: "Dear Dick: This is to express my thanks and appreciation for your efforts in behalf of the speech I made before the NAB [National Association of Broadcasters] Convention. You put the speech beautifully on the track in your first draft, and, in so doing, relieved me considerably of my anxiety about whether I had a speech at all. Also, you helped keep it on the track and your judgment about questions of content were of great help and comfort to me."

news and Paley. Fortunately, Stanton, too, had an enormous interest in and great aspirations for the network news operations. He had the same insistence on integrity, high standards, independence, and the importance of broadcast news was maintained. Although Bill Paley stepped back somewhat from news activities, he never lost his pride, ambition, and interest in CBS News.

3

Stanton: Renaissance Mentor

It was the explicit, announced Paley-Stanton policy, of ines-
timable importance to network news, that the News Division
was not regarded as or expected to be a profit center, as all
other CBS divisions were. We fulfilled those expectations.

—Washington University, Seattle, May 5, 1986

T HE PHRASE "RENAISSANCE MAN" is tired and overused. But in
his breadth of interests and expertise, and in his thoughtful development of a personal and professional philosophy of what broadcasting
should be, Frank Stanton came as close to being a Renaissance man as
anybody I have ever met.

Frank Stanton was the president and chief operating officer of CBS
during the period of its explosive growth—from 1946 until 1971. Brilliant and innovative, he was a doctor by virtue of his Ph.D. in psychology.[1] Frank had an extraordinary sense of order and style, and he became an acknowledged leader in a variety of fields—art, architecture,
design, the social and behavioral sciences, and photography. He had an
intense interest in the American political process.[2]

---

[1]Frank had come to CBS in 1936 as an audience researcher for $50 a week. RCA-NBC
had turned down his application for a job the same week that RCA-NBC had also rejected Peter Goldmark's job application. For $100 a week, NBC could have had both
Stanton and Goldmark.

[2]When I worked with him in the early days, Frank was fascinated by automobiles—
fast ones. He used to go out to the Detroit testing grounds to watch, and drive, the new
experimental models. Once, on a Sunday, while we were working at the old CBS head

Frank was, above all, a person of principle—a man of the highest standards of integrity who threw his enormous energies and brilliant and precise mind into struggles which involved much more than business considerations. He was indefatigable; he never seemed to need sleep. His integrity was uncompromising, yet it was gentle. He nursed his associates along and taught them by osmosis and example, not by forbidding and righteous moralizing (or demoralizing) lectures. Stanton was a listener—a patient listener.

Unlike many in broadcasting, he was cerebral rather than emotional or instinctive. He had to work with many who worked from the gut and from instinct—"those with fire in the belly, which seared the gray matter in their brain," as someone put it. He was patient with them—after all, that was the nature of the business.

And he was a reserved man. He had learned, in his rapid rise at CBS, how painful it sometimes was to be the boss, particularly when he had to fire or pass over his friends at CBS. Early on, he made the intensely difficult decision to avoid close social ties with those who worked at CBS.

These circumstances—his orderly, analytical mind and his distance-keeping—led some who did not understand him to believe that Frank was remote and cold, an automaton. But the portrayal of Stanton as distant and unaffectionate is belied by the loyalty he engendered among those who worked for him—especially in News. Long after he had retired in 1973, whenever he appeared at industry meetings and CBS News people were present, there was a standing ovation when he was spotted and asked to rise. And even today, Frank has a constant stream of old colleagues, both news and non-news people, who come to him for advice or commiseration—or just to see him and say hello.

Remote, cold people do not engender that kind of long-lasting affection and respect.

At CBS, Frank always had to work in the shadow of Bill Paley. At meetings attended by Paley, at least when others were present, Frank almost never disagreed with Paley. He usually made a few quiet comments and for the rest was silent.

---

quarters at 485 Madison Avenue, he asked me whether I would like to take a drive with him in his new sports car, which he had parked outside the building.

His new car was a Muntz—a super sports car made and sold by Madman Muntz, whose main business was the manufacture of television sets. Frank got behind the wheel and said that the car could accelerate to sixty miles an hour in nine seconds. Then he proceeded to demonstrate. (The statute of limitations has long since run out, and on a Sunday in those days, Madison Avenue was empty of traffic.) It felt as if it did—I don't know for sure, because my eyes were closed.

As CBS grew and diversified and Paley focused on other company matters, Frank Stanton, by natural inclination, focused more and more on news. He understood its importance. He understood how crucial broadcast news, with its enormous public reach, was to our society. He understood, from the outset, its special dangers: the imperative need that it be responsible and honest, free of personal bias.

He also understood, long before anybody else (and many seem since to have forgotten), that it was essential that news be kept separate from entertainment. Because the news is surrounded by entertainment in the broadcast schedule, and indeed is supported by broadcast entertainment revenues, Stanton felt it should be distinguished from entertainment both in technique and in nomenclature.

Hence, he insisted that there be no staging, no faking, no music in news broadcasts. He insisted that news reporters not participate in entertainment programs; that news broadcasts be the exclusive province of professional journalists and not entertainment producers. He insisted that while the entertainment people produced "shows" or "programs," the CBS News Division did no such thing: It produced "broadcasts."

And while advertisers could sponsor news broadcasts, no news broadcast could ever be said to be presented solely by one sponsor, because it was not—CBS News presented it. News broadcasts were on the schedule because CBS so decided, not a sponsor.

All this was not a matter of fussy detail. It was a matter of deep principle to keep broadcast journalism pure. The crossing of the lines—by entertainment into information, and by news into entertainment—which became so marked in the 1980s and 1990s was a matter of deep distress to Stanton. It never would have happened—at least at CBS—had he still been there.

•   •   •

Stanton had multiple major roles at CBS which required delicate tightrope walking. He had to deal with advertisers. He had to be responsible for the operations of other CBS divisions—both broadcast and nonbroadcast—and each division had strong ideas about what CBS News should be and what it might do for, or to, them. However, most difficult were his responsibilities in Washington. Frank Stanton passionately believed that the free press guarantee of the First Amendment means what it says—that Congress (and any government authority, at any level) may not abridge the freedom of the press—and that broadcast journalism was part of that protected press.

When, to Frank's outrage and horror, the producers of the quiz shows rigged them in the late 1950s, it was Stanton who went down and took his lumps at House hearings in the early 1960s—and issued policies and rules which ameliorated the crisis. When the FCC forbade broadcast stations to editorialize, it was Stanton who fought in Washington, successfully, to restore the right which all the rest of the press enjoyed.

When the Equal Time Law barred debates between the major presidential candidates, Stanton, almost single-handedly, persuaded Congress to suspend Section 315 for the 1960 campaign, making the Nixon-Kennedy debates possible. Thus began what now seems to be a tradition presidential candidates cannot avoid—campaign debates. And when we broadcast "The Selling of the Pentagon" and infuriated the Nixon administration and some members of Congress, it was Frank Stanton who held his ground before a House subcommittee and risked going to jail to vindicate broadcast journalism's First Amendment right to protect its notes and outtakes from congressional scrutiny.

Print publishers and proprietors can, if they choose to, stay away from Washington except for occasional visits—like attending White House dinners or the annual Gridiron Club festivities. Broadcast network executives, however, have no such option. Certainly uniquely among American press organizations—broadcasting was dependent on, and vulnerable to, Washington. The White House, congressmen, and senators were not hesitant to threaten us with legislative punishment and even extinction if we didn't do what they wanted us to do— or if we did do what they didn't want us to.

Frank Stanton spent a lot of time and energy in Washington because it was an important part of his job. He cultivated friendships with powerful legislators, like the Senate majority leader and later president of the United States, Lyndon B. Johnson. It was Frank, a superb woodworker, on whom President Johnson called to design and fix a desk in the White House. Frank did, working on the desk on his hands and knees.

It was one of the glories of being head of CBS News during Stanton's tenure that he managed so successfully to keep his Washington functions separate from his relationships with me and the News Division. I cannot recall, and I do not believe, that there was a single instance when Frank's discussions with me ever, to my knowledge, stemmed from what must have been constant criticisms and "deals" emanating from Washington.

Senior management performed what was nearly a miracle. It kept me, and my CBS News associates, completely insulated from the Washington pressures to which it was subjected. Indeed, I was unaware of them. And I did not know of the brutal arm-twisting to which Stanton and Paley were subjected during the Nixon administration until I read the White House memoranda and tape transcripts after they finally became public through the Watergate hearings. Stanton saw to it that we at CBS News were able to live in a protected world of ignorance of these pressures. It was truly heroic.

•   •   •

My files and my recollections covering the years when Frank Stanton was at CBS and I was with the News Division are remarkably free of memoranda or other instructions and inquiries from Frank. He did, from time to time, when crises arose or urgent matters emerged, circulate "The President's Notes," addressed to all of CBS, including CBS News and the news departments of the CBS-owned radio and television stations. They reminded the entire CBS organization of, and reaffirmed, long-standing policies.

It was in the wake of the quiz scandals that his "Notes" laid down the rule that whatever went on the air—whether entertainment or news—must be what it purported to be, with no false staging, no representation of spontaneity when in fact there had been prearrangements or questions and answers in advance.[3]

Several instances were typical of Frank's remarkable, and useful, eye for visual detail and clarity. This vintage exchange between Frank Stanton and me occurred after he had become vice chairman in 1971. By memorandum dated January 2, 1973, Frank wrote: "Am I wrong or didn't we show Tip O'Neil [*sic*] with his hair parted on the right with

---

[3]It was this articulation of policy, first announced by Stanton in a public speech when he learned of the chicanery in the quiz programs, which led to the most unfortunate breach between Stanton and Ed Murrow.

Jack Gould, the *New York Times* critic, called Stanton to ask whether the policy applied to news, and particularly to Murrow's soft feature series involving interviews of celebrities in their homes. Since *Person to Person* necessitated prearrangements and blocking out questions in advance, Frank had to say that the policy applied across the board and that if questions were put in advance, that fact had to be disclosed on the air. It was an unexpected question; it seems to me that Stanton had no choice; he could not exempt news or Ed Murrow.

By the time news of Stanton's quick answer to Gould reached Murrow in London, Ed, without the context and background, understandably reacted furiously and attacked Frank. Both sides lost their tempers. It never should have happened. It was a misunderstanding and caused an avoidable breach between two very great men who had the same love, respect, and aspirations for broadcast news.

After Ed left CBS News for the United States Information Agency, it was a priority of mine to heal the breach and to bring Ed back to CBS News. Frank, and senior management, agreed. I believe Ed would have come back, but his fatal illness intervened.

[Dan] Rather and on the left with [Roger] Mudd—on the *Evening News* tonight?"

Stanton was referring to the still pictures which we used in the upper corner, behind the correspondent. Frank, of course, had spotted an error; he was right. By memorandum, I replied:

> What can I say after I say I am sorry? Yep—the slide we used on the January 2 *Evening News* had O'Neill's part on one side, and the film of him during the Mudd piece had the part on the other side. I wish I could say that the good congressman just likes to vary by veering from left to right, but the more accurate and shameful explanation is that the Graphic Arts Department reversed the slide in order to make the subject look in the best direction for design purposes . . . I love you to watch our broadcasts, and I'd be heartbroken if you didn't. But sometimes I wish you'd watch them with your eyes closed.
>
> P.S. I will not—I swear I will not—point out that Tip spells his last name with two l's. (Or, more probably, you just do that to make me feel better?)

To the public, the CBS eye was just a logo they saw on the screen at every station break. To me, it was Frank's own impeccable eye, reminding us that we should be accurate even on the little items that people with less sharp eyes and full attention might miss. In all, he was my mentor for many years before I even knew that there was such a thing.

•   •   •

In June 1990, when it came time to write notes for some remarks about Frank for the Emerson Radio Award to be given at the Plaza Hotel in New York, I found, after much struggling and tossing out of drafts, that Frank outran the wit or the vocabulary that would do justice to his extraordinary genius. So I went through my files, where I found the precise words for which I was groping. Frank Stanton had retired in 1973, and in November 1974, Eric Sevareid made these remarks about Frank:

> Frank Stanton did many things for me and there was nothing I could ever do for him.
>
> That is apt to be the fate of men of his character. As the ancient Greek said, character is fate.
>
> So it was Frank Stanton's fate to do always for others. To be still on his feet when others were down; to be cool when others were in a fever. To make the hard decisions when others could not make up their minds. He was where the buck stopped. . . .

No man in broadcasting more readily accepted the public responsibilities of this technically private enterprise. He made uncounted decisions that cost the business in order to profit the people.

This learned man knew that liberties can be defended only as long as we still have them; that they are our own, and sole, defense . . .

I have received nothing but honorable treatment from Frank Stanton in all these years. I am aware that he intercepted many arrows directed at me; I am aware that there must have been many others I am not aware of, because he never told you about such things, himself.

In this business it is extremely rare that any man sitting far up there in the executive suites becomes a hero to those sweating down there in the bear pit. Not by grandiloquent acts of heroism. But by sheer endurance, steadiness, unalterable support. He was there, in season and out.

As usual, Eric had it exactly right. He spoke for all of us—most certainly including me. Frank Stanton surely was, as I so often have stated, the best nonpracticing journalist who ever lived. And when, in 1973, he was no longer at CBS, in season or out, I sorely missed him.

4

President, CBS News

I don't like the network news's tendency of aiming at the senses, the emotions, the feelings rather than aiming for the mind. Too often, we are left with impressions, paint splashes, rather than ideas and thoughts which are the important currency of mankind's progress.

—*Benton Lecture, University of Chicago, March 3, 1988*

I TOOK OVER AS PRESIDENT OF CBS News in February 1961. It was a foolish, or crazy, or courageous step for Paley and Stanton to take. I never did ask them why they did it, and I suspect the people in the great CBS News organization were bewildered, suspicious, and surprised, too.

I had spent my first nine years at CBS working directly for Frank Stanton, who brought me along on the whole range of broadcasting matters. But above all, Frank steered me into what interested and stimulated him the most: broadcast journalism. I was involved, with Paley and Stanton, in the aftermath of Ed Murrow's broadcast on Senator Joseph McCarthy and the policy issues which it raised. Frank also took me to the major news events which CBS News was covering and which he attended, such as the presidential conventions.[1]

---

[1]The fact that I had no real function, in respect of the News Department, however, was brought home to me when I was hanging around CBS News headquarters at the Democratic Convention in 1956, the first one I attended. I was sitting on some stairs, doing nothing, when one of the producers motioned for me to come over. I thought he wanted me to join the group to discuss some journalistic issue, but I was wrong. Instead, he told me to get eight coffees—three black, three sugar and cream, two sugar. I did. But to spare him embarrassment (I had been a vice president at CBS for four years by then), I borrowed a red armband marked "Page" from one of the pages when I came back with the coffee.

By the end of the 1950s, I had become acquainted with Ed Murrow, Fred Friendly, Eric Sevareid, Charlie Collingwood, David Schoenbrun, Bud [Burton] Benjamin, and other great journalists who later became my associates. Indeed, Fred Friendly used to invite me over to screen, with him and Ed and their associates, episodes of *See It Now* and, later, *CBS Reports*, before they were broadcast. They were not asking me for my opinion or for suggestions; they only wanted to share their enthusiasm for the finished work with me. But I was pleased; I began to think I was almost inside CBS News—a fine place to be.

When Stanton told me that I had been kibitzing long enough and it was time for me to try my hand at actually doing something, I was delighted. But I was also scared. Network news organizations are serious, professional organizations run by experienced journalists. I was hardly qualified to be president. I had neither the credentials nor the track record. As the new president of CBS News I knew I already had three strikes against me.

Strike one: I was not and never had been a journalist.

Strike two: I was a corporate type and the rule was that corporate types were laymen who just did not, and could not, understand the news profession. I was of a different breed. After all, a corporate type's job was to make money; a newsperson's nobler calling was to make democracy work by informing the people—which cost money.

Strike three: And perhaps worst of all, I was, or had been, a lawyer. My past as a lawyer was a cross I had to bear those first years as I tried to learn my trade.

On the day of my appointment to my job as CBS News president, I was sitting in my new office on the twentieth floor of 485 Madison Avenue—the CBS corporate floor. The door swung open and Ed Murrow walked in. It felt ridiculous to think I was to be this great journalist's boss—even nominally.

Ed congratulated me—and then looked at me. "What's the matter?" he asked. "You look scared."

"I am scared," I said. "What do I know about journalism?" One of Ed's talents—one which made him such a fine reporter—was his sensitivity; he not only knew, but he also *felt*, what was going on in other people's minds and hearts. He sat down and hitched his chair next to mine.

"Come on, Dick," he said, "I didn't start in this business as a reporter, either—I had no journalistic training. You only have to have two things to be in this business. You have to love the news—I do, and I know you do, too, and you have to have a deep respect for the human race."

That was all the encouragement I needed. But I did ask Ed whether he had any advice for me.

"Only this," he said, "and it comes from Elmer Davis: 'Don't let the bastards scare you.'"

And then Ed put his hand on my knee. "One more piece of advice, Dick, which I must pass on to you. Watch out for Fred Friendly." (Friendly was the executive producer of *See It Now*, *CBS Reports*, and other great Murrow documentaries, and generally considered to be Ed's partner and alter ego.) "Fred does have fire in his belly. And he's a great producer. But watch out—he doesn't know a fact when he sees one."

• • •

CBS senior management, of course, recognized that I was uncooked indeed when I became president of the News Division. Wisely, Frank Stanton suggested that I choose from within CBS News a number two person who was a knowledgeable, experienced broadcast journalist and who was respected by his colleagues for his ability and integrity. The man we chose, recommended by Ed Murrow, among others, was Blair Clark. Blair had been producer and anchor of the CBS Radio Network's *World News Tonight* which, with the *World News Roundup*, was among broadcasting's very best news series.

Blair shored me up. He initiated me into the mysteries of broadcast journalism. He patiently counseled me and frequently steered me from mistakes. It was typical of his impatience with organizational bureaucracy and hierarchy that he usually dropped "vice president" from his title.

My first years with CBS News involved the most intensive on-the-job training that any newsperson has ever had. News judgments are hard to explain and define, and my colleagues were patient and tolerant as I wandered through the newsrooms and parked myself in the control rooms, trying to learn and understand.

I used to drop into the area where the *CBS Evening News* was prepared and ask why a particular story was chosen as the lead, or why we included one story but excluded another. This was a delicate business. No matter how hard I tried to indicate to the contrary, it was the kind of question that could easily be misinterpreted as criticism of the judgment of my associates who were responsible for the *Evening News*. It was the kind of question that was likely to be heard as "You idiot—Why in heaven's name did you lead with that story?" not "Why?—Explain and teach me."

When I asked why this story and not that one, the executive producer of the *Evening News*, whose time was precious because he had a dozen urgent matters to attend to in preparing for the evening's broadcast, would look at me as tolerantly as he could, and with the least possible scorn in his voice, if not in his heart, he would reply, "News judgment."

"What's that?" I would foolishly press on.

"It's just something you feel here," he would reply, sometimes pointing to his belly, sometimes to his heart, sometimes to his head. Then, the executive producer would patiently explain that news judgment wasn't anything that could be reduced to written rules or a meaningful statement of principles. What one has to do, I ultimately realized, is simply to be in the business long enough so that one gets the true feel of it—it comes just from being in journalism. If one is lucky, it comes by osmosis.

5

Half-Hour Evening News

We didn't pick Walter to anchor the Evening News *because of his hairdo—he didn't have one. We didn't pick Walter because he was beautiful—he wasn't. We didn't pick Walter because . . . a focus group, wired up to a machine, palpitated at the sight of him. They didn't have things like that in those prehistoric days, so we were on our own. We picked Walter for the only sound reason to choose an anchor: He was a real pro, a superb reporter—a newsman who always gave his audience an honest account, no matter what his personal beliefs. It was the right assignment.*

—*Museum of Television and Radio dinner,*
New York, December 5, 1988

ONE OF THE FIRST DECISIONS Blair Clark and I made was to replace Douglas Edwards with Walter Cronkite as anchor of the *CBS Evening News*. Doug had been a fine radio journalist for a long time. In fact, many years earlier, he and Mike Wallace together did a local news broadcast for a radio station in Detroit, sponsored by the Cunningham Drugstore. Doug and Mike were then known as the "Cunningham Aces."

When that newfangled thing called television came along, most of the CBS News correspondents thought that it was just a temporary—and forbidding—toy which would not last long. Besides, while there were tens of millions of radios out there, very few homes had a television.

Doug Edwards knew that television was not just a fad. He agreed to move to television to become the anchor of the weekday *CBS-TV*

Evening News. His only network competition then was NBC's John Cameron Swayze. In deference to its sole sponsor, Swayze's broadcast was called the *Camel Caravan.*[1]

But by 1961, Swayze was gone, replaced by an able and interesting pair of reporters, whom NBC, almost by accident, had put together to anchor the 1956 political conventions. The reporters were Chet Huntley and David Brinkley. They were very good together. Their contrasting styles—Chet deep-voiced and serious, David light and wry—were just right for the 1956 conventions, and the evening news.

Their success was due to more than just excellent chemistry. It was a happy combination of two fine journalists. Chet Huntley, in appearance and delivery, was as close as NBC could come to Ed Murrow (who never much liked television and was more comfortable with his nightly radio broadcast than he would have been with a nightly television broadcast). Brinkley, I believe, was the first broadcast journalist to master the art of writing words for news to be heard, as they are in broadcasting, rather than for the eye, as they are for print.

The new style which Huntley and Brinkley brought to the network evening news also brought NBC dominance in the ratings. At the same time, Doug Edwards was fatigued after fourteen years of his nightly television broadcasts. During this early period, the mechanics of television, both in the studio and in the field where everything was shot on film, were cumbersome, primitive, and unreliable, so that each evening's broadcast was a hairy adventure. We concluded that in these circumstances, we ought to make a change.

•   •   •

Walter Cronkite took Doug Edwards's place on April 16, 1962. And that was the first time that I learned how angry and articulate the people out there—the viewers—could be. Letters and postcards—even telegrams and phone calls—came from people all over the country. They all adored Doug and were angry at me for replacing him. All this was a new experience for me, and a shattering one. Doug took the move far more graciously than his constituents did. And in the years following, he effectively and successfully continued to broadcast for CBS News both on the radio and television networks.

Walter Cronkite was almost the stereotypical, traditional hard-nosed, no-nonsense wire-service reporter. He had worked for many

---

[1]Three decades make a great deal of difference. Today, there are no sole sponsors of network news; no self-respecting news organization would permit a sponsor to attach its name to its broadcast.

years for United Press—in Kansas City and other domestic bureaus—
then covered the Normandy invasion and other events in World War
II. He finally became UP's bureau chief in Moscow. He had done some
radio broadcasting for American radio stations, and ultimately, he was
persuaded to join CBS News.

One program he anchored, *You Are There*, was a re-creation of historical events with actors portraying the historical figures and CBS
News correspondents "interviewing" these figures and "reporting"
the events as they unfolded. ("General Washington, it's terribly cold;
your men are hungry and freezing. Do you think you can last out the
winter?" "Yes." "This is John Jones, CBS News, reporting from Valley
Forge.") *You Are There* was a popular series. Later standards would
have precluded it because it intermingled fact and drama and used actors and CBS News Division correspondents on a program produced by
the entertainment arm of CBS Television, not by CBS News.

Cronkite closed each of the *You Are There* shows with: "And that's
the way it was, July 4, 1776," or January 1, 1 A.D., or whatever.
"That's the way it was"—followed by the day and date—became Walter's signature sign-off (sometimes he called it the equivalent of his
masthead). He kept it throughout his *Evening News* anchoring career,
modified to "And that's the way it is, Friday, February 7, 1967."

Walter and I had a running discussion over the years about his tag
line. I argued that for Cronkite (whom surveys showed to be the nation's most-trusted person) to say "That's the way it is" five times a
week would injure his credibility. The reason I felt that way was because it was untrue: "The way it is" could not be accurately reported
in a fifteen-minute or thirty-minute (less the commercials) television
broadcast.

In 1969, and thereafter, I raised questions about Cronkite's use of his
closing line. I wrote a memo to Gordon Manning, vice president in
charge of hard news at the time, explaining why the phrase troubled
me. Gordon scrawled a handwritten note on my memo to him characterizing my questioning as nitpicking and suggesting that I must have
been acting on somebody else's behest. Sometimes I abandoned my
light, mild memo style, and this was one such occasion:

> I would be less than candid if I did not tell you that I am angry and dis-
> tressed by your note responding to my memorandum in which I ques-
> tioned "That's the way it is." I know we are all under pressure here, but at
> least among ourselves, we would be a lot better off if we took a deep breath
> before we emit angry reactions. And I particularly resent your rather clear
> implication that I was acting on behalf of somebody else. I was not. The tag
> line bothered me and continues to bother me. I don't think this is nitpick-
> ing at all. I think that this is just as bad as—and because we are in news,
> perhaps worse than—the most atrocious huckstering by Madison Avenue.

> Because I don't want to be dictatorial even about matters about which I feel very strongly, I do not propose to eliminate the tag line, but unless you can come up with more reasoned persuasion, I am going to show my memorandum to Cronkite and discuss it with him.
>
> Incidentally, I cannot find many things that are more important than "soul-searching the precision" of what CBS News says every night on the most widely looked at news in the United States.
>
> If I sound angry, it's because I am.

But Walter argued that I was being much too literal; he did not believe that people really thought that he had presented a complete and comprehensive picture of the way things were, so no harm was done. Sometimes, in the course of these discussions, Walter and I were on the edge of a compromise: Once we decided that after "That's the way it is," Walter would add, "For further details, read your favorite local newspaper." But then we looked at a sampling of local daily papers and found that more and more of them were relegating most of the national and international news—which is all that network news deals with—to one double column on an inside page. Thus, we would be jumping from the frying pan of one untruth into the fire of another.

Of course, the tag line remained throughout Cronkite's anchoring career. Curiously, even those most critical of television news never raised any serious question about "That's the way it is." I figured that if the *New York Times* could stretch the literal truth with its "All the News That's Fit to Print," Walter was entitled to a little poetic license, too. Until Walter retired two decades later, "That's the way it is" is the way it was.

● ● ●

Another priority was to persuade CBS senior management, my associates in the Television Network Division, and the CBS Television Network affiliates to permit us to expand the network evening news from fifteen minutes to a half hour. In the early 1960s, public opinion surveys disclosed the awesome fact that a large part of the public relied on television news as its primary source of information. In the circumstances, expansion of the evening news from fifteen to thirty minutes seemed obvious, logical, and imperative. But it took two years to accomplish.

Senior management was all in favor of expansion, and most of the CBS Television Network people were, too. But it is an unavoidable fact of broadcasting life that there are only twenty-four hours in each day. If newspapers and magazines want to expand, they can add pages, and if they have enough ads, they do. But broadcasters can't expand their pages because their pages are time—hours and minutes. All broadcasters can do is substitute. To make room for a new program or the expansion of an existing one, a broadcaster must remove another. Even that might be doable without a maximum dustup except that not only do programs compete for time but so do two other entities— the network and the affiliated stations.

There was the rub. The time adjacent to the fifteen minutes occupied by network news was time used by stations for their own programs. And not surprisingly, affiliates did not want to yield the time they were occupying to the network. Without affiliates carrying network programs, a network cannot exist. Therefore, the CBS network, and particularly the Affiliate Relations Department, was reluctant to get the affiliates angry, and few things were more likely to get them angry than taking away "their" time.

There was other nervousness at the network level. Some uneasy foot-draggers expressed doubt whether there was enough news for us to fill a half hour. Others did not think viewers would sit still for a whole half hour. This was finally resolved, and the logjam was broken thanks largely to two very disparate people, Bill Hylan and Ernie Leiser.

Bill Hylan was the CBS Television Network's senior sales vice president. Enlightened and straightforward, and a superb sales strategist, Bill listened to all the arguments. Then with his no-nonsense mind, he decided we could never know whether the half-hour news would work until we tried it. Besides, it would give him more advertising time to sell—and that's what a sales executive likes best to do. That breath of fresh air did it. We got the green light.

But then we had to bring the thirty-minute news into being. This took careful and creative thought. The broadcast could not have just twice as many stories as there were in the fifteen-minute news, nor could it have the same number of stories, each twice as long. A quarter of an hour may not seem like much in a person's lifetime, but for network television news, it was a revolution.

That's where Ernie Leiser came in. An experienced journalist—as a foreign correspondent and a producer in charge of the evening news— Ernie had a vision of what the half-hour news should be.[2] He wrestled with his idea. He analyzed it. He reduced it to a detailed written plan—complete with hypothetical dry runs based on the actual news

---

[2]*Editors' note:* "In a long and detailed brief he prepared for presentation to the corporate brass and the network's reluctant affiliates, Leiser wrote that 'we see it as an entirely new kind of broadcast with a new feeling and a new scope.' The new format, he added, would go beyond the 'compressed, tabloid treatment' of the fifteen-minute program and present 'more news of more kinds, and we will give that news more meaning.' Leiser asserted that 'we will not only have a front-of-the-book, we will have a back-of-the-book as well.'" Gary Paul Gates, *Air Time: The Inside Story of CBS News* (New York: Harper and Row, 1978), p. 139.

flow of sample days. The half-hour news was his more than anybody else's besides Walter Cronkite's.

It is in the nature of television network scheduling that when the News Division gets something, it usually has to give up something. To get the half-hour news, we had to give up *Eyewitness to History*, a fine and valuable series which I continually and unsuccessfully tried for the next seventeen years to restore to the television network schedule. *Eyewitness* was a half-hour prime-time series, broadcast each Friday, reporting the week's major story in greater depth and cohesion than was possible through the bits and pieces scattered over the week's evening news broadcasts. It was our equivalent of a newsmagazine's cover story. Anchored by Charles Collingwood, produced by Les Midgley, it was a distinguished series. Trading *Eyewitness* for the half-hour news was a high price to pay, but the half-hour news was so important we had to pay it.

On Monday, September 2, 1963, at 6:30 P.M. EST, the first network half-hour evening news was broadcast. To mark the occasion, that first broadcast included a Cronkite interview of President John F. Kennedy, on the lawn of the Kennedy compound in Hyannis, Massachusetts. It was more than a celebratory interview. It was a substantive one, focusing on Vietnam, with the president already trying to distance himself and this country from the war. He stated that it was not our war but a war for the South Vietnamese to win or lose.

One week later, NBC, with Huntley-Brinkley, also went to a half hour. NBC's evening news had been, like ours, only fifteen minutes long. NBC's initial half-hour broadcast also included a special interview with the president. Somehow, NBC's imaginative press relations people, taking advantage of what was then an often supine and ingenuous trade and general press, managed to create the public impression that NBC had pioneered the half-hour news and that all we at CBS News did was to proceed under forced draft after NBC had made the decision, so that we could beat NBC to air by a few days. In fact, it was the other way around.

I minded that only a little. The important thing was that we finally did it; we doubled our time for the network evening news. It was not until several years later that ABC, then a struggling third commercial network, finally went to a half-hour evening news.

It is also part of mythology that CBS's real motive for expanding to a half hour was to close the continuing ratings gap between it and NBC's Huntley-Brinkley news. I cannot exclude the possibility that it was a factor which persuaded some affiliates, and some of my brethren at the CBS Television Network, and maybe even some in senior management, that our going to a half hour would do the trick. But that was not my motive—for two strong reasons.

First, I felt—passionately—that fifteen minutes was inadequate time for us to do the job of informing the public in a way that a democracy had a right to expect us to do. Expanding the news to a half hour was a matter of principle. Second was a matter of realism: It would have been just plain dumb to expect that expanding our news to a half hour would carry us ahead of NBC in the ratings. Dumb because it was obvious that NBC, to maintain its then leading position in network news, had to expand as soon as we did. In fact, it took five years, until 1967, before "Uncle Walter," as he came to be known, won the ratings war and the *CBS Evening News* became the nation's dominant news broadcast.

• • •

Whether it was Cronkite on CBS or Huntley and Brinkley on NBC, the half-hour network news had profound significance. The late Theodore White has said that because of the expansion, the American political process was revolutionized, not only in respect of choice of candidates and campaigning but in respect of the political party structure itself. Others have written that it played an important role in major societal changes.

It is difficult to be certain of direct causal connections between any aspect of television programming, including news broadcasting, and political or societal events and movements. But it is clear that the half-hour news had significance vastly beyond the addition of fifteen minutes. Network evening news became not just twice as long and twice as important; it was a quantum jump. Certainly, it immensely increased the public reliance on television news. Unfortunately, I would guess that it contributed to much of the public's mistaken belief that the half-hour network news was all that it needed to be informed about national and international news.

By hindsight, the news expansion came at a propitious time. The civil rights struggle; the Kennedy and Martin Luther King assassinations; the urban riots; Vietnam; Watergate and the first resignation in history of a president of the United States—all lay ahead. It is conventional wisdom that television news played a major role in all of these—certainly in Vietnam, the first "living-room war"; in civil rights; in Watergate. But unquestionably, whatever impact television news did have, it was greater because of the half-hour news. Television could not have reported these momentous events and political and societal movements as effectively as it did if network news had remained confined to fifteen minutes.

6

Cronkite and Sevareid

I believe that the most important lesson Eric Sevareid taught television journalists is that even in television in the beginning is the word. Only a very few television journalists today seem to accept that. . . . This new breed of producers are verbophobes—people who fear talking heads on television as the ultimate turnoff—and photophiles—people who lust for pictures at all costs. But only rarely is a picture worth a thousand words—if your cameras happen to be there at assassinations, ten-alarm fires, hurricanes, volcanoes blowing their tops. What Sevareid demonstrated night after night was that a couple of hundred words are worth a thousand pictures when the thoughts are those of a penetrating mind, accompanied by a brilliant ability to put those thoughts into just the right words.

—**Men's Club, Westport, Connecticut, October 15, 1992**

SOON AFTER THE INAUGURATION of the half-hour *CBS Evening News*, we made two more changes which defied convention. One was to appoint Walter Cronkite as managing editor—making him broadcasting's first anchor *and* managing editor. The other was to appoint Eric Sevareid as an analyst on the *Evening News*, giving up 10 percent of the broadcast to a "talking head." Both, I believe, contributed significantly to the ultimate success of the *CBS Evening News*.

Making Walter Cronkite managing editor stemmed from my conviction that an anchor must do more than provide lead-ins, lead-outs, and deliver the five minutes or so of "tell" stories.[1] I believed that the anchor should share major responsibility for the content of the entire broadcast: the choice and order of stories, the development of the stories, and their treatment. After all, to the viewing public, it was not the *CBS Evening News with Walter Cronkite*, its official name. Rather, it was the "Cronkite News"—or just plain "Cronkite"—as in "Did you see that story on Cronkite last evening?"

Of course, giving an anchor the role of managing editor would be disastrous foolishness if anchors were chosen because of their hairdo, or beauty, or pear-shaped tones, if for no other reason than that it is perpetrating something of a fraud on the viewer or listener who believes anchors know what they are talking about. News is too important to leave to actors, declaimers, or announcers, no matter how gorgeous. Sooner or later, their lack of journalistic skills will catch up with them and so will the public's perception of their credibility.

Cronkite was completely credible because he was a professional journalist. He was tough, passionately insistent on objectivity and fairness. Above all, he was always checking to make sure the facts were right. (He often used to insist that if wire-service copy was to be used, it first be checked for accuracy.) He was, in short, both a great reporter and a great editor. That is why he was the ideal person to try the radical notion of serving both as anchor and managing editor.

Within the news broadcasting profession, there was considerable skeptical eyebrow raising and giggling among the competition at what we had done. We were, they said, putting the monkeys in charge of the zoo. But I believe we made the right decision. Walter did not just drop in to the newsroom at midafternoon, read over the five or six minutes of script which he was to deliver, and then recite it on the broadcast.

Instead, most days, he was in by 9:00 or 9:30 in the morning, working the telephone to the bureaus and correspondents in the field, checking with his sources, reading the rolls of wire-service copy. He would meet with the producing staff to shape the lineups—the tentative list of stories for the evening's broadcast. As the day progressed, he reviewed stories as they came in, often questioning and checking facts, and then writing or rewriting his own script for the broadcast. The result was that the evening news became the joint product of the executive producer and Walter, the anchor and managing editor, where previously, it had been the executive producer who controlled the program. Public perception of responsibility, thus, was matched by the fact of responsibility.

Sometimes this dual responsibility caused a certain amount of tension between anchor and executive producer. But a strong anchor with

---

[1] "Tell" stories are the stories for which there is no film or tape, or no time for them, that are told on camera, usually with graphics, by the anchor.

exacting standards, which Walter had, working with a strong executive producer (and each one who occupied that position was), made for a stronger news broadcast. The tension was journalistically creative. Each was good discipline for the other.

• • •

Our second innovation was to appoint Eric Sevareid to provide analysis four times a week. His pieces were from two and a half to three minutes each. (Walter always wanted them shorter because he had to squeeze in so much important news; Eric often wanted a little more time because he had to squeeze in so much important thought.) Eric worked on them all day—researching, talking to his sources, writing, and polishing and buffing them until, with remarkable frequency, they shone. He was an artist among craftsmen. I owe a great debt to Eric, because by his work, he taught me what journalism should be— that there is no substitute for a thoughtful journalist on staff with a regular slot and whose last sentence of his piece cannot be predicted from his first sentence.

Eric was a veteran correspondent who had been hired by Ed Murrow during World War II. Some people write beautifully; some people think clearly and brilliantly. Few can do both. Eric was one of the few. He was ideally suited to do broadcast analyses. His only flaw was his tendency to feel ill. When Fred Friendly was president of CBS News and Eric begged off a Friendly assignment, Fred angrily told Eric that he was the worst hypochondriac that he, Fred, had ever met. Eric, his blue eyes wide, his voice soft, replied, "But Fred, even hypochondriacs get sick sometimes."

It wasn't anything as minor as occasional illnesses, real or otherwise, however, which led many of my colleagues in broadcast journalism to question our wisdom in devoting so much broadcast time each evening to Eric's analyses. After all, the scornful critics argued, this was television, and television was pictures. We did not decorate Eric's pieces with graphics, or maps, or pictures. It was just Eric sharing his excellent thoughts with us. For many in our business, that was a high crime—it was nothing, heaven forbid, but a talking head.

In television, we tend to be bemused by the business of pictures. But over and over again, at every opportunity, I reminded my colleagues that in journalism, words are of prime importance. This is a hard lesson for television journalism to learn. The result has been that the primary objective is to seek pictures rather than the essence of the story. Further, the words are written, both in content and timing, to fit the pictures, which gives the pictures even more control of the story. And in my mind, most damaging of all is the tendency to use pictures that have only remote relationship or relevance to the story.

I came to believe that too often pictures did not add to a story but subtracted from it. Unless the words and the pictures match, the frenzy for pictures is in fact counterproductive, diminishing understanding, blocking out the message. If the purpose of journalism is to transmit messages to permit understanding, our practice may sometimes be fatal.

Of course, there was no such problem with Eric Sevareid and his analyses. It was just Eric talking to the viewer at home. The only distractions were those which might arise in the kitchen or living room or wherever the viewer was. We did not make it harder for the viewer—or for Eric—by sending out distracting pictures at the source. I confess, however, that Eric's pieces may have been helped by a picture—the picture of Eric talking. As somebody wrote years later when Eric retired, many people believed that if God ever came to visit this planet, he would look a lot like Eric Sevareid.

• • •

Broadcasting is an imitative and derivative business. Success breeds imitation—never mind finding the elements that underlie the success and determining whether or not they can be replicated. Because of Huntley-Brinkley's success there was a theory that I should find a partner for Walter Cronkite. But I did not go to the double anchor for a number of reasons. The first and perhaps overriding one was that I felt that Huntley and Brinkley had a unique chemistry which could not be captured and repeated. David was David; Chet was Chet; and David and Chet together were something very special. It was not that there was magic in having two anchors. It was that there was magic in these two men.

In the early days of the fifteen-minute broadcast, there was limited time for the actual news. With the two anchors, after subtracting for commercials and lead-ins and lead-outs, and for passing the wand back and forth between them, what time was left had to be allocated almost completely to Huntley and Brinkley and divided between them with reasonable equality. Almost all the reporting had to be done through them if their styles, characters, and personalities were to be strongly established, as they had to be for the broadcast to work.

But this meant that in the fifteen-minute broadcast there was no time for the rest of NBC's correspondents, and there were some very good ones. In the long run, NBC ultimately paid for this. Possibly even more precious to a reporter than a salary increase is a byline, and broadcasting's equivalent of a byline is the reporter's appearance on air. The need to establish Huntley-Brinkley deprived many NBC reporters of their bylines. It was bad for morale. And important as anchors are, an anchor cannot be successful in the long run without a strong group of contributing reporters and producers.

I have always felt that the adverse effects of double anchors on NBC News were long lasting. It was never able to build up a strong corps of reporters with sound bench strength, as CBS News did from the outset—and as ABC News, under Roone Arledge, finally did beginning in the late 1970s.

The fact is that historically, for a news broadcast of a half hour in length (the considerations are quite different for a news broadcast which is an hour or longer), no double anchor has come close to matching Huntley-Brinkley's success.

When Huntley retired, NBC tried it with John Chancellor and Brinkley and then with Roger Mudd and Tom Brokaw. *ABC World News Tonight* abandoned Peter Jennings as sole anchor and replaced him with Harry Reasoner and Barbara Walters. When that proved catastrophic, however interesting, ABC tried triple anchors (nothing exceeds like excess) with Frank Reynolds in Washington, Max Robinson in Chicago, and Peter Jennings in London.

That just did not make sense to me. I had chosen Cronkite as the evening news anchor because he was simply the right person for the right place. A further reason for staying with the single anchor was that a double anchor, for all practical purposes, precludes the managing-editor concept, which, as I have noted, is valuable to a cohesive and sound news broadcast. It is not practical to have two managing editors, particularly if they are working in different cities.

Among the difficulties I had with double anchors, therefore, was the lack of logic which dictated the division of stories—a lack of logic which I suspected that, instinctively, the viewers would feel even if they never analyzed it. And that might well rob the news broadcast of its most precious ingredient—its credibility. The illogical batting back and forth between anchors would, I felt, cause the viewer to feel that we were playing games. Broadcast news cannot afford that.

And so, even though Huntley-Brinkley continued to dominate the ratings through the first half of the 1960s, I stayed with single-anchor broadcasts. It was not until 1982, almost two decades later, that both NBC and ABC abandoned multiple anchors in favor of single anchors—ABC with Peter Jennings and NBC with Tom Brokaw. Both broadcasts, I believe, were stronger as a result. And both moved toward the managing-editor concept.

7

Friendly Takes Over, Temporarily

There are limits beyond which good journalism cannot and should not go in pursuit of circulation, ratings, or credibility. Sometimes unpopularity and people's refusal to believe what we offer as truth can be badges of honor. That's why we still commemorate great and courageous editors like William Lloyd Garrison and Elijah Lovejoy.

—World Affairs Forum, January 10, 1988

COURTEOUS AND GENTLE AS ALWAYS, Frank Stanton did not tell me I was being fired when he called me upstairs to his office in February 1964. Frank said that policy matters at the corporate level, especially those involving Congress, which had always been hostile to the networks, had become so urgent that he needed me back to work with him.

When Stanton told me of my reassignment, I asked him to look me in the eye and tell me that this was his decision and nobody else's. He said it was. I asked him whether the real reason was that he wanted me back to work with him. He said it was.

I was skeptical. I knew that Bill Paley, as well as some affiliates, accustomed to being in first place, had become impatient that the *CBS Evening News* remained behind Huntley-Brinkley in the ratings. I had been head of the News Division for three years, and I had little to show for it. Douglas Edwards had been replaced with Walter Cronkite; we had expanded the evening news to a half hour—but so far as the Nielsen ratings were concerned, nothing had happened.

Fifteen years later, several years after Frank Stanton had retired and on the eve of my own mandatory retirement from CBS, I asked Frank again whether the decision to take me out of the News Division had really been his—and why. This time, he confirmed that the decision had not been his. Paley had concluded that the News Division was on dead center and that it needed bolder and more dynamic leadership.

Paley chose to replace me with Fred Friendly, the energetic and intense executive producer of *See It Now* and *CBS Reports*, who had worked closely and effectively with Ed Murrow. And indeed, if management was looking for boldness, energy, and dynamism, Fred was their man. He had, to use one of Fred's own favorite phrases, "fire in his belly." He worked, and spoke, from the gut. Fred, as one of his associates used to say, "never had a nervous breakdown, but he sure was a carrier."

To provide the leadership qualities which Paley decided I lacked, so the rumors went, Fred was offered the number two position in CBS News, as head of documentaries, among other things. According to reports of some of his *CBS Reports* producers, Fred returned to his office after the number two position had been offered to him and told his associates he was not inclined to accept—it had to be the presidency of CBS News or nothing. His producer associates recommended that he stick to that position. He did, and he replaced me.

When Fred delivered an inaugural talk to the CBS News staff, he told his CBS News associates, in his typically sweeping and flamboyant cadences, that I had succeeded in getting the time on the television network that CBS News needed to do its job and that, thenceforth, his focus would be the pursuit of excellence. I was grateful for the first part of his statement. As to the second half, I had thought that I had been persistent in that pursuit.

If Fred concluded that serving as my number two man would not work, he was right. Fred and I had had some run-ins during the three years of my presidency. He was often unenthusiastic if I made suggestions after prescreening *CBS Reports* and even threatened to resign unless I stopped insisting on changes.[1]

In addition, there were sharp contrasts in our style and approach to management. That difference was vividly, if bizarrely, illustrated when CBS management fulfilled one of my dreams and gave CBS News an hour every week of regularly scheduled prime time—from

---

[1]One day I wrote out an undated memorandum addressed to Fred and signed by me, stating that effective on the date of the memorandum, his resignation was thereby accepted. I put the memo in my desk drawer and told Fred that the next time he tried the resignation ploy, I would fill in the date of the memorandum and hand it to him. He never threatened me with resignation again, although in 1966, two years after he became president of CBS News, Fred's tactic backfired.

10:00 to 11:00 on Tuesday evenings. Naturally, some of those Tuesdays were to be occupied by Fred's *CBS Reports*.

Fred was only a part—although a highly autonomous part—of CBS News's Documentary Department. The Documentary—or Public Affairs—Department was headed by a brilliant, soft-spoken, innovative man named Jack Kiermaier, who had been responsible for some remarkable and off-the-beaten-path broadcasts.[2] I did not want Kiermaier and his documentary units to atrophy by disuse, and I thought that a weekly *CBS Reports* would be too much even for Fred's extraordinary energy and ability. So I insisted that Fred and Jack alternate Tuesdays.

Fred was unhappy with that notion. He was adamant that he would not share; I was adamant that he would. We had lunchtime meetings at Blair Clark's home in the Turtle Bay section of New York City, where we negotiated and we bargained. Finally, Fred and I struck a complicated agreement, and I reduced it to a written memorandum. To make sure that we understood each other and that the bargain would stick, I signed the memorandum and initialed each page, and I had Fred sign the memorandum and initial each page.

But as we approached the new season, it became apparent that Fred was planning on his programs for more than half the Tuesdays and that Jack Kiermaier was being squeezed out. I called Fred in and tossed the signed, initialed memorandum at him—the document had become known as the "Treaty of Turtle Bay." He waved it aside. "Agh," he said, "that's nothing; it's only in writing."[3]

I had a hard time understanding Fred; he had a hard time understanding me. Or maybe our problem was that each of us understood the other too well.

• • •

I was away from the News Division for two difficult years while Fred Friendly was president. Except for a few occasions, I had little to do with broadcast journalism, although I was still a news junkie and a

---

[2]Jack's work was, and remains, underrated and unsung; someday, a museum will hold a Kiermaier retrospective and his imaginative work will be recognized.

[3]Postscript to the Friendly-Kiermaier issue: Soon after Fred replaced me as president of CBS News, he fired Kiermaier. Jack became head of the noncommercial station Channel 13 (WNDT at that time) in New York City. When Fred, in turn, left CBS News in 1966, he became the television consultant to the Ford Foundation, which at that time was providing large grants to noncommercial television, including the New York City station. Fred, as a result, had very considerable influence over noncommercial television operations. Soon, Jack Kiermaier was no longer head of the New York station. Jack believes that he is the only person whom Fred Friendly fired from two different jobs in two entirely different organizations. Jack ultimately wound up back at CBS.

passionate booster for my former colleagues. There was one frustrating episode, however, involving Friendly and CBS News. It happened during the summer of 1964, a few days after the Republican Convention.

Walter Cronkite had been the CBS anchor at the convention; Huntley and Brinkley had anchored NBC's coverage. Most of the television critics had written that NBC's coverage was superior to CBS's, and NBC's ratings were ahead of CBS's by a large margin. A few days after the convention had ended, I was sitting in my office on the corporate floor of Black Rock when the door was flung open, followed immediately by Fred. Pale and agitated, he said, "I have to talk to you; I need your advice."

I was flattered. I closed the door and invited Fred to sit down. "No," he said, "not here"; he did not want anyone to interrupt or overhear us. He asked me to walk with him from Black Rock to the new CBS News headquarters on the West Side, near the Hudson River, on West 57th Street.[4]

As Fred and I walked northwest among the crowds of pedestrians, he told me that Paley and Stanton had been dissatisfied with the performance of CBS News at the Republican Convention. They had insisted, or strongly suggested, that Cronkite be replaced for the Democratic Convention, scheduled in a few weeks. Fred did not make it clear whether he had been given a command, but I believe he had. Bill Paley was a master of making what he wanted done perfectly clear, but he stopped just short of commanding it—there was a fine line, more symbolic than actually leaving the addressee much discretion. Fred asked me what he should do.

I told him that I could not answer until he told me what he wanted to do. Fred replied that what he wanted to do was irrelevant, it was Paley's candy store. I answered that there was nothing for me to advise him about if he felt that his views were irrelevant. If he was obliged to carry out whatever the orders (or strongly expressed wishes) were, that was that. If, on the other hand, he felt that it was still possible for him to make the decision, first he had to make up his own mind whether it was right to keep Cronkite as anchor or to replace him. If he thought Cronkite should not be removed, then he should resist management's suggestion. But first he had to make up his own mind.

---

[4]CBS had by then moved from 485 Madison Avenue to the stunning Saarinen-Stanton CBS office building known as "Black Rock," located at 52nd Street and Sixth Avenue. The design of the building was Stanton's; the gourmet restaurant on the ground floor of the building was Paley's—he used to drop in late many mornings to taste the soup.

This conversation took only a few blocks; we were less than halfway to West 57th Street, but Fred still insisted that I had it wrong, that how he felt was not the point, since it was Bill Paley's company. We were talking past each other, and since there was nothing further for us to talk about, I turned around and walked back to my office at Black Rock.

The next day, Fred and Bill Leonard, who was in charge of the campaign and election coverage, flew to the West Coast to tell Walter that he was to be replaced for the next—the Democratic—Convention. He was replaced by Roger Mudd and Bob Trout, who served as double anchors for the convention that year. Both were superb reporters. But once again, the delicacies of double anchors were painfully demonstrated. It just did not work; the ratings were even worse than they had been for the Republican Convention.

Although prodded by the press, Walter never said a word criticizing senior management or Friendly. It was a superhuman exercise in restraint and graciousness in the face of immense temptation. I know that he never forgot it. Walter went on about his business as anchor of the *Evening News*; but he never missed anchoring another convention until he retired as a regular correspondent in 1982.

• • •

In early 1966, there was a reorganization at CBS, which, in an indirect way, brought about the resignation of Fred Friendly.

For many years, CBS had operated through divisions—the Television Network Division, the Television Stations Division, the Radio Division, the News Division, the Records Division, and so forth. Each division had its own president, who reported directly to President Stanton and Chairman Paley. But these divisions had grown so large and CBS had diversified so widely that Paley and Stanton could no longer give each one the attention it needed. It was not practical for so many and such varied divisions to report directly to them.

The company, accordingly, was divided into umbrella groups—the CBS Broadcast Group was one—which combined all CBS broadcast activities. The broadcast divisions remained, each with its own president, but instead of reporting to Paley and Stanton, the division head now reported to the new Broadcast Group president, Jack Schneider. Schneider was young, but he was a veteran broadcaster who had come up through the sales ranks at the stations, and then had been the president of the CBS Television Network Division. Under the reorganization, Friendly was to report to Schneider. This was not a combination made in heaven.

In early 1966, the Senate Foreign Relations Committee began holding hearings on Vietnam—the first official public examination of the administration's Indochina policies. The television networks made their decisions about providing live coverage of the hearings based on the newsworthiness of particular witnesses. Live coverage meant that the regular daily network schedules, which consisted mainly of reruns of popular situation comedies in the mornings (such as *I Love Lucy*), a few game shows, and then soap operas, had to be preempted. Preemptions were costly for the network because advertising revenues were lost.

On February 4, 1966, at 8:30 A.M., both NBC and CBS began live coverage of the hearings and continued coverage for two full days. This set the stage for the crisis several days later involving coverage of the hearings on Thursday, February 10. The witness on that day was former ambassador and expert on U.S.-USSR relations, George Kennan. On the days following Kennan, other witnesses, including General Maxwell Taylor and Secretary of State Dean Rusk, were also scheduled to testify.

In a memo, Friendly strongly recommended to Schneider that there be full live coverage of the Kennan testimony, as well as the Taylor and Rusk testimonies scheduled for the following week. His memorandum concluded that while he was aware of the financial burden that would be placed on the CBS Television Network, "I consider these hearings as a matter of conscience for this company and this executive. This is public service in the most basic sense. I am sure you will agree."

Fred was always a passionate advocate. And often, he did not fit his strategy to his particular target. In this case, his memorandum gave the appearance of talking—or shouting—down to his new president. Jack Schneider, who had seen so much of the profitable daytime schedule preempted in recent days, did not enjoy being lectured to on the importance of news and the public obligations of CBS, all of which he already thoroughly appreciated. The "I'm-sure-you-will-agree" climax of Fred's eloquent memorandum to Jack may have looked more like a challenge. Jack did not agree, and he promptly proved Fred was mistaken.

Only NBC News covered the Kennan testimony live, while the CBS Television Network broadcast its regular morning situation comedy reruns, including what seems to have settled in television history as the seventeenth rerun of *I Love Lucy*. Schneider defended his decision on the ground that the "opinion makers," those who would have a particular interest in the Kennan testimony and the burgeoning issue of Vietnam, were not at home, while the housewives who comprised the daytime audience would not be particularly interested anyway.

It was generally believed at the time of the controversy, and is now embedded in history, that Fred resigned in anger because his recommendation that Kennan's testimony be carried live was rejected. That was nice and clean-cut, simple and obvious—the good public service guys against the bad bottom-line guys. But it was more complicated than that. It is a reasonable guess that if Bill Paley, or even Frank Stanton, had rejected Fred's recommendation, Fred would have been angry, but that would have been the end of it. The real issue was less the substance of the decision than who decided it.

In an attempt to resolve the issue, Fred met with Schneider, then tried to reach Bill Paley, but Paley refused to intervene. Without Paley, Fred had to "work it out" with Stanton. According to Fred's later account, meeting with Stanton gave him no satisfaction; he would have to continue to report to Schneider.

Stanton's recollection is quite different. According to Frank, Fred and Frank met on a Friday to try to explore a reporting arrangement which might satisfy Friendly. They reached no conclusion and adjourned until the following Monday. During the meeting on Monday morning, Winnie Williams, Stanton's secretary, came into Stanton's office to tell him that Jack Gould, the *New York Times* television critic, was in the outer office and urgently wanted to talk to him. When Stanton stepped out to see Gould, Gould showed Stanton a long, detailed, and eloquent letter from Friendly. It was a letter of resignation, and Friendly had sent Gould a copy.

That, as Stanton later described, "blew it." He went back into his office and ended the meeting. Two hours later, Fred's lawyer came to see Stanton and told Stanton he wanted to continue to try to find a reporting arrangement satisfactory for both Stanton and Friendly. Stanton told him it was too late.

Fred, I am sure, did not really want to resign—as he later wrote; he loved the job. But the letter was out; it was too late—the point of no return had been passed. Friendly had used the resignation tactic once too often, and he was—and henceforth would forever more be—Fred Friendly, former president of CBS News.[5]

It was clear that questions of decisionmaking, scheduling, reporting, and reorganization unhappily converged on Friendly—and CBS senior management—simultaneously. The Kennan issue came up at the same time that the reorganization occurred, and there was no time for either Friendly or Schneider to learn how to live with the new situation.

---

[5]*Editors' note:* Fred W. Friendly died on March 3, 1998, at the age of eighty-two. He was recalled at a memorial service as a man who brought great integrity and courage to broadcast journalism, both as a producer and president of CBS News and as a prominent teacher at Columbia University's Graduate School of Journalism. *New York Times*, April 24, 1998.

• • •

On February 16, 1966, the day Fred Friendly's resignation was announced, Stanton called me to his office and asked me whether I wanted to return as president of the CBS News Division. Of course, he already knew what my answer would be.

Jack Schneider and I went to Broadcast Center to meet with CBS News personnel. Arrangements were made to carry our remarks to the Washington Bureau by closed-circuit radio. Jack made the announcement that I was returning; I have no recollection of what I said, but I am sure that I told my news colleagues how glad I was to be back.

The reception was cordial. I learned, long afterward, that Walter Cronkite and Eric Sevareid had gone to Black Rock to meet with Stanton and urge him to reappoint me News president; and that Charles Kuralt was particularly helpful in easing my return, telling the news staff that after the Friendly turmoil, my return was welcome and constructive. By the afternoon of February 16, I was in my new office at Broadcast Center.

I was, of course, delighted to come back. But at the outset, I returned as acting president, not as president of the CBS News Division. I insisted on this because I was concerned about an important matter with potential adverse effects on how effectively I could serve as the head of News: It was the troublesome problem of the relationship between Bill Paley and Frank Stanton.

Paley and Stanton were two men of immense contrasts: Frank—orderly, precise, methodical, cerebral—by choice, a loner; Bill—a showman, an extraordinary salesman, a bold gambler. Paley was, when he chose to be, warm and charming, where Stanton was perceived to be cold and aloof. In a way they complemented each other, and it could have been, it should have been, a perfect fit.

For a while, it was. Paley went off to World War II, working with General Eisenhower as a colonel in Eisenhower's European headquarters. After the war, Paley did not devote as much time or energy to CBS as he had before he left, yet this was a period of great CBS growth and increasing reputation. Stanton became president of CBS in 1946 and was universally recognized as the industry leader and statesman because of his frequent appearances in Washington. People at CBS believed that Bill Paley came to feel uncomfortable about Frank Stanton's prominent role. When, eventually, Paley finally came back to CBS full-time, there was tension—palpable to many of us—between them.

The climax came in 1966 when Paley reached sixty-five—the mandatory retirement age at CBS. Paley and Stanton had earlier agreed that when Paley retired, Stanton would succeed him as chief executive officer—a move Stanton had long looked forward to. As Paley's sixty-fifth birthday arrived, all that remained for the succession was the formal approval of the agreement at a meeting of the Board of Directors on February 9.

On the day of this meeting all the board members, including Frank Stanton, were at their places in the boardroom—all except Paley. After a delay, Stanton's secretary finally came into the boardroom and whispered to him—he left the room. We waited longer. At last, both Paley and Stanton came in. Stanton was even paler than usual, and he was flushed in the back of his neck, as happened when he was very angry. The board meeting proceeded. Nothing was said about the new arrangement.

As soon as I could after the meeting, I asked Frank what had happened. He told me that Paley could not go through with his resignation.

What had happened was that Stanton had insisted on a new contract before the change in positions was made. (He felt that an earlier contract had not been observed.) But Paley had done nothing to arrange a new contract or even to discuss a new salary. He told Stanton that he would take care of that later. When Stanton insisted on a new contract first, the deal was off. Paley never came back to the question of a new contract, and Stanton never became CBS's CEO.

The Paley-Stanton schism widened and deepened as a result of this episode. But this was only a dramatic measure of the uneasy relationship which permeated the company. I had felt it in my term as News president in 1961 to 1964—and before. Particularly when I was fired in 1964, I felt that I was caught in the middle between these two extraordinary and talented men. Life was too short, and running the News Division was complicated and exacting enough without adding the pervasive context of the Paley-Stanton problem.

For this reason, and joyful as I was to have a second chance at the presidency, I agreed to Stanton's offer on a temporary basis only. Friendly's departure was sudden; it left a puzzled, worried, and headless News Division. The void had to be filled quickly, but I did not want the job on a permanent basis until Paley and Stanton had worked out a more satisfactory modus vivendi between them.

By mid-April 1966, Stanton, concerned that my title as "acting" president had caused confusion and uncertainty within the News Division, assured me that they had. My associates were not quite sure where I stood. Was I a temporary visitor, a lame duck, while senior management looked for someone else? I also badly wanted to believe that the Stanton-Paley problem had been solved, and so I believed it was—more or less.[6] The "acting" was dropped, and I officially succeeded Fred Friendly, the man I had preceded, as president of CBS News.

On returning to CBS News, I found things pretty much as I had left them just two years before. Blair Clark was gone as vice president of News, replaced by Gordon Manning. Gordon, who had been editor at *Newsweek* magazine, had a hundred ideas a week, and he never gave up trying to do the impossible. Bill Leonard, steady, professional, witty, who had spent his entire adult life in broadcast journalism, was still vice president of political coverage and documentaries. David Klinger, a uniquely patient, organized, prudent, and soft-spoken man, was vice president of business affairs—and an associate on whom I could always rely for special assignments. The more complicated and difficult the assignments were, the more he thrived on them, and the more I could be sure that there were no t's uncrossed, no i's undotted. It was a strong management team on whom I could and did rely—and, they were fun to work with.

There had been few other changes in CBS News personnel. Pretty much the same correspondents, producers, editors, and writers who had carried me the first three years were still there; still ready, willing, and able to carry me again, as indeed they did for thirteen more years.

Although Friendly wrote in his book *Due to Circumstances Beyond My Control* that in the final days before his departure, Paley told him that CBS News "was back in first place," I found that the ratings of the *CBS Evening News with Walter Cronkite* were still behind Huntley-Brinkley, although the gap had narrowed during 1965. Throughout 1966 and 1967, the ratings were virtually equal, although by the third quarter of 1967, the ratings for the *CBS Evening News* had begun to edge ahead. Its clear ratings dominance emerged in 1968, and remained, even after Cronkite retired in 1982.

---

[6]It was not until 1982, long after Stanton had retired from CBS and after Paley had retired as chief executive officer and chairman of the board, that the breach between Paley and Stanton was finally healed. Paley made the first gesture when he arranged for CBS to contribute a half-million dollars—to be matched by funds raised from other sources—to establish a Frank Stanton Chair on broadcasting and the First Amendment at Harvard's Kennedy School of Government. (Stanton was a Harvard overseer and the chairman of the Kennedy School's Visiting Committee.) I had rarely seen Frank Stanton visibly excited, but when we had lunch, right after the chair had been announced, he was both excited and pleased.

8

The True Story of
60 Minutes

*I have a singularly undistinguished track record in divining
the future. In 1964, I bet $100 that Barry Goldwater would be
the next president. In 1963 and again in 1966, when two of my
CBS News colleagues proposed a new type of news broadcast
series—a prime-time hour-long informational news magazine
called 60 Minutes—I turned them down; I told them it would
never work.*

—**Benton Lecture, University of Chicago, March 3, 1988**

IT IS TRUE THAT THE HALF-HOUR *CBS Evening News*, the regular
Eric Sevareid analyses, and *60 Minutes* all were begun while I was
president of CBS News. Yes, they all happened on my watch. But *60
Minutes* happened more in spite of me than because of me, and the
spectacular success it attained was not what I had contemplated at all.

• • •

The story of *60 Minutes* began in 1963 during my first term as president. One day, Bill Leonard, our vice president for documentaries, and
Don Hewitt,[1] one of our most energetic and innovative producers,

---

[1]Hewitt, a journalist-showman, did not just give instructions in a control room, he
conducted the *1812 Overture* there, complete with sweeping gestures and his own
sound effects of cannons and fireworks. *Editors' note:* Hewitt is still the executive producer of *60 Minutes*, and Mike Wallace still anchors the program with four additional
coanchors.

dropped in to see me. Bill told me that Don had a great idea for a new series. We have, they explained, documentaries—the broadcast equivalent of a book. We have the evening news broadcasts—the broadcast counterpart of a newspaper. But we had no counterpart of a magazine, and that was what they were proposing. They even had a name for it: We would call it *60 Minutes*.

Many stories, they explained, were too important and complex to be dealt with in the minute and a half or two minutes available on the evening news but still did not need a full hour—the customary documentary length. In fact, Don and Bill pointed out, some of our documentaries would be better if they did not have to be padded to fill an hour. There was precedent: Some of the earlier Ed Murrow *See It Now* broadcasts dealt with several subjects.

Although Bill and Don made a persuasive and passionate pitch, I was not buying. I told them I thought that viewers were too accustomed to the documentary and hard news forms; that they would not like being jerked from one subject to another. And each of the three or four or five segments would have to be compelling or else the viewer would abandon the channel as soon as one segment did not grip them.

Printed magazines, I pointed out, did not have that problem: A magazine reader almost never reads a magazine from beginning to the end, reading every word in between. The reader picks and chooses, and if a story is skipped, that does not mean that the rest of the magazine is lost to the reader as a broadcast would be lost to the viewer.

Those were arguments with a certain amount of sense. But decades later, I now confess that they were only part of the reason for my negative answer. What really turned me off was the prospect of a 50 percent increase in the internecine warfare between the hard news and the public affairs/documentary departments of the News Division. Each tended to regard the other as not quite respectable or "serious." Each fought the other for time on the air; for available producers, writers, editors, and correspondents; and each laid immediate claim to a story idea the minute it was a gleam in anybody's eye.

I had a hard enough time trying to bring cohesion and unity to the News Division. I did not relish the prospect of a third unit—the magazine people—fighting for turf, personnel, and news subjects, leaving me one more gung ho gang whose claims I would have to mediate. I had my hands full trying to figure out a way to beat out Huntley-Brinkley. Coping with Don Hewitt and the gaggle of tigers with whom he would inevitably surround himself, while fending off Cronkite and Friendly, was just too much for me.

I told Don and Bill that they had a lousy idea and it would never work. For such ignoble reasons, I delayed *60 Minutes* by several years.

In all candor, I cannot claim that this was my only colossal mistake as president of CBS News. But in the case of *60 Minutes*, as it turned out, I had another chance. Not very graciously, or even sensibly, I seized it.

•   •   •

There are two versions told by Leonard and Hewitt—and by me, for that matter—of how I came, in 1966 after I returned as president, to reverse my 1963 decision and give *60 Minutes* a green light. This is one of those circumstances where the passage of time makes me uncertain how much of the versions we tell are apocryphal or whether they—or one of the versions, anyway—were rooted in fact.

The first version goes like this. Very shortly after I came back to the News Division in February 1966, Hewitt and Leonard laid siege again, pressing for my approval. I continued to be reluctant, expressing doubt that it would work. Finally (and this is the version Leonard likes to tell), Bill, in exasperation, said, "Dick, you sound just like Fred Friendly. Fred said the same things you're saying when he turned down the idea." I am alleged to have replied, "Fred said 'No' to *60 Minutes*? OK, then, let's go ahead."

If Fred did reject the idea of *60 Minutes*, he may have had sound reasons. As executive producer of the landmark *See It Now* and *CBS Reports*, he was widely regarded as the greatest of contemporary documentarians. To one whose lifeblood had gone into full-length documentaries, a collection of fifteen- or eighteen-minute segments (especially if orchestrated by maestro Hewitt, for whom Fred had no great affection) may have appeared a trifle frivolous.

Worse yet, management over at Black Rock would probably follow its usual course of extracting a price in exchange for approving the insertion of *60 Minutes* into the network schedule. The inevitable price might well be a diminution of the number of *CBS Reports* and other full-length documentaries. If that was a basis for Fred's negative response to Don and Bill, he was prescient. Cutting down on documentaries was just what ultimately happened—permanently, it appears.

This is the second version. Don and Bill knew that while other people's weaknesses might be for fine wine, or great martinis, or gorgeous and companionable women, I was impervious to any such ordinary temptations. What I liked was desserts: rich, gooey, and all chocolate. At our regular News Division management luncheons in the private dining room at Broadcast Center, I would often collect—and eat—all the desserts which my associates had the good sense to decline.

Wise strategists that they were, so the story goes, Don and Bill took me out to lunch at an expensive restaurant and arranged for my meal to be placed on the table before we arrived. The meal awaiting me consisted entirely of desserts, mostly chocolate ones. As I worked my way through this meal fit for the gods, Bill and Don went to work on me. My reluctance finally overcome, supposedly I said, over the remains of the last dessert, "OK, let's give it a try."

Actually, the restaurant part is true, but I have persuaded myself that the inauguration of *60 Minutes* didn't really turn on my weakness for chocolate desserts or my competitiveness with Fred Friendly. I prefer to think it was due to my conviction that an essential component of a news division president's proper management style is that he not impose his own ideas on his associates but let them try whatever they thought was right and about which they were enthusiastic. I always tried to remind myself that the odds were good that they were right, and I was wrong; that they were entitled to give their ideas a try. Which is just what they did.

• • •

Once I had given the green light for *60 Minutes*, I put my initial doubts behind me and pushed for its success as hard as I knew how. I realized that we were engaging in a pioneering effort—much was at stake. As the time for the first *60 Minutes* broadcast grew closer, I became increasingly nervous about what seemed to be Don's and Bill's lack of planning. Early in 1968, I wrote Bill a critical memo deploring what I saw as the inchoate state of the planned series. The concept, I insisted, had not been crystallized.

It was my idea that the entire CBS News organization would contribute to *60 Minutes* and the pieces would come from correspondents who had stories that could not be properly reported in two or three minutes on the *Evening News*. These would be supplemented by stories from the documentary unit when its people working on full-length documentaries thought the subject matter could better be handled in fifteen or twenty minutes. Since, as I visualized it, the anchor would only introduce and lead out each segment, and perhaps add a small essay at the end, I saw no reason to have more than a single anchor who, it was planned, would be Harry Reasoner.

The suggestion that there be a double anchor—Mike Wallace added to Harry Reasoner—was all wrong. There was no reason for a double anchor—what was each one supposed to do? Also, Wallace and Reasoner were not a good combination—the "chemistry" was not right. Above all, since all CBS News correspondents were supposed to be contributing to *60 Minutes* from their existing beats, I thought Don Hewitt should just build up a small producing and editing staff. I most certainly did not want a separate *60 Minutes* enclave, a large separate principality devoting itself solely to the series.

Bill and Don, thank goodness, patted me on the head, said, "There, there; we know what we're doing, wait and see," and went their own way. They were right; I was wrong. If my concept had prevailed, it would have failed, just as some of the later television magazine efforts, using my concept rather than Don's and Bill's, failed.

With my concept the cohesion, the unique character which marked *60 Minutes*, would have been absent. It had to have its own pair, or trio, or quartet, or quintet of reporter-anchors. It had to have its own group of producers and editors. It could not depend on whatever others within the organization happened to have the time and appetite to produce. What I was expecting was the equivalent of having the regular staff of the *New York Times* turn out the Sunday *New York Times Magazine*. So the only credit that I can claim for the ultimate success of *60 Minutes* is that I did not cut it off at the pass in the first place and that I did not insist on my mistaken ideas about what it should be.

• • •

In 1968, with Mike Wallace and Harry Reasoner as its correspondents, Hewitt as its executive producer, and Leonard as its supervisor, *60 Minutes* went on the air on alternate Tuesdays at 10:00 P.M.

Either in content or in ratings, *60 Minutes* was not an overnight success. In its first years, it tended to be soft with rather trivial pieces, and the early reviews were lukewarm. Its ratings were low. We blamed the low ratings on the great popularity of the programs which NBC put on against *60 Minutes*. In the beginning, we had to admit to ourselves that the only hits for which *60 Minutes* could claim credit were for the programs opposite it.

But as *60 Minutes* found its rhythm and its style and Wallace and Reasoner proved me absolutely wrong, I began a campaign to persuade Black Rock that a regular weekly schedule was the one thing which would really cause *60 Minutes* to break through. I argued that being on every other week broke viewer habit and that *60 Minutes* would be more successful if it were on the schedule at the same time every week.

It did finally become a weekly series on Sundays at 6:00 P.M.—not exactly in prime time, but close. But there were problems here, too. First, Sunday at 6:00 P.M. is not a very desirable time period. During much of the spring and fall and all of the summer when the nation is on daylight saving time, many people are not at home at 6:00 on Sunday evenings watching television.

Second was the problem of professional football—the season stretched from late summer to January, and an inordinate number of broadcast games started at 4:00 P.M. EST. And even when professional football was over for the season, the CBS Sports Division would schedule golf, basketball, tennis, or some other sport which spilled over into *60 Minutes*'s time period or eliminated it altogether.

Obviously then, when it began as a weekly series on Sundays at 6:00 P.M., *60 Minutes* was struggling under a variety of handicaps, but it was resilient. Although its ratings were still marginal, it showed considerable signs of life.

I was the Oliver Twist at CBS—always taking my plate across town to Black Rock asking for more. And so I began nagging to move *60 Minutes* to the 7:00 P.M. time period on Sundays. This would not only relieve us of the sports overrun problems most of the time but would also give us an hour when more people were watching television, especially during daylight saving time. I begged; I cajoled; I invented all sorts of arguments.

Our break came in October 1975. As the new season began, the networks were required to devote Sundays from 7:00 to 8:00 P.M. either to "family hour" or to public affairs programs. But low ratings in this time period began to suggest that adults were rejecting the programming in the required family hour.

In a memorandum, I pointed out that the low ratings CBS received for Sundays evenings at 7:00 must be due in part to the unpopularity of *Three for the Road*, the program which then occupied the 7:00 to 8:00 time period. I concluded tentatively:

> The question which occurs to me and which no doubt has already occurred to you is whether . . . there is a sizable adult potential in the Sunday 7 to 8 P.M. period that is not now being reached, and whether, conversely, the ABC and NBC programs in that time period have not already pretty well captured the nonadult viewers. If the answers to these questions are affirmative, it might indicate that *60 Minutes*, with its track record of adult attraction, is just what the doctor ordered to bring in, or bring back, the adult audience not now being served in that time period. Just asking.

Programming chief Oscar Katz came to our rescue and shocked our colleagues by agreeing that *60 Minutes* might do reasonably well at 7:00 P.M. Jack Schneider leaned toward Katz's optimism: He felt that as an alternative to Disney on NBC and *Swiss Family Robinson* on ABC, *60 Minutes* might well go higher than its projected rating.

It did. Nobody—not Don Hewitt, not Bill Leonard, not I—dreamed how much higher it would go, almost immediately. And since then it has consistently been among the five most popular network series on television. In some seasons, it has been the highest rated of all program series. No series out of a network News Division had ever done any such thing. And it was commonly believed that the huge ratings of *60 Minutes* were responsible for the high ratings of the rest of the entertainment programs on the CBS schedule on Sunday night. This was often referred to as CBS's "blockbuster night," without which, it was said, CBS would not have maintained its prime-time domination for so long.

Good luck, a fine program, and patience, it turned out, can work wonders. Patience is the key. It took a long time from the beginning of *60 Minutes* in 1968 to its spectacular breakthrough eight years later. In today's frenetic climate, it is reasonable to speculate that *60 Minutes* would never have been kept on long enough to become the enormous success that it did, at last, in 1976.

• • •

The success of *60 Minutes* had a number of far-reaching consequences. The most immediate in 1975 was that it saved the News Division's budget in the nick of time.

It had always been a basic—and for us, wonderful—policy, established by Bill Paley, and consistently observed by him and Frank Stanton, that while all other CBS divisions (with the possible exception of the CBS Laboratories Division, which engaged in research) were expected to be profit makers, the News Division was not. The News Division's budget consisted solely of its expenditures.

I assume that the financial measurement standards now applied by CBS corporate management are much more stringent. Indeed, not only is the News Division as a whole expected to be profitable, but even more dangerous, each individual news series or group of broadcasts is expected to yield a profit, too. But in the good old days—including the mid-1970s when Arthur R. Taylor was president—the way I have described it was still the way it was.

Late in 1975, when we submitted our proposed budget for 1976, it showed a deficit of more than $15 million for the news operation for the coming year. Reluctantly, and somewhat apologetically, I thought, Taylor told me that although he believed news was the most important part of CBS broadcast operations and while he entirely agreed that the News Division should not be expected to make a profit, there were limits to the amount of money we could drain from the company.

Each year, he said, News was costing CBS more than the year before. Somewhere there had to be a cutoff point—a point where News had to tighten its purse. We had not reached that point yet, he said, but when we reached a deficit of $20 to $25 million, he would have to rein us in.

I could not quarrel with the principle that there had to be some limit on the amount News cost the corporation, given the fact that the method of estimating what we cost was pretty generous to us. But we never were faced with the limits which Arthur Taylor set, because the spectacular success of the very profitable *60 Minutes* made all that academic.

What made *60 Minutes* such a remarkable business phenomenon in network television was its combination of top ratings and low costs. In the mid-1980s, the average costs of a single hour of an entertainment series approached $1 million. But programs produced by network news divisions—whether hard news, news specials, documentaries, or magazine-type programs—cost less than half of what entertainment programs of comparable length cost. As a result, *60 Minutes* was the most profitable program in the history of network television. Estimates of the program's annual profits are in the $60 to $70 million range—in some years that was around a quarter to a third of the total network profits, even in the days when the networks were very profitable.

The first remarkable consequence of *60 Minutes*, therefore, was its hugely beneficial economic impact on the News Division itself, because it deflected the serious budget cuts that threatened our effective operations. It had an equally beneficial profit impact on the CBS Television Network and CBS, Inc.

It is a cardinal principle in television programming that nothing succeeds like success: If a particular program is a hit, there will be dozens of attempts to clone it. Therefore, the second major consequence of the success of *60 Minutes* was a frustrating—and costly—ripple effect. Promptly, there came the clones.

NBC had already tried its first newsmagazine—*First Tuesday*—which, despite several tries, did not succeed. In the mid-1970s, after *60 Minutes* had become a hit, ABC added its weekly newsmagazine—*20/20*—broadcast on Thursday evenings, from 10:00 to 11:00. Transported by our own success, in 1977 we, too, tried a clone.

We called it *Who's Who*.[2] It did not work—or at least, it did not work well enough. We never found the magic, and *Who's Who*, to my great sadness, was canceled. Some of the toughest moments of my sixteen years with CBS News were those when I assembled the fine people responsible for *Who's Who* to tell them we were going off the air. Perhaps—we like to console ourselves with the thought—if it had been the less frenetic and impatient times which permitted the nur-

---

[2]*Editors' note: Who's Who* profiled celebrities and other well-known figures. Dan Rather was the host, and Charles Kuralt and Barbara Howar were the profilers. Edward Bliss Jr., *Now the News: The Story of Broadcast Journalism* (New York: Columbia University Press, 1991), p. 295.

turing and flowering of *60 Minutes*, *Who's Who*, too, might have found its rhythm and character. But that was not to be.

Besides rescuing CBS News from what might have been fatal budget cutbacks and from causing the spate of attempts by all three commercial networks to vainly clone it, ironically, perhaps the most profound consequence of the great financial success of *60 Minutes* was that it spoiled management. By 1976, CBS had a new breed of senior managers who came from the ranks of hard-nosed nonbroadcasting business enterprises. More absorbed in traditional bottom-line profits, they tended to dismiss the concept that a news division was not expected to be a profit center. They saw that idea as impractical and unbusinesslike, as just a rationalization of the belief—indeed the fact, until 1976—that the drain on profits from news was inevitable.

Then along came *60 Minutes*. If *60 Minutes* could make all that money, why not everything else in the News Division? The program raised expectations and suggested a new criterion for news organizations—profitability—which had not existed before. The corporate rules and demands of news were never the same.

•   •   •

I was never able to define exactly what the ingredients of *60 Minutes*'s success were. Perhaps the most common—and easiest—explanation was its "protected" time period. Indeed, in the beginning, *60 Minutes* was protected, as only public affairs programs and entertainment programs particularly suitable for children were permitted in the Sunday evening time slot. But as the years wore on and the time period became less and less "protected," the popularity of *60 Minutes* did not diminish no matter what the competition threw at it. Nor can the answer for its continued success be that *60 Minutes* became such an ingrained viewer habit that its longevity was guaranteed: Television audiences are known for their cyclical preferences, and a great hit one year can disappear the next.

The popularity of *60 Minutes* was also attributed to its lead-in—the National League football games. But the audience for *60 Minutes* did not depend on the caliber of, or the public excitement about, particular football games, nor were its ratings lower after the football season ended. In fact, in a large part of the country—in the Pacific time zone—*60 Minutes* did not immediately follow the game, which ended somewhere around 4:00 P.M. PST, yet its ratings were as high on the West Coast as they were in the East.

I must conclude that the success of *60 Minutes*, like that of Huntley-Brinkley and so many other creations and enterprises which succeed while others fail, was a product of happy, but elusive and mysterious, congeries of both tangible (like time period and competition) and intangible factors. Although program experts and market research specialists keep trying to predict what will succeed and what will fail (down to predicting the exact rating and share number), public response is unpredictable.

The fact is, we do not really know what makes a hit. And I take comfort that nobody has yet found a way to analyze the process, identify the factors and ingredients that make for success, and then create assured hits by computer. Although people will keep on trying, I hope they will never succeed.

Part Two

Outside Pressure: The Nixon Years

CBS Memorandum
From: Richard Salant
Re: News Judgments
Date: May 23, 1973

I suspect that you were somewhat grieved by reading the UPI story on the first page of the *New York Times* on Saturday about the statements which Mrs. [Martha] Mitchell had made on Friday in front of her apartment—statements highly critical of President Nixon's role in Watergate. The UPI story credited the interview to NBC News. I understand ABC had substantially the same material on its local news.

We did not broadcast this, although we had it on film, because [the producers] felt that Mrs. Mitchell was so obviously not in control of herself that it would have been unfair to have broadcast it—unfair both to Mrs. Mitchell and to the president. . . .

Whether or not I would have made the same decision, I am pleased and proud that our associates make judgments like these and are ready to sacrifice a rather sensational film clip for the sake of restraint and a nice sense of ethical fairness.

9

War Against the Media

Two of the most common propositions that we hear are that (1) television news is so immensely influential that it brainwashes the nation—everybody except you and me, because we are too smart for that; and (2) network television journalists are left-of-center liberal Democrats whose politics slant our reporting. The hitch is that these eternal truths—our pervasive power and our pervasive left-of-center bias—can't both be true. If they were, we'd be reminiscing about the administrations of Presidents Stevenson, Humphrey, McGovern, and Mondale. The fact is neither proposition is true—we're not biased, and our impact on people's minds is limited.

—World Affairs Forum, January 10, 1988

IF RICHARD NIXON HAD FOLLOWED my advice, I would not have written the following chapters. My advice came in a letter I wrote for *Esquire* magazine in October 1968 before that year's presidential election. *Esquire* had asked me, among others, to write letters of advice to the president-elect. As the presidential campaign was still going on, I did not know if my letter would be to Richard Nixon or Hubert Humphrey, so I addressed it to "Dear Mr. President-elect." The letters were published in the January 1969 issue of *Esquire* under the title "You Didn't Ask Us, Mr. President, But. . . ."

In my letter, I asked that the new president "be tolerant of us, for you will not be satisfied with the way we report you. Nobody ever is— least of all, presidents." My letter continued, "In the long run, all Americans will be better off with a minimum of muscled news management and a maximum effort of all the press to resist both management and seduction. Let us keep it a game and not a war."

I laid particular stress on the vulnerability of broadcast journalism; and I closed:

> Above all, protect us, protect the people's right to know, and protect the truth by not using the gratuitous fact that broadcasters are licensed to try to guide our hands and voices as we seek light in the darkness of the tunnel.
>
> Let us, Mr. President-elect, work together to restore tranquillity and tolerance. We must all accept the fact that government plans and programs—even government leaders—are expendable. A free press and the truth can never be.

My hopes, expressed in that letter, were never realized—Richard Nixon did not follow my advice. In fact, the new president embarked on a course of conduct precisely opposite from the course I had urged. What, historically, had been occasional, presidential spasms of exasperated loss of temper at the press became with Nixon a deliberate orchestrated White House campaign against it.

•   •   •

At the threshold I should emphasize that my own direct experiences with the Nixon White House were insulated and limited. I never met with Nixon when he was president. I met him just once, on the eve of his running in 1968. He was working with a New York City law firm, laying the groundwork for his comeback campaign. Bill Paley, Frank Stanton, and I met with him in a New York apartment, and he talked quietly about his life's crises and his past experiences. There was no mention of his planning to run for the presidency, but it was obvious he planned to do so, and the meeting was a minor part of that plan. It seemed to me that he just wanted to let us know that he was still around and that he really was a nice guy. The real Nixon, I came to learn, however, was not the Mr. Nice Guy of that 1967 chat.

We had every reason to expect that Nixon and his associates would be very conscious of television—how it treated him and how he could use it. Nixon knew that television was partially responsible for President Lyndon Johnson's "credibility gap," and it was Johnson's inability to gain public support for the war in Vietnam that caused him not to seek reelection. Nixon was determined that the press, including television, would be so managed that no such fate would overtake him. Also, television's coverage of the 1968 Democratic Convention in Chicago, with its demonstrations, riots, and disarray, left ineradicable scars on Hubert Humphrey's campaign for the presidency. Some observers thought it was the negative impression of the convention that allowed Nixon to win the election.

We knew, then, that Nixon would be very conscious of television, but we did not realize the lengths to which he was willing to go to coerce and control it.

• • •

In order to recount what actions the administration took, it is necessary to fast-forward from the beginning of Nixon's presidency in 1969, to 1973 and 1974 when Senator Sam Ervin's committee investigated Watergate. It was during these investigations that White House memos, as well as the transcripts of Nixon's tapes, were made public. The memos and tapes finally provided the context for all the individual episodes of press intimidation which occurred during the Nixon years.

They also established that Walter Cronkite was right when in a speech on May 17, 1971—several years before we learned of the transcripts and the memoranda—he said, "Many of us see a clear indication on the part of this administration of a grand conspiracy to destroy the press." He also said, "The evidence today buttresses the suspicion that the administration has . . . conceived, planned, orchestrated, and is now conducting a program to reduce the effectiveness of a free press, and its prime target is television."

At the time, when I read Cronkite's speech, I thought that he was being a little paranoid. I was unwilling to believe that a president of the United States would embark on any such course; I was ready to assume that the events of the early Nixon years were just more of the same old presidential criticism of the press which had marked our nation's entire history.

As usual, Walter proved to be right. The only thing he was wrong about was his qualification that his charges could not be proven "short of documents which probably do not exist." This was understandable, since nobody in his right mind would have imagined that there were all those White House tapes and memoranda. But the documents *did* exist, and the congressional Watergate hearings put them in the public record.

As the Senate Committee began its Watergate investigation in 1973, a number of press-related documents surfaced. For example, one was an important memo written in 1969 to H. R. Haldeman from Jeb Magruder, special assistant to the president, which suggested ways the Nixon administration could orchestrate press coverage. Magruder wrote that the administration should not be "unwilling to use the power at hand to achieve our long-term goal, which is eight years of Republican administration."

Referring to "unfair coverage," Magruder urged the administration to use a broad approach "to get to this unfair coverage in such a way that we make major impact on a basis which the networks, newspapers, and Congress will react to and begin to look at things somewhat differently."

He made five proposals in the memo. The first was to "begin an official monitoring system 'of network news' through the FCC as soon as Dean Burch is officially on board as chairman." With such FCC monitoring, Magruder wrote, "we then have legitimate and legal rights to go to the networks, etc., and make official complaints from the FCC."

Magruder's second proposal was to "utilize the antitrust division to investigate various media relating to antitrust violations. Even the threat of antitrust action I think would be effective in changing their views."

Third, Magruder proposed "utilizing the Internal Revenue Service as a method to look into the various organizations that we are most concerned about. Just a threat of a [sic] IRS investigation will probably turn their approach."

Fourth, "Begin to show favorites within the media."

And fifth, "Utilize Republican National Committee for major letter-writing efforts of both a class nature and a quantity nature. . . . I think that by effective letter writing and telegrams we will accomplish our objective rather than again just a shotgun approach to . . . one specific news broadcaster because of various comments."

A second document example was a memorandum, dated February 4, 1970, and stamped "High Priority," from Haldeman to Magruder. It instructed Magruder to mobilize "the Silent Majority" to "pound the magazines and the networks" concerning Vietnam. Haldeman told Magruder to "concentrate this on the few places that count, which would be NBC, *Time*, *Newsweek*, and *Life*, the *New York Times*, and the *Washington Post*.[1] Sure enough, a group calling itself the "Silent Majority" picketed one of the networks.

Proposals to plant columns with specific named sympathetic conservative columnists were suggested; a number of columns by those named duly appeared. In other memos, Jeb Magruder proposed a letter-writing campaign to editors, complete with twelve model letters. I suspect that I received some of them—the models looked familiar after I saw them in the White House memoranda. This, presumably, was the public mood to which Agnew had insisted we be "responsive."

---

[1]Haldeman made no mention of CBS—he knew how to hurt.

Beyond the memos and transcripts, there was another expression of the administration's state of mind that ultimately came to light—the ruminations of Frank Shakespeare, Nixon's director of the United States Information Agency. An articulate, intelligent, dedicated conservative, Shakespeare was a former CBS television executive.

He had frequently and publicly expressed concern that most journalists, and especially network journalists, were liberals. His remedy involved subjecting journalists to a political litmus test. Shakespeare proposed that news organizations balance their staffs by affirmatively hiring conservative journalists.

When Joe McGinnis's book *The Selling of the President 1968* was published, we learned that Shakespeare had recounted a "fantasy" to McGinnis, who wrote that Shakespeare had said to him:

> Now listen to this, here's what I thought I'd do. I thought I'd go to Walter Scott (then NBC's board chairman)—this would be in private, of course, just the two of us in his office—and say here are the instances . . . where we feel you've been guilty of bias in your coverage of Nixon. We are going to monitor every minute of your broadcast news, and if this kind of bias continues, and if we are elected, then you just might find yourself in Washington next year answering a few questions. And you just might find yourself having a little trouble getting your licenses renewed.

Shakespeare, reported McGinnis, paused, smiled, and said, "I'm not going to do it because I'm afraid of the reaction. The press would band together and clobber us. But goddammit, I'd love to."

Shakespeare, I assume, never paid his "fantasy" call on Scott. But Charles Colson did act out the fantasy in a call on Frank Stanton in 1972. A memo from Colson on September 25, 1970, made clear that his purpose at such meetings was to threaten and intimidate. "They are very much afraid of us," he reported to Haldeman.

Stanton swore in his 1974 affidavit, "I met . . . with Mr. Colson on September 15, 1972, at which time he showed me a series of memoranda surveying CBS News on a week-to-week basis which he claimed demonstrated bias in reporting." And, Stanton swore, two months later, just after Nixon's reelection, "Mr. Colson called me on the telephone and said in substance that unless CBS substantially changed its news treatment of the Nixon administration, things will get much worse for CBS." He also said, in substance, since you didn't play ball during the campaign . . . we'll bring you to your knees in Wall Street and on Madison Avenue.[2]

---

[2]Neither William Paley nor Frank Stanton, following their usual policy of insulating us from pressures which the government sought to put on them, told me about these visits. I learned of it only when Colson's memo became part of the Watergate hearings.

It is against this background of White House memoranda, of tapes, and of Nixon advisers' preelection "fantasies" that the Nixon administration's threats, attempts to control the news, and actions against CBS must be viewed. They were not isolated and individual episodes. They were part of a plan, a "conspiracy," as Cronkite had accurately called it, that was led from the Oval Office.

So we go back to the beginning of the Nixon years.

• • •

The administration's serious campaign against the press began— very loudly and with lasting reverberation—during Nixon's first year as president. The shot that was heard, at least around the broadcasting world, was Vice President Agnew's speech given at a regional Republican Party meeting in Des Moines on November 13, 1969.

I vividly recall the afternoon before Agnew's speech. I was across town at CBS headquarters for a meeting. It was 3:00 in the afternoon when somebody brought in an advance text of the speech, scheduled for 7:00 that evening, just four hours later. I quickly scanned it, and we promptly decided to carry it live. So did the other networks. (I had only a moment's hesitation, arising out of the fact that it had always been our policy not to schedule the broadcast of any event, if we could possibly avoid it, which would interfere with our network news broadcasts.) It was an easy judgment, even though it may have seemed to be masochistic. Agnew's speech easily met the test of newsworthiness, and that was that.

Just ten days earlier, President Nixon had addressed the nation on all the television networks. He reviewed the war in Indochina and his efforts to bring it to an honorable end; he rejected U.S. withdrawal, and blamed the North Vietnamese for continuing the war. Each of the networks followed Nixon's address with a few minutes of analysis. This displeased the administration—particularly the analysis of CBS News diplomatic correspondent Marvin Kalb, who did just what a good reporter-analyst is supposed to do: Report additional facts which give context to, and illuminate, the speech which is being analyzed.

Agnew's speech was a strong critique of network television news. First, he attacked news analysis following presidential speeches—calling it "instant analysis and querulous criticism"—and objected on the ground that it might unduly influence the American people, a function which he apparently believed should be reserved exclusively to the president. (He and his associates had never criticized "instant analysis" of speeches by Democratic presidents.) The views of network television newspersons did not, he said, represent the views of the American people. (He did not explain how he knew that, nor did he examine the question of whether that is the proper test of reporting and analysis.)

And then he came to the heart of his message: Network television, Agnew said, is "enjoying a monopoly sanctioned and licensed by government." Blaming television for the Vietnam demonstrations, Agnew proclaimed, "It was time that the networks be made more responsive to the views of the nation." The operative word is "made." The vice president did not specify who was to do the making, or how, but the word was a word of coercion, to be read in the context of his explicit emphasis on the fact that all networks are licensed. (The ominous warning of license vulnerability and antitrust action was thus first publicly sounded as later speeches and actions of the administration would reemphasize.)

To make sure that we in broadcast journalism, and our affiliates who carried our news broadcasts, got the point, Agnew reminded us of what we were already painfully aware: Just a few months before, the United States Supreme Court had held in the Red Lion case that broadcast journalism had considerably lesser First Amendment rights than print journalism. Thus, broadcast journalism could be regulated in ways that were unthinkable when applied to print.

•   •   •

Agnew's assault in Des Moines was not a single shot. A week later, in Montgomery, Alabama, Agnew broadened his attack to include the *New York Times* and the *Washington Post* as well; both had been critical of the Nixon administration's handling of the war in Indochina. Not forgetting network television news, he said that when "the network commentators go beyond fair criticism, they will be called upon to defend their statements . . . and when their criticism becomes excessive or unjust, we shall invite them down from their ivory towers to enjoy the rough and tumble of public debate."

Again, Agnew was not specific. He did not spell out who would "call" the commentators or before whom they would be called. He did not identify the "we" who would issue the "invitations" or with whom the "debate" was to take place. He did not explain by whose standards the fairness or justness of the newspersons' comments were to be judged or who would be the judges. But against the backdrop of his Des Moines speech, I do not believe that the press was being paranoid in guessing that "we" was the federal government and the administration which were to do the calling and the judging. Agnew insisted in his Des Moines speech, and repeated three times in his

Montgomery speech, that he was not advocating censorship, but that gave us small comfort.

Agnew's speeches did strike a responsive chord with many Americans, who made it clear that they thought the press had it coming. And he did make some valid points in his call for fairness, accuracy, and objectivity; for searching journalistic self-examination; for a greater recognition by journalists of their own fallibility; for a greater receptivity to criticism; and for a less stubborn resistance to admitting error when error occurs. But Agnew did not invent these points: Many within journalism had made the same points before Agnew, and continued to make them after Agnew. They are points still to be emphasized.

• • •

I never met Bob Haldeman, or Ronald Ziegler, or John Dean, or Charles Colson. I did meet twice with Herbert Klein, the president's director of communications—and once with John Ehrlichman, White House counsel and assistant to the president. Although the Nixon White House made calls to Stanton and Paley, there were only a few calls made to me at CBS to complain about CBS News stories. These relatively trivial incidents did not affect CBS News reporting. They were minor irritants, nothing more than mild attempts on the part of the White House people to influence us.

I met Klein after Nixon made his first trip to Europe, shortly after he was inaugurated in 1969. Nixon visited with heads of state and made a number of public appearances. On his return home, CBS News broadcast a one-hour news special summarizing and evaluating the trip. A major segment was devoted to a discussion by leading journalists from each of the nations Nixon had visited, reporting their, and their country's, reactions. On balance, they were not favorable.

As soon as the broadcast ended, Herb Klein called me. Klein, a journalist, was soft-spoken and amiable; he had none of the hardness which characterized most of his White House colleagues. He (or the president, or both) was unhappy about that segment; Klein told me that it was wrong to turn to foreign journalists for evaluation. I told him that since he was new at his new job, I would let it go this time, but that in the future, any such complaining call from the White House or other government officials would be on the record.

Two years later, *60 Minutes* did a piece on the early life of Vice President Agnew. The report included a reference to Agnew's student years; he was, reported Mike Wallace, an indifferent student and the record of his marks at high school had disappeared. A few weeks later,

Klein came to see me in my office. He told me that Mrs. Agnew was unhappy and upset by the piece. (The visit was at Agnew's request, Klein wrote in his book *Making It Perfectly Clear*.)

It was a minor matter, but as I had told Klein in 1969 that I would make such a communication public—I did; it found its way into some newspapers. In his book, Klein referred to this incident, writing that "I had long regarded personal discussion such as that with Salant as private and helpful for both sides . . . But somehow, the Salant discussion was leaked to the media, and I never felt after that I could speak in confidence to Salant."[3]

I regret that Herb Klein had forgotten that I had explicitly told him in 1969 that all such communications would be on the record. That is a wise policy in case adventurous presidential associates or anyone else in a position of power over the press attempt to influence the news.

Years later, Jody Powell, President Carter's press secretary, called me at home to complain about my decision not to carry live a speech by President Carter. Powell urged me to reverse my decision. I told him that our conversation would be on the record. He replied that that was fine; he was going to record the conversation. That, I believe, is the best way. I did not reverse my decision.

I met with John Ehrlichman, in New York City on April 29, 1971, after he had been interviewed by John Hart on the *CBS Morning News*. I joined Ehrlichman, Hart, Phil Lewis, the *Morning News* executive producer, and Harry Griggs, a *Morning News* producer, at breakfast at the Plaza Hotel. I was curious to see what sort of man Ehrlichman was.

In the course of a good deal of polite small talk, the subject of Dan Rather came up. Ehrlichman criticized Rather's professional abilities and objectivity. I mentioned that we had hired Rather after his excellent reporting for our Houston, Texas, affiliate. In response, Ehrlichman asked me whether we needed a correspondent in Austin, Texas. We then went on to other bits and pieces of conversation. It was all low-key; Ehrlichman was smiling pleasantly—all gums—throughout.

I was not exercised until I returned to my office. After reviewing what I thought had happened, I became angry. I had decided that the conversation constituted an ominous threat. Ehrlichman had, as I

---

[3]It was typical of the gentle kindness of Herb Klein that he concluded the sentence by adding, "although I regard him as an able news executive, doubtless one of the best."

pieced it together in my office, deliberately initiated an unwarranted attack on Rather and then proposed that Dan be removed from the White House beat and sent back to Texas.

And so I used the most readily available weapon: I leaked the story to a reporter. I told the reporter that Ehrlichman's comment had assured that Rather would stay on the White House beat as long as he chose. (As he did—he outlasted Nixon at the White House and was not transferred to New York as anchor of *CBS Reports* until Ford had become president.) The story as I had leaked it appeared, with some embellishment, in several newspapers and, ultimately, in books.

Before I leaked my version, I should have checked with my CBS colleagues who had been at the breakfast. It was not until Ehrlichman's book *Witness to Power* was published in 1982 that I learned that my impression of that breakfast conversation eleven years earlier was different from his. Ehrlichman wrote that it was I, not he, who had raised the question by asking him how he thought CBS News people at the White House were doing. Since I had asked the question, wrote Ehrlichman, he answered. He confirmed that he had said that Dan was consistently critical of the administration's domestic policy initiatives and that he failed to check his stories either because "he had a bias or he was lazy."[4] Ehrlichman wrote that he thought it was the latter.

Then, according to Ehrlichman, after I recounted how we had hired Dan from Houston after we had seen a superb story he had done about the rescue of a horse stranded in a hurricane, he replied that "it had always seemed a long jump from covering a horse stranded in a flood to covering the White House."[5]

After I read Ehrlichman's account, I asked John Hart for his recollection. He confirmed that, indeed, it was I who raised the subject with Ehrlichman. John wrote me: "My memory . . . is rather clear, as is the memory of the astonishment I felt." He wrote that I "astounded" him

---

[4]Paradoxically, a few pages after his account of the Plaza breakfast and his admission of his distaste for Rather's reportorial talents, Ehrlichman turned to a discussion of press conferences, and, in the course of explaining that Nixon held few of them because the reporters asked "a lot of flabby and fairly dumb questions," Ehrlichman had said that "it seems to me a great deal more . . . could be developed as interesting news and valuable for the people out of a one-on-one with Dan Rather."

[5]That was hardly an accurate summary of Dan's reporting career. By the time Nixon became president, Rather had been a CBS News correspondent for seven years, had distinguished himself in his reporting of President Kennedy's assassination in Dallas in 1963, had served as White House correspondent during the Johnson administration, and had reported from London for six months.

by asking Ehrlichman, "How do you feel our people at the White House are doing? Or, what do you think of our coverage at the White House?" John also wrote, "the memory of the shock that you asked is still fresh." When John returned to his office with Phil Lewis, the executive producer, he said to Phil, "Do you believe it? The president of CBS News asking the White House what it thinks of us?"

John also remembered that after Ehrlichman listed his complaints about Rather, Ehrlichman "grinned a big grin and said, 'don't you need a correspondent in Austin?' It didn't occur to me that this was a serious effort to get Dan out of the White House. I saw it as his attempt to make a light exit from the subject."

John Hart is a fine reporter. I accept his version of my meeting with Ehrlichman. I do not know what had impelled me to ask Ehrlichman such a dumb question; it invited the reply I got. To John Ehrlichman—and to Dan Rather, for that matter—my regrets.

• • •

There were other ways the White House tried to manipulate news coverage. In one instance, the administration complained about allegedly unfair reporting. Clark Mollenhoff, special White House counsel, who had once won a Pulitzer Prize, attacked a story which Don Webster had reported on the *CBS Evening News*. Webster had witnessed and filmed an atrocity committed by a South Vietnamese soldier.

A Vietcong was lying on the ground, apparently dead or unconscious, with his rifle lying nearby. Don saw, and the film showed, a South Vietnamese soldier approach the Vietcong's body, kick it, and shoot it. In the background, a helicopter was visible. Don reported that the helicopter was ours and that American soldiers had witnessed the incident but had done nothing about it.

Mollenhoff planted stories that the incident was staged. (They were published, no doubt because of Mollenhoff's high, and deserved, journalistic reputation.) This planted version asserted that as the South Vietnamese approached the Vietcong soldier, the latter made a sudden movement reaching for his rifle, that the South Vietnamese had shot in self-defense, and that the helicopter and the troops who were watching were not American but Australian.

We rechecked the story and satisfied ourselves that it happened exactly as Webster had reported it. Cronkite replayed it on the *CBS Evening News*, slowing or stopping the film at crucial points, establishing that the Vietcong had made no motion and that the rifle was lying out of his reach. We made a still picture of the helicopter and had it enlarged. It clearly showed American markings and the insignia of the unit involved. Cronkite, in replaying the story, explained that the incident was an example of the lengths to which the administration would go to distort and cast doubt on accurate journalistic reports.

White House reporters were also subject to personal harassment. CBS newsman John Hart received a letter from Frank Shakespeare criticizing a story John had reported; shortly afterwards, he was audited by the IRS for the first time in his life. Dan Rather, returning to his home from a vacation earlier than expected, found that his files in the basement of his home had been rifled.

These episodes were, at the least, ambiguous. It might have been a burglar at Rather's; it might have just been John Hart's turn with the IRS. But both correspondents had been major targets of administration criticism. That we were suspicious of harassment at all was an indication of the climate which had been created by the administration.

There were no such ambiguities in what happened to Marvin Kalb and to Dan Schorr. Both were on the White House's enemies list, as we learned later from testimony at the Senate Watergate hearings. Marvin Kalb's desk at the State Department was broken into and his papers scattered about. (Kalb was told by State Department officials that a cleaning lady probably did it.) Kalb was also placed under surveillance and, along with Washington reporters from other news organizations, was wiretapped.

Schorr, too, was on the enemies list—number eighteen on a special list of twenty. The ubiquitous hatchet man Charles Colson, who drew up the enemies list, included the notation next to Schorr's name: "a real media enemy."[6] In the summer of 1971, an FBI agent called me at home early in the morning. He told me that Schorr was being considered for an important job with the administration; he asked me questions about Dan. I immediately called Schorr to notify him. He was completely surprised and assured me that he knew nothing about it, did not know what job, if any, he was being considered for, and was not even looking for a job.

In the days following, the FBI questioned other CBS people, as well as Schorr's relatives, friends, and neighbors. The FBI told each interviewee that they were investigating Schorr in connection with a job

---

[6]*Editors' note:* Schorr found out he was on the enemies list while reporting live on the air for CBS. He was on the air when he was handed a just-released copy of the list. As he was going through the names one by one, he was startled to see, and report on the air, that his own name was number eighteen (from Schorr's statement, made at Harvard's Kennedy School of Government, November 6, 1997).

with the government. Ronald Ziegler and Frederick Malek, White House head of personnel, answering queries about the Schorr investigation, leaked a story that Schorr was being considered as special assistant to the chairman of the Council on Environmental Quality.

In 1972, Senator Sam Ervin, chairman of the Subcommittee on Constitutional Rights, held hearings on the episode. It was established that the administration had never contemplated offering a job to Schorr—a fact that was confirmed in the Nixon impeachment proceedings before the House Judiciary Committee in 1974. In an interview on the Dick Cavett show on March 22, 1973, Pat Buchanan, then a White House special assistant, said that the plan had been to offer Schorr a job in order to get him off the air. On August 1, 1973, testifying at the Senate Watergate hearings, Haldeman admitted that he had requested the background investigation of Schorr.

When news of the investigation appeared in the press, some viewers were outraged, not by the investigation but by Schorr. In August 1973, a Scottsdale viewer wrote me condemning our coverage of Watergate and equating it with the guilt-by-association techniques of McCarthyism.

Our reporting, he wrote,

utterly demolishes any credibility you might have had with the public to assign Dan Schorr as a major Watergate reporter when he was allegedly a primary target of the White House; how any rational person could expect him to render anything approximating an impartial reporting—let alone interpretation, as he is prone to do—under the circumstances is beyond me. Schorr himself shows his own lack of professionalism by refusing to disqualify himself and you compound the abuse of reportorial responsibility for objectivity by not compelling him to do so. . . . What monumental gall it takes to refuse to render such an elementary accounting!

I answered:

Your letter hardly identifies you as a model of restrained objectivity. Whatever our lapses, I trust that we do better than you do—but then our professional duty requires such objectivity, while as a nonjournalist, you have the luxury and right to be as biased and illogical as you choose.

Your reasoning is quite extraordinary. You say that Dan Schorr should have disqualified himself, or we should have disqualified him, from reporting on Watergate (or presumably on any other activities relating to the administration) because "he was allegedly a primary target of the White House." Stop and think about this extraordinary contention that you make:[7]

What it comes down to is that all any administration—not necessarily this one but some future . . . Democratic one or even a Socialist one—has to do to get a reporter whom it doesn't like off its back is to order an FBI field investigation of the reporter, then lie in stating that the purpose of the investigation was because a job was offered to him, then admit that it lied—and so achieve exactly what the administration sought to do: Require the reporter or the reporter's employer to make him stop reporting. That's really what you are contending—that because the administration outrageously and without just cause had Schorr investigated by the FBI (and then lied about it) Schorr should be disqualified from his normal beat. Talk about lifting yourself up by your own bootstraps!

Incidentally, I would note that William Safire later wrote that Dan Schorr, despite the excusable anger he might feel because of the outrageous FBI investigation, has distinguished himself by his restrained and objective reporting on Watergate.

• • •

Sometimes, coming events are foreshadowed in strange and unexpected ways—and are seen as warnings only upon reflection much later. Such a warning signal, foreshadowing the sinister and conspiratorial atmosphere which prevailed at the Nixon White House, occurred at the Republican Convention at Miami in the summer of 1968. I remembered this episode, which I had dismissed from my mind as unworthy of being taken seriously, only after the Watergate hearings finally obtained the Nixon tapes and other White House memoranda and made them public.

At the convention, my office was in a trailer outside the convention hall. One evening, we planned to begin our broadcast coverage with a live Cronkite interview of Nelson Rockefeller. He and his wife, Happy, arrived early; they came to my trailer to wait. We chatted for a bit and then Mrs. Rockefeller motioned me over to a corner, out of earshot of the others. She told me that the convention was giving her an uneasy feeling. When I asked her what she meant, she told me that she was convinced that the hotel suite where they were staying was bugged by the Nixon people.

---

[7]A Phoenix viewer made an identical argument; I answered, "Do you seriously contend that all the federal government has to do to require a reporter to be taken off the air is to designate that reporter as an enemy. I earnestly recommend that (1) you read the First Amendment of the Constitution and (2) you look up the *Encyclopedia Britannica*, under 'Peter Zenger'—[whose] government also regarded [him] as an enemy."

In the conspirational climate disclosed in the tapes at the Watergate hearings, I recalled Mrs. Rockefeller's whispered statement. The irony was that Nixon had not only bugged others but that he had also bugged himself.

10

"The Selling of
the Pentagon"

There are many things we can do to help our credibility. Basic, of course, is accuracy, fairness, balance, and it would help if we were not so reluctant to admit error when we err, as inevitably we sometimes do. . . . But the awful paradox is we can never achieve total credibility; we cannot be believed, or seek to be believed, by everybody—not if we are honest reporters. . . . It's a harsh lesson which every editor learns sooner or later. I sure learned it when we were covering the Civil Rights movement, Vietnam, and Watergate stories.

—*World Affairs Forum, January 10, 1988*

THE 1971 INVESTIGATION BY THE House of Representatives into the broadcast of "The Selling of the Pentagon" went to the heart of the question of where the rights of broadcast journalism stood under the First Amendment. The episode clearly crystallized the issue; it caused many members of the print press—and others—to be acutely conscious of the issue for the first time. But it did not resolve it.

All previous episodes of Congress's attempts to exercise its muscle in respect to CBS News broadcasts had just nibbled around the edges. As a continual pattern, at best, they were annoyances and distractions; at worst, they added to the climate of official intrusion into the conduct of our operations. This investigation, however, came close to sending Frank Stanton to jail. It caused me to seriously consider resigning from my beloved job as president of CBS News. And it reminded us that congressmen, too, are capable of the fury of the scorned.

• • •

Probably none of it would have happened had it not been for my compulsive practice of watching not only all the programs produced by CBS News but those of ABC and NBC News, as well. In January 1970, I watched an NBC News documentary about atomic energy. I was surprised to see an excerpt in that documentary which was, in effect, a film clip praising the glories of atomic energy and the beneficial role it would play in the future of energy resources.

NBC News identified the excerpt as being from a film prepared by the U.S. Atomic Energy Commission. That startled me. I wondered why the government was spending money on propaganda—on a public relations effort justifying the policies it was pursuing and huckstering for an industry it was supposed to regulate. It seemed to me that it would be worthwhile to look into how widespread the practice was and how much of our tax money the government was using to persuade us, rather than inform us. So I suggested to my colleagues at CBS News that we investigate to see whether this might be a subject for a *CBS Reports*.

Over the years, I was constantly coming up with what I considered to be brilliant ideas for documentaries. Most of them struck no sparks among my colleagues who would have to develop and produce them, and so nothing happened. But this was one of the rare exceptions. Bill Leonard, the CBS News vice president in charge of documentaries, decided it was worth looking into, and he assigned the project to Peter Davis, a brilliant young documentary producer. They came back to me and explained that the subject was so big, and spread among so many federal government activities, that the right way to get at it was to focus on the agency with the most elaborate and expensive public relations apparatus. That was the Department of Defense—the Pentagon.

In an early stage of researching the documentary, Peter, or one of his associates, found vivid confirmation of the view that the Pentagon had been engaged in public relations activities for a long time. They found an article in the *New York Times* quoting Democratic congressman F. Edward Hebert from Louisiana:

It is about time the American public be informed as to the identity of individuals and what it costs the taxpayers to maintain and support this gigantic and colossal propaganda machine on the banks of the Potomac. . . . Since the exposé of waste in the military and its effect on the taxpayers' pocketbook has been so vividly brought to the attention of the American people by the committee I head, all the faucets have been turned on by the Pentagon propagandists, alibi artists, and apologists.

The date of this statement was February 26, 1952. The reference to the "gigantic and colossal propaganda machine" and to the "exposé" was not to our "The Selling of the Pentagon," of course, because it was not broadcast until nineteen years later. Rather, it was in reference to the results of an investigation by the House Armed Services Subcommittee on Military Waste. Congressman Hebert was the chairman of that subcommittee.

Ironically, two decades later, it was this same Congressman Hebert who filed a fairness complaint with the FCC against "The Selling of the Pentagon"; the same Congressman Hebert who condemned CBS News and the documentary as "un-American" and "Goebbels-like"; and the same Congressman Hebert who was so instrumental in persuading the Investigations Subcommittee of the House Commerce Committee to undertake its investigation of CBS in the spring of 1971.

• • •

After about a year of research, filming, and editing, "The Selling of the Pentagon" was first broadcast on February 23, 1971. It focused on the Pentagon's public relations efforts, which ranged from distributing propaganda movies to holding military demonstrations around the country. As is usual with television documentaries, relatively few viewers (only several million) watched the initial broadcast.

The *New York Times* reviewer and many other television critics praised the broadcast. (It was given all the major awards that year.) But others criticized it—including Congressman Hebert, Vice President Agnew, and Melvin Laird, the secretary of defense. CBS News, in its regular news broadcasts, reported these criticisms.

The controversy it engendered was so great that we decided to rebroadcast it a month later. This time, the audience was half again as large as it was for the first broadcast. At the end of the second broadcast, we included a twenty-two-minute addendum, which included statements by some of the documentary's main critics, and a five-minute reply by me. In it I said:

No one has refuted the essential accuracy of "The Selling of the Pentagon." You have seen and you have heard Pentagon activities for yourselves: the manipulation of news, the staging of events, and the selling of the Pentagon's points of view. None of our critics has said that these things didn't happen or weren't done—and so the validity of the broadcast stands unscathed.

The critics were not moved. *Barron's*, a Dow Jones weekly, published a full-page editorial demanding that CBS's licenses be "forfeited"; and Republican senator Robert Dole from Kansas—with approval—put the *Barron's* editorial in the *Congressional Record*. The *Martinsburg* [West Virginia] *Journal*, published in Democratic Congressman Harley Staggers's home district, supported a congressional investigation and stated that networks should be regulated since they were not entitled to the protection of a free press.

Air Force Magazine published an article by its senior editor, Claude Witze, attacking "The Selling of the Pentagon" in lengthy detail. (Jack Anderson later charged in his column that the Pentagon had planted the article with Witze, who had not, alleged Anderson, checked the story out.) Even the *Washington Post*, which emphatically defended our First Amendment rights and condemned the House investigation, sharply criticized the documentary's editing.

• • •

Meanwhile, two of the main congressional critics, Congressmen Staggers and Hebert, discovered an even more sympathetic and cooperative forum than the FCC for their complaints against "The Selling of the Pentagon"—their own fellow members of Congress. On April 7, 1971, Staggers's Special Subcommittee on Investigations of the House Interstate and Foreign Commerce Committee issued a subpoena to Frank Stanton, directing him to appear before the subcommittee to testify and to bring "all film, work prints, outtakes, and sound-tape recordings, written scripts and/or transcripts" relating to the preparation of "The Selling of the Pentagon."

On April 20, CBS furnished a film copy of the broadcast and, as it does for anybody who requests it, a transcript to the subcommittee. But it respectfully "challenged the subcommittee's power to inquire by compulsory process into the editing of the broadcast." Accordingly, Stanton declined to produce materials not actually broadcast.

On April 30, CBS submitted an opinion of its counsel that the subcommittee's compulsory demand to produce material not broadcast was beyond the subcommittee's power because of the First Amendment, and so CBS was under no duty to comply. On May 26, the subcommittee rejected this contention. Staggers told a reporter that a print reporter's notes could not be subpoenaed but a broadcast reporter's could.

The subcommittee then issued a modified subpoena, still calling for outtakes—material which was not broadcast because it had been edited out—but disclaiming any interest in transcripts and filmed materials of "interviews or events which did not appear, even in part, in the actual broadcast." This meant that the subcommittee wanted all the outtakes relevant to those segments which were actually broadcast. Obviously, it wanted to compare what parts of particular interviews and scenes were kept in the final broadcast and what portions of those interviews and scenes had been left out.

Usually, in the preparation of documentaries, somewhere between twenty and fifty times more film or tape is shot than is actually used. Even in hard news broadcasts, an hour interview may result in much less than a minute on the air. (The process is no different in respect to print: Lengthy interviews by print reporters often result in only a sentence or two of quotes.)

• • •

When Stanton appeared before the subcommittee on June 24, 1971, he stated that the purpose of the investigation was to "make an official governmental inquiry into the editing process employed in producing the documentary." He told the subcommittee that it was the opinion of outside counsel for CBS that the subcommittee "may not constitutionally compel CBS to produce the subpoenaed materials or give oral testimony for such a purpose."

Stanton testified in his opening statement that

clearly, the compulsory production of evidence for a congressional investigation of this nature abridges the freedom of the press. The chilling effect of both the subpoena and the inquiry itself is plain beyond all question. If newsmen are told that their notes, films, and tapes will be subject to compulsory process so that the government can determine whether the news has been satisfactorily edited, the scope, nature, and vigor of their news-gathering and reporting activities will inevitably be curtailed. . . .

[T]his subcommittee's legislative purpose—to prove "distortions" or to control "editing practices" in broadcast news reports and thereby engage in official surveillance of journalistic judgments—has no constitutional warrant and therefore no benefit that can be balanced against the chilling effect of this subpoena, let alone outweigh it. . . .

Based on advice of our counsel and our own conviction that a fundamental principle of a free society is at stake, I must respectfully decline, as president of CBS, to produce the materials covered by the subpoena of May 26. For the same reasons, I must respectfully decline, as a witness summoned here by compulsory process, to answer any questions that may be addressed to me relating to the preparation of "The Selling of the Pentagon." . . .

We take this position as a matter of conscience, because of our obligation to uphold the rights guaranteed by the First Amendment. That amendment embodies our national commitment to freedom of the press. It protects the rights of journalists, not to make them into a privileged class but to safeguard the liberties of us all by preserving one of the most indispensable elements of responsible democratic government—to report freely on the conduct of those in authority. In Judge Learned Hand's famous phrase: "To many this is, and always will be folly; but we have staked upon it our all."

There can be no doubt in anyone's mind that the First Amendment would bar this subpoena if directed at the editing of a newspaper report, a book, or a magazine article. Indeed, the chairman [Congressman Staggers] has been quoted as having specifically conceded this point. However, it is urged that because broadcasters need governmental licenses while other media do not, the First Amendment permits such an intrusion into the freedom of broadcast journalism, although it admittedly forbids the identical intrusion into other press media. If broadcasters must comply with such subpoenas, broadcast journalism can never perform the independent and robust role in preserving those freedoms which the Constitution intended for American journalism.

After Stanton had completed his eloquent opening statement, Chairman Staggers began the proceedings:

THE CHAIRMAN: Do you realize that as a result of your refusal to comply with the subpoena you may be found in contempt of the House of Representatives with all the consequences that flow from such contempt?

STANTON: Yes, I do.

THE CHAIRMAN: Knowing this, do you persist in your refusal to provide the subpoenaed material?

STANTON: Yes, I do.

THE CHAIRMAN: Does the decision not to provide the subpoenaed materials reflect a decision of the management of CBS?

STANTON: Yes, it does.

THE CHAIRMAN: So that the record may be clear on this point, speaking as the chairman of this subcommittee, I hereby order and direct you to comply with the subcommittee subpoena and to provide forthwith the materials therein described. What is your response?

STANTON: I respectfully decline.

THE CHAIRMAN: At this point, Dr. Stanton, it is my duty to advise you that we are going to take under serious consideration your willful refusal to honor our subpoena. In my opinion you are now in contempt.

The chairman thus concluded that Stanton was in contempt, but for four more hours, the subcommittee members persisted in trying to elicit from Stanton the materials and testimony which they knew he would not provide. Each had to have his satisfaction in lecturing and scolding Stanton. They refused to recognize that any First Amendment issues were involved. This, they insisted, was broadcasting, and Congress could do whatever it pleased in overseeing broadcast journalism's accuracy and its news and editing judgments. Congress had a right and a duty, they said, to engage in such oversight.

Frank Stanton, as always, was unflappable and cool for most of the four grueling hours of testimony. But near the end, he lost his temper when Staggers tried to separate him from the CBS News Division. Staggers said that he had known Stanton for a long time, and "I respect you as a man. I don't blame you, I blame your organization."

Stanton responded, "Please, Mr. Staggers, don't separate me from the organization, because the men in the organization are the men I put in the organization." Staggers replied, "But Jesus picked twelve disciples and one sold him for thirty pieces of silver, another denied him on the night that he was crucified, and another doubted him when he came back. Now that is the kind of men we have today and that we had then."

At that, Frank Stanton got mad. He replied, "I think that is most unfair to refer to our news organization that way." Staggers asked, "Being prophets and disciples of Christ?" Stanton replied, "No, as being traitors." Staggers retreated: "I didn't call them traitors or anything like that; no sir, I would not do that."

In fact, as I learned later, Frank Stanton did believe that there had been some flaws in the editing of "The Selling of the Pentagon." But that was between him and us, and not between him and Congress. He would not let Staggers relieve him of responsibility and shift it to us in the News Division, even if it involved the risk of jail for contempt. That's the kind of boss reporters and editors dream of.

Chairman Staggers concluded his hearings with his statement that

> this [television] is the most powerful media [sic] we have in America today, and you talk about chilling effects. This runs chills up and down the spine of every person in America. When there is untruth put over these networks they can control the land, and you know they can if we allow this to go on. Anything I say or you say can be distorted and made to be a fact, and they can ruin every president, every member of this Congress, or anybody else if we allow this to go on. We must have those outtakes.[1]

---

[1]Doubtless, Chairman Staggers did not realize that similar fears of a new means of communications had also been echoed four centuries earlier—then it was Gutenberg's invention of that frightening object called the printing press. That fear led to the licensing and government control of the press in England, which Milton, and then our Founding Fathers, repudiated.

Four days later, on June 29, the subcommittee voted five to nothing to recommend that Frank Stanton be held in contempt. The next day, the full Commerce Committee, also chaired by Congressman Staggers, met to vote on his subcommittee's recommendation. It voted twenty-five to thirteen to recommend to the House of Representatives that Stanton be held in contempt.

The full House had never rejected a recommendation for contempt in its entire history.[2] It seemed to me that the odds were against us and that Frank Stanton would be held in contempt for a documentary for which I was responsible. I felt that I was risking Frank's freedom. I was holding his coat while he went to battle and ran the risks.

Mindful of Staggers's closing dialogue with Frank when Frank refused to permit Staggers to shift the blame from himself to us in the News Division, I wrote a note and passed it to Peter Herford, a good friend and associate at CBS News. Peter was related to Brock Adams, a congressman from the state of Washington. Adams was one of the thirteen who had dissented from the Commerce Committee's recommendation.

I asked Herford to pass the note on to Adams. It said, "What would be the effect of the House vote on contempt of RSS's [my] resignation from CBS News? Is there a reasonable possibility that such a resignation would swing the vote *against* contempt?" (Except for Peter Herford, nobody was aware of my note. Until he reads it here, Frank never knew about it. I did not want Frank to have to pay for whatever misdeeds I had committed.)

A few days later, Peter relayed the word back to me: Adams advised against my resignation. He felt that it would not do much good, and could even do harm, since it might look like a confession. It would have made Frank's refusal to comply with the subpoena look even worse to Staggers and his friends. They might have thought Stanton was hiding something.

I cannot say that I was unhappy about Adams's advice. Had I any indication that my resignation might turn the House vote in Stanton's favor, I would have gone forward with it. But when Adams said it would be futile, I was glad that I did not have to leave a job which I enjoyed so much.

•   •   •

The tension of the investigation also affected the operations of CBS News. As we were waiting for the House vote, CBS lawyers collected

---

[2]Although in 1879, when a committee voted to hold George Seward, the U.S. minister to China, in contempt, the House adjourned before acting on the recommendation.

affidavits from CBS News people. Bill Small, the chief of the CBS News bureau in Washington, swore in his affidavit, filed with the House members, that the activity in Congress had already had a profound effect on CBS News and could lead to an unseen congressional presence in the newsroom, with investigators peering over the shoulders of journalists as they made their decisions. Small said journalists were already cautious and nervous when it came to dealing with key members of Congress:

> There is a feeling which I share with many of my colleagues that outtakes of film will not be the end. Frustrated as investigators will become with this single source of raw material, they will seek a mandate to go beyond it to internal memoranda and individual memory of the editing process.
>
> Investigations ex post facto are injurious to a news organization. Each time we conduct our own examination of a single story or a documentary, we tie up many men for many hours. Each time government does this, in the acts of federal agencies or congressional committees, the hours are multiplied and attentions distracted from the fundamental job of news gathering and presentation. It saps the energy of CBS News . . .
>
> Courage is the essential ingredient of my craft. It will be replaced with caution. Public service is the heart of what attracts good men to journalism. It will be blunted with concern for the intrusions of investigators and inquisitors. I am convinced that the end result will be the loss of most good men. They will run for newspapers where the First Amendment is yet to be corrupted. Those who remain will no longer operate freely . . .
>
> My colleagues are professionals in their craft and it is a high calling. If there were deception, deceit, fraud, or even the merest fudging of the truth, they would speak up strongly and forcefully. They now do when they suspect even honest error. I dread the day when they fear to speak up. This effort on the part of the Congress brings that day closer.

• • •

As the recommendation that Stanton be held in contempt was pending, cracks in the dike began to appear for the committee majority's position.

Other than Frank Stanton, the only witness to appear before the Investigations Subcommittee was Dan Henkin, the assistant secretary of defense for public affairs. The charges that "The Selling of the Pentagon" had so edited interviews and speeches as to distort their meaning centered, in large part, on the editing of Roger Mudd's interview with Henkin.[3] When Henkin, a man whom my colleagues in the Washington Bureau respected and liked, testified, he continued to contend that the editing of the interview had distorted his meaning. (Of all the criticisms of this broadcast, the editing of Henkin, I believe, raised the most legitimate questions; the issue was ambiguous. While I am convinced that the editing was not intentionally mischievous and that it fairly reflected Henkin's statements, it is possible that the editors misunderstood him.)

While critical of "The Selling of the Pentagon," Henkin also testified, "I have never questioned the integrity of CBS News, and I do not do so now." He told the subcommittee, "I am certain that the members of this committee share with me my unswerving belief in the sanctity of the First Amendment for all information media."

He testified that as a former newsman, he would not have produced his notes in response to the subcommittee's demand. He was asked by a subcommittee member whether he thought that giving the outtakes of the documentary's interview with him to Congress would be "doing any violence to the First Amendment." Henkin replied, "No, but there is a matter of principle here."

Newspapers and newspaper editors—even those most critical of "The Selling of the Pentagon"—publishers' associations, and journalists' associations all condemned the attempt to force CBS to produce the outtakes. *Barron's* and Staggers's hometown newspapers were lonely exceptions. Perhaps influenced by this overwhelming support for Dr. Stanton's position, the Nixon administration disassociated itself from the subcommittee's and the committee's efforts.

At the White House, Herb Klein said, "I believe that in going beyond what was broadcast, and asking to get, in effect, notes of programs that they infringe on the ability of broadcasters or print media to develop a story." He called the subpoena dangerous to a free press. Ronald Ziegler, Nixon's press secretary, also questioned the subpoena; he pointed out that it was a Democratic majority of the committee and a Democratic chairman who had issued the subpoena.

President Nixon himself said that while network commentators and newspaper reporters were not above criticism, "when you go, however, to the question of subpoenaing the notes of reporters, when you go to the question of government action which requires the revealing of sources, then I take a very jaundiced view of that action."

• • •

---

[3]One of the more illogical aspects of the congressional demand for outtakes was that Henkin himself, as was the custom in the Pentagon, had the entire interview audiotaped. He made a transcript of the complete interview available, and it had been entered into the *Congressional Record*. Therefore, Congress already had the outtakes for the material on which much of the criticism had focused, and a subpoena was unnecessary.

On July 22, the day before the contempt vote, Congressman Wilbur Mills, a Democrat from Arkansas, who at that time was considered by many to be the most powerful congressman in the House, spoke on the floor of the House. Mills was the chairman of the House Ways and Means Committee—and had been for thirteen years. "Mr. Speaker," he said, "I have some serious questions in my mind about the citation with all due respect to my good friend from West Virginia, the chairman of the [Commerce] committee." He said that he had tried to inform himself on the matter and that he had read the affidavits from CBS newsmen. He put those affidavits in the record, leading off with Bill Small's. Mills then sat down.

On the next day, July 23, the contempt citation came to a vote in the House of Representatives. I had remained in New York, and I went into our newsroom to stay abreast of what was happening.

Chairman Staggers spoke at length. He said that the committee needed the outtakes. He charged that "there might be twenty or thirty or forty different places where they misquoted or misplaced these things, we do not know . . . We want the facts. That is all we want."

Congressman Hebert spoke:

They cry "First Amendment." I believe in the First Amendment, and there is nobody in this room who can challenge my standing on that. They have had their First Amendment. They have had their chance to lie under the First Amendment. If it were not for the First Amendment, they could not have practiced the deceit that they have practiced. . . . I agree that the public has a right to know. How is the public to know if we do not make them show what they have under the table and up their sleeves?

Perhaps most persuasive with his colleagues, however, was Democratic congressman Emanuel Celler of New York City. Celler was eighty-nine years old; he had served in the House for twenty-five consecutive terms; he was the senior member of the House; and he was chairman of the House Judiciary Committee—the Constitution was his special field. He spoke against the contempt citation.

Celler recognized how unusual it was for the chairman of one House committee to speak in opposition to the chairman of another on an issue like this. "I counter my fellow chairman," he said, "and that counter leaves an ashen taste in my mouth." But he was doing so, he said, because "the First Amendment towers over these proceedings like a colossus."

Celler continued, "No esprit de corps and no tenderness of one member for another should force us to topple over this monument to our liberties, that is, the First Amendment." He declared that the First Amendment did apply to broadcasting and that government subpoenas could not reach outtakes. Celler stated that interference with the media had a chilling effect. And he predicted that if the House should vote contempt, the courts would not sustain it.

Chairman Staggers brought the debate to a conclusion, criticizing "the greatest lobbying effort that has ever been made on the Congress of the United States." Pointing to the motto on the inscription behind the Speaker's chair, he said, "Mr. Speaker, the slogan up there says 'In God We Trust.' Are we going to change it to 'In the Networks We Trust'?"

A motion to recommit—which would in effect bury the contempt citation recommendation by sending it back to the Commerce Committee—was then offered by Republican congressman Hastings Keith of Massachusetts. The House voted on the motion—and the vote was 226 to 181 to recommit.

The House had voted not to hold Frank Stanton in contempt.

•　　•　　•

Congressman Harley Staggers was most unhappy about his defeat by the full House. After the vote, he said, "Lord, I'm disappointed." "The networks," he said, "now control the Congress." And he added that something had to be done about television's "calculated deception." But he did not leave it to somebody else to do that "something."

Ten days after the vote, on August 1, I received an urgent call from a man on the West Coast who had worked as a freelancer for CBS News as part of a technical crew. He told me that he wanted to talk to me about conversations which he had had with a special investigator of the House Investigation Subcommittee of the House Commerce Committee—Staggers's committee.

When he came from the West Coast to see me, he told me that the subcommittee investigator had called him to "discuss CBS editorial practices." The investigator had asked him to tell of any cases of staging or manipulation, "no matter how small." The investigator told the freelancer that he was talking to as many technical people who worked for CBS News as he could. He was looking for stories from them which "would wipe out" the contempt vote; his purpose was to establish such widespread malpractice that ultimately, the House vote on outtakes would be reversed.

Shortly after the meeting with the freelancer, the CBS News Los Angeles bureau manager telephoned. He reported that a CBS News film editor and a CBS News cameraman had been approached by Staggers's investigator, who asked to meet with them to discuss our "news-gathering practices." A CBS News correspondent on the West Coast also called to inform us that the investigator had telephoned

him on his private line and told him that the subcommittee had assigned six investigators to work on the inquiry.

We sent word to our Los Angeles bureau to tell all those who had
been approached that they should cooperate fully and honestly with
the investigators and that if they wanted a lawyer, we would pay for
lawyers of their own choice. But the investigators apparently failed to
find what they were looking for, and the matter died. Not for lack of
trying, Staggers struck out again.

• • •

Leaving some scars, the congressional investigation of "The Selling
of the Pentagon" ended. It had raised, dramatically, the issue of the
Constitution's guarantee of a free press as it applied to broadcast journalism—the part of the press on which a majority of American people
relied.

Although I was, of course, pleased and relieved that Congress had
turned back the contempt citation against Frank Stanton, I will admit
that I have sometimes had a gnawing regret that the case did not
ripen into a court proceeding. A contempt citation against Frank
Stanton would have been an ideal case to test the issue of broadcast
journalism's status under the First Amendment, once and for all. Had
the Congress voted contempt, the matter would have had to be
turned over to the Department of Justice to seek a court ruling that
Stanton was in contempt. The defense would have been the First
Amendment.

Ours would have been a clean-cut case. Whatever the criticism of
"The Selling of the Pentagon," there was no question of its essential
validity. It involved a news investigation of the workings of an important part of the U.S. government—precisely the kind of watchdog role
which the First Amendment was designed to protect. But the House
vote cut off the possibility of a court proceeding, and the pervasive and
injurious uncertainty still persists.

Perhaps, of course, it is just as well that the episode of "The Selling
of the Pentagon" ended where it did. A majority of the House presumably based its vote on First Amendment grounds (although that would
not necessarily serve as precedent in a future case in Congress; a future Congress might vote differently). And if we had lost in the
Supreme Court—it was by no means certain that we would win—not
only would our second-class citizenship have been set more firmly in
concrete than ever, but Stanton might also have gone to jail.

So, probably, it was just as well—for Frank Stanton, and for the issue
of law which I wanted so badly to vindicate—that the case reached a
happy ending in the Congress, instead of risking an unhappy ending in
the Supreme Court.

• • •

I found two consolations in the affair. The first and most important was that my mentor, friend, and boss, Frank Stanton, had stood up for us, and for the First Amendment, at great risk to his personal freedom—and the House of Representatives refused to cite him for contempt. The second satisfaction was for me of quite a different nature. "The Selling of the Pentagon" had focused on a variety of the Pentagon's public relations efforts, which included:

• Holding military demonstrations in towns and cities, at which young children were encouraged to fight with each other and to play with the military weapons which were being exhibited;
• Sending officers from the Industrial War College on tours of the country to discuss and espouse policies relating to the Indochina War;
• Putting on elaborate demonstrations, with live ammunition, of military weapons for invited VIP civilians;
• Circulating old Cold War propaganda films for free public showings;
• Assigning five of its own film crews to Vietnam (at least one crew shot, and released, film of a "battle" which admittedly was staged).

In the midst of the Pentagon's attacks on our documentary, all of these activities were "deferred," cut back, or eliminated. A Pentagon spokesman conceded that the Pentagon had learned something from "The Selling of the Pentagon." Perhaps we at CBS News did, too.

• • •

A postscript: Vice President Agnew had been selected, or elected himself, as a point man to lead the attacks on "The Selling of the Pentagon." During the Christmas season that year, Agnew announced the gifts he was giving for Christmas. He was giving to me, so his press release said, a desk with two legs partially sawed off—because all my work was tilted.

When reporters told me about the gift and asked me what I was giving to Agnew in return, I replied that I wasn't giving him anything. "What," I asked, "can you give to a man who has nothing?"

I'm still waiting for the sawed-off desk.

11
Watergate Reports

I strongly believe that responsible journalism cannot have as its central objective giving people what they want—or avoiding displeasing them. The objective must not be merely to interest and titillate—to grab an audience—but to provide the information they need. And so if journalism is to perform the function which a democratic society has a right to expect, there will inevitably be some, usually the most vocal, who will be displeased.

—Haas Foundation lecture, Seattle, May 5, 1986

M Y ONLY TRUE CONFRONTATION with Bill Paley involving news content, during my sixteen years at CBS, was over our lengthy and powerful two-part report on the Watergate scandal. This report was broadcast on the *CBS Evening News* in October 1972, shortly before the presidential election in which President Nixon was running against George McGovern. Designed as a summary and update of the Watergate story which the *Washington Post* had broken so dramatically in the spring of 1972, it had been weeks in preparation by *Evening News* producers Stan Gould and Linda Mason. It concerned the continuing succession of new revelations and allegations which indicated that the Watergate break-in was much more than the "third-rate burglary" described by White House press secretary Ron Ziegler.

I had discussed the concept and approved it. Since the story was breaking rapidly on an almost daily basis, I thought it would be good journalism to try to put it all together in a cohesive story—as far as it had gone—adding whatever new facts our correspondents could find. As they worked on preparation of the reports, which were to include pieces by our correspondents who had been covering the story, I told my *Evening News* colleagues that they had better finish their work promptly. I thought it would be unfair to broadcast our reports on, or just before, Election Eve, since it was important to give the Nixon people a chance to react. (All the major administration figures had declined to be interviewed on camera in the course of preparation of the pieces.)

On Friday, October 27, 1972 (any further delay and I would have had to pull the plug), the *CBS Evening News* broadcast the first of our two-part series. Walter Cronkite introduced Part One this way:

> At first it was called the Watergate caper—five men apparently caught in the act of burglarizing and bugging Democratic headquarters in Washington. But the episode grew steadily more sinister—no longer a caper, but the Watergate affair escalating finally into charges of a high-level campaign of political sabotage and espionage unparalleled in American history. Most of what is known of the Watergate affair has emerged in puzzling bits and pieces, through digging by the nation's press and television newsmen. Some of the material made public so far is factual, without dispute—those men caught in the act at Watergate, for instance. Some is still allegation, uncovered by the press but as yet legally unsubstantiated. We shall label our sources carefully as we go along. But with the fact and the allegations, we shall try tonight to pull together the threads of this amazing story, quite unlike any in our modern American history.

The report then traced the history of Watergate, beginning with Dan Schorr's account of the break-in itself and then proceeding to a report tracing the political sabotage aspects of Watergate. In covering this part of the story, Cronkite very carefully noted which news organization was the source for which allegations of who was involved.

In fact, when Cronkite noted that the *Washington Post* had reported that H. R. Haldeman, Nixon's chief of staff, "was one of the men who controlled a fund for political intelligence," Cronkite also emphasized that that charge had been "denied by the White House in most heated terms." Cronkite quoted Ziegler as calling the *Washington Post* story "character assassination, and the shoddiest kind of journalism." But Cronkite did not leave it hanging there. He concluded, "We at CBS News cannot at this point substantiate any Haldeman involvement. The *Post*'s editor says the paper is sticking by its story."

Cronkite closed with the statement, "In our next report—the money behind the Watergate affair."

Of the slightly more than twenty-two minutes available for news content in the *CBS Evening News* that night, after the commercials and station breaks, we had devoted fourteen minutes—64 percent—to Watergate.

Four days later, on Tuesday, October 31, eight days before the election, the *CBS Evening News* broadcast Part Two of the report. We had originally planned to broadcast it the day before—on Monday, October 30—but, as I shall describe, much happened in those four days between reports. Part Two, as Cronkite had said, focused on the source of funds for the Committee to Reelect the President—funds which were used for the political sabotage and intelligence-gathering which led, among other things, to the Watergate break-in.

After Cronkite's introduction, Dan Schorr reported that a large secret cash fund—probably more than a million dollars—had been assembled by the Nixon campaign organization. It was collected immediately before a new campaign contribution law went into effect; the contributions were anonymous. Schorr described how the money found its way to the campaign and noted that four Mexican checks for $89,000, part of $700,000 flown on a Pennzoil Company jet from Houston to Washington, found their way into the Miami bank account of Albert Barker, then under indictment for his part in the Watergate break-in. The four Mexican checks, Schorr reported, were signed by the Mexican attorney of Gulf Resources, which, through a subsidiary, had transferred the money to the attorney.

Schorr reported that in another instance, a Minnesota banker gave $25,000 in cash, on a Miami golf course, to the Nixon campaign's Minnesota finance chairman, who, after converting the cash into a cashier's check, turned it in to the chairman of Nixon's finance committee. That $25,000 also turned up in Barker's bank account. Barker withdrew the total, $114,000, the day before the preparations for the break-in began, according to the indictment of Barker.

Schorr reported that the "secret fund" was kept in a safe in the campaign chairman's office. He then identified the men who controlled the fund, noting, however, that the *Washington Post* had published a broader list which included the president's lawyer, Attorney General John Mitchell, and Bob Haldeman. All of this, as Schorr reported, was denied by the White House.

Cronkite then reported that the *Washington Post* had said that Hugh Sloan Jr., a White House official, had implicated Haldeman in grand jury testimony, but that Sloan had denied it. Cronkite stated that "while there is no substantive evidence linking Haldeman to the fund, the *Post*, saying it has other sources, stands by its story."

Next, Dan Rather's report dealt with the men involved and the White House reaction. "The question is," Rather began,

> if any or all of what is alleged to have been going on is true, how high up in the White House does it go, and is the president himself involved? Of-

ficial denials claim that the whole affair is a political smear. The president's men also claim that CBS News, in passing along the allegations of others, is being politically unfair to Mr. Nixon by spreading the smear.

Rather then described the three men—Mitchell, Haldeman, and Dwight Chapin—and their authority in the White House. Rather reported that two high administration sources had told CBS News that no campaign money could be spent without Mitchell's specific authorization. Haldeman was described by Rather as "the president's right arm," who, along with Mitchell, was in charge of the reelection campaign. Chapin, Rather reported, was "Haldeman's right arm." None of the three, said Rather, would be interviewed by CBS News; to answer the published charges, they said, would only "spread untrue charges." Rather's report concluded, saying that

until and if Mitchell, Haldeman, and Chapin choose to publicly answer specific allegations, the answer to the question, if what is alleged is true, how high up in the White House does it go, cannot be answered. The president's men keep on insisting that in our system, everyone is innocent until proven guilty. They keep issuing general denials. They are depending upon that and silence to make the allegations go away.

Cronkite closed the two-parter this way:

There's a long history in American politics of election year shenanigans. Some did little damage and came under the head of pranks. Some have been more serious and have involved stolen and forged documents to disconcert the opposition and confuse the people. But the allegations in an important segment of the nation's press this year suggest a plan in high places to disrupt the normal processes of election politics beyond any such schemes in recent memory. The Nixon administration calls these allegations false, in some cases; overblown, hearsay, and misleading, in others. But apparently this segment of the press, and those disturbed at the possible injury done to the country's delicate election process, will not be satisfied with mere denials, will not put their suspicions to rest unless, or until, some impartial body examines the case and renders its verdict.

Cronkite then went to his customary closing: "And that's the way it is, Tuesday, October 31st, 1972." Part Two had taken about seven minutes—31 percent—of that night's *Evening News* broadcast.

• • •

Perhaps because of all that was later revealed about Watergate in the following months, and what became known, the reports now seem tame. I thought that they were a fine piece of journalism—an important contribution to public knowledge about a major story in American history. I was pleased that it had been done with such restraint and had been so carefully crafted, distinguishing what was known—relatively little—with what had been alleged elsewhere.

But wisely, and as we soon came to realize, presciently, it reported, at that early stage of the unfolding story, that there was still much to be known and to be resolved. It served—and I was delighted that it did that and nothing more—as an early warning sign of a piece of history which was yet to develop—one way or the other. The reporting was fair; it was careful; it was, if anything, understated, as it should have been at that stage.

There was heavy viewer response—a majority of it favorable. *Time* magazine said that "CBS's willingness to go beyond superficial coverage of daily charges and countercharges was the lone bright picture in network television's spotty campaign coverage." John O'Conner, the *New York Times* critic, wrote,

> The one major exception to coverage-as-usual was ventured on the *CBS Evening News with Walter Cronkite*. With the help of several reporters, including Daniel Schorr and Dan Rather, Cronkite presented two multipart series—one on the U.S.-Soviet grain transactions, the other on the Watergate bugging affair—that attempted to explore complex stories in a depth and with a cohesion rare, if not unprecedented, for TV newscasts . . . [T]he CBS decision to proceed took at least a modicum of guts. . . . More significantly, though the series demonstrated that network evening news need not be limited to providing little more than a super glossy headline service. . . . [Despite their length] the viewer was not deprived of any important item in the rest of the day's news. The results were . . . impressive enough to put a sizable dent in the familiar argument that TV news . . . can be nothing but a headline service.

Not everybody agreed with *Time*, the *New York Times*, or me. Bill Paley and Charles Colson certainly did not. It turned out that much had happened between October 27, when Part One was broadcast, and October 31, when Part Two was broadcast. Some of it I only learned about later—some, much later. Some of it I learned when I went back to the office on the Monday morning after Part One and before Part Two.

Several days before Part One was broadcast, I met with Frank Stanton. He told me that he had been told that Cronkite was preparing, and CBS was offering to advertisers, a half-hour special described as a "hatchet job" on Nixon. (I learned later that it was Charles Colson who told Stanton this.) I told Frank that the story was wrong; we were doing no such thing. But I did tell him that we were preparing a special Watergate report, the first part of which we were planning to include in the *Evening News* beginning that Friday.

I later learned that Stanton watched Part One with a friend in his office as it was broadcast on the first feed at 6:30 P.M. EST. His friend thought it was a fine piece. Frank called Mr. Paley at his home and told him that he should watch it when it was broadcast by our New York station on the second feed at 7:00 P.M. When the second feed was over, Paley called Frank, but, I am told, he did not seem to be angry or upset by the broadcast, although Stanton later said Paley thought it was too long.

I did not learn until long after the episode what occurred next. On Saturday morning, the day after Part One had been broadcast, Charles Colson telephoned Frank Stanton's home, but Stanton was out. (In 1970 Colson had previously visited Paley and Stanton to make threateningly clear White House displeasure with the network's treatment of Nixon; Colson claimed that Paley or Stanton had told him that he should call them when he had specific complaints.) Colson then reached Paley and attacked the Watergate piece.

When Stanton came back home that Saturday morning, he returned Colson's call and was told that Colson had already spoken to Paley and that there was no need for Colson to discuss the matter with Stanton. Stanton then called Paley, who told Stanton about the Colson call and Colson's anger about Watergate Part One. Even then, Stanton later told me, Paley did not seem particularly angry or disturbed by the piece. Stanton has no recollection that he discussed the merits of the piece during this phone call or that he had any substantive discussion with Paley at any other time.

But by Monday, October 30—the day when we had planned to broadcast the second part of the Watergate report—Paley was upset and angry. I was called to a meeting at Black Rock that Monday morning with Paley; Stanton, who by then had become CBS vice chairman; Arthur Taylor, president of CBS; and Jack Schneider, the president of the CBS Broadcast Group.

Paley was emphatic in his critical view of Watergate Part One. It was, he said, contrary to CBS standards and policies. It was unfair, unbalanced, derivative, inaccurate, based on hearsay, mingling rumor with editorial opinion, implying guilt from the Nixon officials' refusal to be interviewed, and so inordinately long that it caused the *Evening News* to shortchange much of the other news which occurred that day.

In short, Paley did not like Part One. He made it clear that he would be unhappy indeed if we went forward with Part Two. But as was his invariable practice, even when he made his views—and wishes—perfectly clear, he did not order me to spike Part Two. Had he done so, I would have quit on the spot—there are times when the weapon of resignation must be unsheathed. Had Mr. Paley ordered me to eliminate Part Two, this would have been such a time of fundamental principle and conscience for me.

The others attending the meeting said very little one way or the other. Paley had spoken, and there was no need for them to speak. Frank Stanton and, I believe, the others attending the meeting felt it was Paley's case. Paley, doubtless aware of my affection and respect for Frank Stanton, repeatedly associated Stanton with his criticisms. He said that "Frank and I feel that . . ." or that ". . . and Frank agrees." Frank expressed neither agreement nor disagreement. It would not have been proper for Stanton, at such a meeting, in the presence of others, to have contradicted Paley's insistence that he and Frank were as one on the issues—or that Frank disagreed with the chairman on the merits. Much later, after I retired from CBS News, Stanton told me that he most certainly did not agree with Paley.

I was pretty quiet myself. It did not seem to me that this was the time, place, or circumstance for me to debate the specific issues—especially without the transcript in front of me. (I had come to the meeting unaware of what the issues might be.) Nor did it seem to me to be useful: It was clear to me that Paley had reached conclusions and my arguments would not move him. At least, I think and hope that these, and not cowardice or timidity, were the reasons for my not counterattacking at the meeting. And so I contented myself with mumbling a defense that I thought the broadcast was fine.

I went back to my office immediately after the meeting and reviewed Paley's criticisms. I felt that one had substantial validity—that given the public's reliance on television news as its primary, or even sole, source of news, our having devoted over half of our news hole to a single story might have shortchanged other news. In fact, some months before, when there was no inkling that we would do a Watergate report in the *Evening News,* I had raised with my associates the same issue—the wisdom of devoting a large part of our small news hole to a single story. It was a question which had been bothering me.

In reviewing the issues which Paley had raised, I focused on that question. I recalled that a portion of Dan Schorr's piece, scheduled for Part Two, traced in detail the source of the secret campaign funds and how they had been shifted from place to place and account to account in what seemed clearly an effort to launder the funds. This information had already been included, early in September, in a special broadcast we had done. Much of what was proposed in Schorr's report in Part Two was repetitious of his earlier report.

It seemed to me, therefore, that we could cut down the Part Two Schorr report without hurting it. But I did not want to reach that conclusion unilaterally. I met with Sandy Socolow, the *Evening News* executive producer, and Stan Gould and Linda Mason, the producers of Part Two. We discussed the issue at some length. Walter Cronkite did not participate. At least, so far as I was involved, he never took a position one way or another.

I proposed cutting a few minutes from the Schorr piece—about three, as I recall. But I was troubled, not by whether it was sensible to cut but what my motivations were. I have been accurately quoted by David Halberstam, in his book *The Powers That Be*, as having said to Socolow, Mason, and Gould that I hoped that I was taking the position I did because I was persuaded of its merits rather than because Paley had so forcefully raised the issue. Finally, with no resistance from the producers, we decided to shorten Schorr's piece. The discussion and the editing forced a one-day postponement of Part Two. As I have noted, however, we did go forward with it the following day—Tuesday.

I believed then, and I believe today, that the decision was mine, not Paley's. It is true, however, that I would not have made the cut in Part Two were it not for Paley's criticism. But the point of length which he made so strongly at the Monday morning meeting was the trigger, not the reason. I do not believe I would have pressed it had I not felt—as my earlier questioning of long pieces indicates—that it had substantial validity.

And, after all, although Paley had so clearly indicated his distaste for the notion of going forward with Part Two—short of ordering that it be killed—we did broadcast it.

Paley was angry that we did so. A day or two later, he asked me to lunch with him. So far as I can recollect, it was only the second of three times that he and I ever met alone together (the first was in 1954 when I worked with him on the preparation of "The Road to Responsibility," the third was when I met with him at his apartment to tell him I was going to NBC). Ours was an employer-employee relationship, as were almost all the relationships between CBS people and Paley. Paley had no social relationships with CBS people—even with Frank Stanton.

I never felt at ease with Bill Paley. There was no chemistry between us. We operated in different worlds, and on different wavelengths. I had always found conversation, or even discussion, with him difficult—neither of us ever seemed to be able to persuade the other, and he worked more from magnificent instinct than I did. He was a superb showman and a great salesman. I most certainly was neither.

Of all my meetings with Paley, our one-on-one lunch the week of October 30 was, for me, the most uncomfortable. He was very angry that I had gone forward with Part Two and that it had the same flaws, as he saw them, which he had called to my attention at the Monday meeting concerning Part One. I defended the reports, but I did not persuade him, nor did he persuade me.

The next day, on November 1, 1972, I received this memorandum from him:

On Monday (30), at a meeting attended by Dr. Stanton, Mr. Taylor, you, and me, I expressed on behalf of Dr. Stanton and myself a serious uneasiness at the devotion of some two-thirds of the *Evening News* broadcast on Friday night to the Watergate affair—an extraordinary length of time for a hard news broadcast; and one seldom, if ever, done before. Our objection also was that it departed from our basic news policy of fairness and balance in that by dealing with a mixture of allegations and facts without the distinction always being clear, it seemed to be showing a distinct bias against one of the presidential candidates.

I pointed out that although the commentary specified at the outset that some of the contents of this long segment was still allegation, this caveat was inevitably lost sight of by the audience in view of the emphasis given the story by the length of time devoted to it, and would, in any case, be forgotten in the long list of charges that followed in such a way as to leave the impression that they were substantiated facts.

Again last night, just a week before the election, the same situation arose. Some seven minutes—a third of the news content of the broadcast—were devoted to a similar mixture of allegations and facts. The use of names and pictures in this context left a strong impression of guilt. This impression was intensified by our clear refusal to accept any of the denials already made because they were not made to CBS News—even though CBS News was the original source of the allegations. Making this kind of demand and obscuring the distinction between facts and allegations, even if unintentional, seems to me unworthy of our fine traditions and ought not to be practiced. I hope very much that it will not be repeated.

It was the most severe memorandum I had ever received from Paley—or anybody else in CBS senior management. I immediately drafted a strong head-on response—but I had the sense first to discuss it on the phone with Jack Schneider for his calmer advice. He suggested eliminating the strong language in my draft, and to try to let things cool down. It was wise advice.

Richard Salant with his daughter Linda, while he was in the U.S. Navy in Washington, D.C., 1943.

Salant poses for a CBS publicity shot, looking over the film of a documentary with Edward R. Murrow, about 1961.

Salant visited the White House on a number of occasions. Here he is in the Oval Office with President John F. Kennedy for an award ceremony, about 1962.

Salant on the set of a roundtable discussion for CBS News in 1963, one of the relatively few times he was before the cameras.

Salant speaking at the Denver University Law Center, where "Years of Crisis" was filmed in December 1963.

Salant, as president of CBS News, meets in December 1963 with some of his far-flung correspondents before the filming of a year-end roundtable discussion about the state of the world. The annual CBS broadcast was part of a distinguished series called "Years of Crisis." The attendees are, from left to right, Stuart Novins, Peter Kalischer, Alexander Kendrick, Salant, Eric Sevareid, Daniel Schorr, Marvin Kalb, Winston Burdett, and Blaine Littell.

Salant with his wife, Frances, during a safety drill on the SS Statendam *in March 1963 en route to Greece, where Salant planned to oversee an Eric Sevareid documentary on democracy, filmed at the Acropolis.*

On behalf of CBS News, Salant presents Jacqueline Kennedy and Robert F. Kennedy with film of CBS's 1963 coverage of the funeral of President John F. Kennedy for the Kennedy Library's film archive.

After a memorial service for Edward R. Murrow, President Lyndon Johnson met with a delegation, including CBS executives, among them Salant. Murrow died on April 27, 1965.

Salant with correspondent Alexander Kendrick in Saigon in 1966, where he had gone to examine firsthand the network's much-criticized Vietnam War coverage. In public, Salant strongly defended CBS's coverage of the war, but privately he worried that "it is not a well-reported war."

Salant in his office on "mahogany row" at CBS News headquarters on West 57th Street in New York City, in March 1966.

Salant enjoys a hearty laugh with Harry Reasoner at an International Radio and Television Society dinner. The button on Salant's lapel reads "Bring Back Zenker." Arnold Zenker was the twenty-eight-year-old program administrator who anchored the CBS Evening News, replacing Walter Cronkite when Cronkite refused to cross the picket line during a strike in March 1967 by the American Federation of Television and Radio Artists (AFTRA).

Fischetti

©1971 Chicago Daily News

For Richard S. Salant with admiration for a great show put on by Roger Mudd and all there at CBS News — John Fischetti 1971

PENTAGON · SELF-GLORIFICATION · COSTS

CBS EXPOSÉ

IN LIVING COLOR — GREEN

The 1971 CBS News documentary "The Selling of the Pentagon," which examined the millions of dollars spent annually by the Department of Defense for its own public relations, was one of the most controversial of Salant's entire career at CBS. The documentary produced tremendous criticism in Congress, and CBS president Frank Stanton was almost cited for contempt. But the broadcast also brought out defenders, such as Chicago Daily News cartoonist John Fischetti, who wrote: "To Richard Salant with admiration for a great show put on by Roger Mudd and all there at CBS News." Reprinted with permission from Karen Fischetti.

On Election Night, November 7, 1972, Dr. Frank Stanton, William Paley, and Salant watch from above, as the CBS News team produces a live broadcast on the outcome of the Nixon-McGovern election for president.

Salant and CBS political correspondent Roger Mudd share a story while working at temporary CBS facilities at a national political convention. Once, when CBS senior management pressed Salant, confidentially, to name who would become the anchor after Walter Cronkite, if that ever became necessary, Salant named Roger Mudd. Salant's statement was later leaked to Variety, reportedly angering Dan Rather, who finally did replace Cronkite after both Salant and the longtime CBS anchor retired.

After a CBS radio call-in program with President Jimmy Carter and Anchor Walter Cronkite on March 5, 1977, Carter and some of his staff met with the entire CBS crew, including Salant, Bill Leonard, Sam Digges, Robert Pierpoint, and Bill Small.

On the next day, November 2, I wrote Paley this memorandum in reply:

I have your November 1 memorandum. I understand and appreciate the points you have made.

I was directly and personally involved in the preparation of the two-part Watergate story, made a number of editing and other suggestions which were adopted, and approved it before broadcast. I share your deep devotion to the keystone CBS policy of fairness and balance; in approving the story and its treatment, I did not believe that that policy was breached. I am distressed and shaken by the fact that you and Dr. Stanton, who have been our best friends and most steadfast supporters, feel to the contrary. . . .

As soon as I get clear after the election, and if you wish me to do so, I would very much like to come over to discuss these points with you.

Just in case Paley should accept my invitation to discuss the issues between us further, I also prepared a detailed twenty-four-page memorandum, with extended exhibits, addressed to myself and dealing with each of the criticisms which had been leveled at our Watergate two-part report.

The memorandum and its exhibits rested in my files. Paley never did invite me over to discuss the matter further. The lunch and the memorandum were his last reference to it. And I remained president of CBS News for six and a half more years—until mandatory retirement.

Throughout this exchange, I was unaware—it did not occur to me—that Colson, or anyone else at the White House, had been in touch with Paley about our Watergate reports. I am uncertain about just when I did become aware of the Saturday telephone call from Colson. I do recall that my antennae started to vibrate shortly after November 11, when Colson made a speech to the New England Society of Newspaper Editors. In that speech, he defended President Nixon, dismissed the importance of Watergate, and attacked the press, and particularly the *Washington Post*, for their Watergate reporting. Included in his speech was an attack on our Watergate two-parter.

"The ultimate coup," Colson said, "was delivered by CBS in the closing days of the campaign. . . . On one program, the unlabeled 'editorial' took fifteen minutes of a twenty-two minute report. The second was ten minutes [sic], one week to the day before election." When I read that, the suspicion crossed my mind that Colson's hand had been in there somewhere. But it was still only a suspicion for a long while after.

During this period, Bill Paley was, in fact, a Republican—and a Nixon supporter. As a colonel in the army during World War II, attached to the U.S.-European command, he became not only an associate but a personal friend of General Dwight Eisenhower. It is widely believed that Paley, as a trustee of Columbia University, played a role in Ike's becoming president of Columbia after the war, before he became a candidate for the presidency.

He was a strong Eisenhower supporter: In fact, it was Paley who, at the beginning of the presidential campaign in 1952, was persuaded by an advertising agency working for Ike to accept, for broadcast on CBS, the first major television political campaign use of spots—one-minute ads. Until then, it was CBS policy to refuse any political ads of less than five minutes in length.

Later, Paley also supported Nixon; published reports identified him as a major contributor to Nixon's campaigns. But subsequently, Paley had second thoughts about the propriety of making political contributions to, or being identified with, political parties or candidates, in the light of his organizational relationship with news. Accordingly, he adopted a policy of not engaging in political activities or making political contributions, although it was not uncommon for publishers to do so. His later recognition of the sensitive issues such activities raise was unusual—and admirable.

I do not know how I would have handled Paley's criticisms—or whether I would have cut Part Two—had I known of Colson's intervention. Perhaps I would not have cut it—perhaps I would have considered Paley's criticism on its merits regardless of its ultimate source—although that would have taken more restraint and patience than I might have been able to summon.

Paley flatly states that he became convinced, on his own, that the Watergate two-parter was seriously flawed and that he did not arrive at his conclusions, or criticize me, or the two-parter, in response to Colson's call. Paley was an honorable man. I believed him. I also believe that if Paley, in his own mind, questioned whether, in a major story, we had not observed CBS's basic policy of fairness, he had a right to strongly make his views known to me.

Two salient points emerge: First, this was the only time that there ever was such an intervention by Paley into news content. Second, we went ahead with Part Two substantially intact, and I was not fired.

12

"When Honesty Was Called Courage"

Letters by the hundreds came across my desk from people who didn't believe the [fire] hoses and the police dogs in Selma; the murder of three civil rights workers in Mississippi; the burning of huts at Cam Ne and the massacre of men, women, and children at My Lai; the break-in at the Watergate and the subsequent cover-up and lies. We made it all up, insisted the letter writers. We should go back to wherever we came from.

—*World Affairs Forum, January 10, 1988*

NIXON FINALLY CAME OUT FROM behind surrogates to personally attack network news at a White House news conference in October 1973. The news conference was held shortly after the "Saturday Night Massacre," when Nixon fired Special Prosecutor Archibald Cox, along with Attorney General Eliot Richardson, and then William Ruckelshaus, who was the next in line, resigned in protest.

During the news conference, a reporter noted President Nixon had written in 1968 that "too many shocks can drain a nation of its energy and even cause a rebellion against creative change and progress." Then the reporter asked, "Do you think America is at that point now?"

The president replied that he thought the American people "can ride right through the shocks that they have," and then he veered off to attack the media:

The difference now from what it was in the days of the shocks, even . . . twenty-five years ago, is the electronic media. I have never heard or seen such outrageous, vicious, distorted reporting in my twenty-seven years of public life. . . . when people are pounded night after night with that kind of hysterical reporting, it naturally shakes their confidence.

Later in the press conference, Robert Pierpoint, a CBS News White House correspondent, asked:

PIERPOINT: Mr. President, you have lambasted the television networks pretty well. Could I ask you, at the risk of reopening an obvious wound. . . . What is it about the television coverage of you in these past weeks and months that has so aroused your anger?
THE PRESIDENT: Don't get the impression that you arouse my anger. (Laughter.)
PIERPOINT: I'm afraid, sir, that I have that impression. (Laughter.)
THE PRESIDENT: You see, one can only be angry with those he respects.

It would appear the president planned this attack. Before he entered the East Room where the press conference was to be held, Nixon noticed Sid Feders, who was standing outside the room. Feders, a CBS News producer, was the producer of the network pool covering the press conference. The president asked Feders who he worked for; Feders told him CBS News. After some small talk about exact timing, the president turned to enter the East Room and said to Feders, "Cronkite's not going to like this, I hope." In a memorandum written a few days later, Feders wrote, "His attack, therefore, came as no surprise."

I issued this statement in response to a press request for comment about the president's remarks:

Our job is to report on the president and his activities. And, therefore, we are professionally obligated to try not to be directly involved in a dispute with the president. We are familiar, of course, with our own news broadcasts—as well as those of the other networks—and we are convinced that none of the network reporting justifies the adjectives the president used Friday night. We have transcripts of all CBS News broadcasts. We believe that any objective examination of these will establish the accuracy and propriety of our reporting.

A week later, the National News Council[1] announced that it had decided to "review and analyze" the president's charges. By unani-

---

[1] I had no connection with the News Council at the time; its chairman was Roger Traynor, the former chief justice of the California Supreme Court.

mous vote of its fifteen members, the council asked the president "for the specific instances on which he based his charges."

Council chairman Traynor stated:

> The charges brought by the president against the media, particularly the electronic media, are so serious that the National News Council believes they warrant a public airing. As an independent body, in a position to make an objective study, we feel that the president's remarks, made publicly before millions of television viewers and reported by the press throughout the world, should be thoroughly investigated.

Accordingly, the council sent a telegram to Ziegler on October 30, 1973, requesting "the cooperation of the executive branch in making available to it specific examples of the reporting complained about in order to assist us in our impartial study and analysis of the charges." At the same time, the council asked the presidents of the network news divisions to make available "any pertinent transcript or tape . . . involving material cited by the president." The network news divisions immediately agreed to do so.

On January 28, 1974, three months after the council had decided to make its study and had requested Ziegler for specifics on which the president had based his charges, the council issued its report.

It summarized two brief meetings its representatives had with Ziegler and with Ken Clauson, and a score of communications to the White House—by phone and by letter. Calls had been unreturned and most letters unanswered. At the first meeting with Ziegler, the council presented abstracts of network news broadcasts to Ziegler with a request that the White House designate specifically which were "outrageous, vicious, distorted." Ziegler replied that the White House "did not have the time or the staff."

At the second meeting, Ziegler said that the file of abstracts would be studied and the White House would get back to the council before the next council meeting scheduled for January 28. The White House did not.

The council unanimously concluded that

> it would be difficult, if not futile . . . for the council to deduce, from the broad and unspecific charges, the particular actions of the television networks that inspired the president's remarks. . . . Under the circumstances, the National News Council cannot proceed with the type of study and analysis it contemplated . . . it is seriously detrimental to the public interest for the president to leave his harsh criticisms of the television networks unsupported by specific details that could then be evaluated objectively by an impartial body.

The president had hit hard, and he had run.

• • •

Meanwhile, as the Watergate story was reaching its climax and Senate and House committees were getting ready to hold hearings, White House supporters continued with a few more efforts to keep a lid on the press. In November 1972, in a speech to the New England Society of Newspaper Editors, Pat Buchanan attacked the *Washington Post* and CBS News for overplaying Watergate after what he termed "an independent investigation in the White House corroborated the findings of the FBI that *no one in the White House was in any way involved in the Watergate affair*" (italics mine).

In a speech to the members of the American Newspaper Publishers Association in March 1973, Henry Kissinger deprecated press coverage of Watergate; he urged the press to stop emphasizing it because, he claimed, it was interfering with the president's conduct of foreign affairs.

On the eve of the Watergate hearings in 1973, the president's supporters took the position that these historic proceedings should not be open to television. In September 1973, Senator Dole introduced a resolution to bar television from the Senate hearings. Dole contended that live coverage of the proceedings "placed . . . a distorted emphasis on them—to the exclusion of nearly every issue confronting Congress. It is time to turn toward such matters as inflation, food prices, boxcars, and gas supplies." (Dole, years later, led the fight to open the Senate floor proceedings to television coverage.) When impeachment proceedings began, one ranking Republican on the House Judiciary Committee objected to the presence of cameras and microphones because, he argued, people were tired of watching Watergate and preferred to watch their regular television programs.

• • •

On the evening before his resignation, August 8, 1974, Nixon said good-bye to the nation in a farewell address. There had been rumors all day that Nixon would announce his resignation in this address, but no one was sure. There were also rumors, passed on to us by Arthur Taylor, that Nixon's announcement would include an attack on CBS News. The climax was at hand.

We decided that the extraordinary events which were unfolding warranted our taking the air at 6:30 P.M. EST, staying on through the Nixon speech at 9:00 P.M., and continuing at least until 11:00 P.M. It was the hardest kind of broadcast journalism—at least four and a half hours of live coverage with no clear idea of what would happen.

Every other kind of journalism—both print and broadcast—has gatekeepers: In usual circumstances, the reporter writes his own copy, and it is reviewed and revised by editors before it is published or broadcast. For live coverage, however, there is only one draft and no checking, no editing, no reviewing. It's tough—and it's dangerous. Even events like political conventions, which until 1984 were broadcast live and in full, had a schedule of planned events and a good outline in advance of how the convention story would unfold—and how it would be covered.

But none of those elements were present on the evening of August 8. Our reporters would have to ad-lib all night except for the half hour or so of the president's talk. All that we in CBS News management could do was to try to set the general tone. So we telephoned the correspondents who would be covering the story that night to remind them that it was not a time, no matter how any of them felt and no matter what Nixon decided to do, for gloating or for editorial attacks. Rather, we told the reporters, if, as appeared likely, Nixon was going to resign—the first presidential resignation in American history—it was a time for national unity and national healing so that the government and the nation could move forward.

• • •

Some of the CBS News correspondents felt it was a time for healing; others felt that their analyses would be incomplete without reference to Nixon's conduct which led to his resignation. Both were right. Among those who felt that Nixon's conduct had to be reviewed was Roger Mudd. In his analysis after Nixon's speech, he did so—toughly and accurately—referring to the damage that Nixon had done to the Office of the Presidency and to the nation.

Many letters of reaction came to me—some praised Roger; some condemned him. The president and general manager of a CBS Television Network affiliate in the South was among those who were critical of Roger's reporting and analysis. He sent me a telegram deploring Roger's postresignation statements. I replied:

> I have your telegram and I am pleased as punch to learn that we generally did an excellent job covering the resignation and that you are proud of Dan Rather. But by the same token, I am distressed that you were disappointed in Roger Mudd and that you felt that his comments were "crude" and "arrogant."
>
> It will hardly come as a surprise to you that we have had an unusually large volume of communications on this subject—just about evenly split, with half of our friends and critics praising Cronkite, Sevareid, and Rather and condemning Mudd, as you did, and the other half terribly critical of Cronkite, Sevareid, and Rather for being sentimental, soft, and unjournalistic and praising Mudd to the skies for being the only one who brought out certain necessary considerations. . . . At least in this case it is pretty clear that our analyses were indeed "balanced."

Having said that, however, I would certainly defend Roger's postresignation analysis as valid, and indeed almost necessary, journalism.

Historical, sad, and traumatic as the occasion was, and one in the reporting of which journalistic restraint was called for, it was important, I believe, in fully performing our obligations as journalists, to include some salt and pepper with the sugar.

In journalism, at least, let there be not only sweetness; let there also be light. I am attaching a transcript of our postresignation analyses; I hope that on reading it you will agree that Roger's comments were not "crude" or "arrogant" and that he brought out certain points which deserved to be brought out if we were to do a complete job. Note that the first comments he made were explicitly from a purely congressional point of view—Roger is after all our congressional correspondent; he reported, entirely accurately, that many in Congress would note that the president attributed his resignation to a disappearance of his "political base," thus putting the blame only, or largely, on the absence of congressional support . . .

The second point which Roger made similarly seems to me to be just what good journalism required to be made—that there were a substantial number of people in the country who will ask, with so many people having been punished, or tried, for their role in Watergate, can one justify the president's going scot-free? Roger did not answer the question; he only put it. And all you have to do is read the debates that are going on now to realize that Roger was correct in articulating that issue. Good journalism requires the recognition of the realities even when the natural instinct may be to go easy. . . . I cannot agree that Roger's phraseology or tone was at all out of line.

•   •   •

Nixon's resignation on August 9, 1974, was an unforgettable moment in the history of our nation.[2] Despite all of the attacks on the

---

[2]Ironically, it was unforgettable for me not only for historical but also for personal reasons. Because it was such a difficult, delicate, and historic broadcast night, I did what no president of a network news organization—or at least this one—should ever do: Work in, and supervise from, the control room. That's the place for the professionals— the executive producer (editor-in-chief of the coverage) and his producers. They knew what they were doing—they were there because they were the best in the business. And except for the broadest kind of basic guidance, they should be left alone.

But that night, with the rumors flying and history being made, I violated all my own principles and stayed in the control room. It was tense. It was dicey. And somebody standing next to me in the control room, seeing me sweating and nervous, handed me a cigarette. (On January 1, 1973, at the constant urging of my wife and my children, my New Year's resolution had been to quit smoking—I had been a more than two-pack-a-day man. And I did quit—for twenty long, painful months.) In the control room, my focus was on other things—the monitors in front of me, the unfolding story. I accepted the cigarette, smoked it, and I was off the wagon with a crash—twenty months undone! And it wasn't until eleven years and one major operation later that I managed to stop again.

press, CBS News had been there from the beginning of Watergate to the end. The day after the Watergate break-in, on June 17, 1972, Paul Greenberg, the executive producer of the *CBS Saturday Evening News*, recognized that there was much more to the story than met the eye, that it was very important. Most newspapers ignored the break-in; the *New York Times* gave it a few inches in its inner pages. But Greenberg led the broadcast with the story—devoting over three minutes (15 percent of its news hole) to the break-in.

A respected journalism professor, evaluating the performance of national news organizations on the Watergate stories, ranked the *Washington Post* first, as it surely deserved. He ranked CBS News second. An editor of the *Washington Post*, at a journalists' conference in 1973, said that our two-part Watergate reports summary and background of the Watergate story on the *CBS Evening News* succeeded in making the story a national one.

Ben Bradlee, the executive editor of the *Post*, credited CBS News, among five others—all print—with having contributed significantly to the story.[3] And Katherine Graham, publisher of the *Post*, told me at a dinner that she had felt lonely on the Watergate story until CBS News began its coverage.

Whatever the evaluation of our coverage of the Nixon years, one thing is perfectly clear: We acted in accordance with the injunction laid down two decades earlier by Elmer Davis: "Don't let the bastards scare you." Senior management never flinched. Nor, to the best of my knowledge, did any one of my thousand associates at CBS News. I know of no story that was ever spiked, no story that was ever softened, because of the pressures.

The fact is, with all the shouting and tumult, while I was sometimes distracted, sometimes made uncomfortable by what seemed to me to be a hostile government, sometimes annoyed with myself for looking over my shoulder, I never felt scared. Paley and Stanton had insulated me from much of the pressure. I never felt heroic; there was

---

[3]*Editor's note:* Ben Bradlee, in his autobiography, tells how important the CBS role was in Watergate. Bradlee quotes Gordon Manning, Salant's hard news deputy, as telling Bradlee, "I'm going to save your ass in this Watergate thing. Cronkite and I have gotten CBS to agree to do two back-to-back long pieces on the *Evening News* about Watergate. We're going to make you famous." Bradlee writes that when the pieces finally ran on October 27 and a few days later, "They had a powerful impact everywhere—on the *Post*, on the politicians (if not the voters), and on newsrooms outside of Washington. Somehow the Great White Father, Walter Cronkite, the most trusted man in America, had blessed the story by spending so much time on it. . . . We were thrilled. No new ground was broken, but the broadcasts validated the *Post*'s stories in the public's mind and gave us all an immense morale boost." Ben Bradlee, *A Good Life: Newspapering and Other Adventures* (New York: Simon and Schuster, 1995), pp. 341–342.

nothing to feel heroic about. It was easy to do what we felt we ought to do.

When a viewer wrote me to praise our courage in our coverage of the Nixon years, I wrote back and quoted Yevgeny Yevtushenko:

> *One day posterity will remember*
> *This strange era, these strange times, when*
> *Honesty was called courage.*

But I was glad that it was over, and at last, all was quiet on the White House front.

13

"Dear Charles": Affiliate Relations

One of the paradoxes of the dialogue Charles [Crutchfield, manager of CBS affiliate WBTV Charlotte, North Carolina] and I had with each other was that each in his own way was, and is, dedicated to a war against advocacy journalism and to the preservation of what he and I both regard as the essence of good journalism—objectivity, accuracy, fairness, and freedom from bias. We both recognized—explicitly—that one cannot achieve those goals, but it is essential to try with all one's energy and dedication. . . . [Crutchfield once wrote:] "Men are never so likely to settle a question rightly as when they discuss it freely." And Charles, you and I certainly did discuss it freely, and so the journalistic questions we asked of each other and of ourselves were decided more nearly rightly.

—Speech to North Carolina Associated Press Broadcasters, October 1977

OUR COVERAGE OF MANY OF THE MAJOR news stories during my tenure—Watergate, Agnew's attacks, civil rights, the war in Vietnam, and the 1968 Democratic Convention in Chicago—was the subject of intense affiliate criticism.[1] During the Nixon years, the vast majority of CBS-affiliated station managers and owners were very suc-

---

[1]Some affiliates cleared all CBS News broadcasts as a matter of principle and policy. Tom Chaucey, the owner of our Phoenix, Arizona, affiliate and a cherished friend, was an outstanding example of 100 percent clearance even when our broadcasts must have outraged him. He was also one of the few who enthusiastically supported my efforts to expand the *Evening News* to an hour, regardless of the economic cost to him.

cessful businessmen and part of the business leadership group in their communities; they were not journalists.[2] Most were conservative, although there were some notable exceptions, and from their angle, CBS News was anti-Republican, antibusiness, and liberal. While many owners and managers actually supported Nixon and his policies in Vietnam, others, nervous about their licenses, were fearful of offending the Nixon administration. Consequently, over the years, many affiliates indicated to me, at meetings, through telephone calls, and by a constant stream of vigorous letters, their disapproval of our news.

In one memorable instance in the fall of 1968, the CBS Television affiliates board summoned me to a special meeting with them, shortly after the Democratic Convention in Chicago. The convention had been marked by ugly anti-Vietnam demonstrations and the Chicago police reaction, which the Walker Commission later characterized as a police riot. Like many other Americans, the affiliates' board members were outraged by what they saw; they could not accept the realities of the confrontation and violence between police authority and the mostly young antiestablishment demonstrators.

Even though each member had been hundreds or thousands of miles away from Chicago, the affiliates knew better than our reporters on the scene what actually happened. At a two-day meeting in Phoenix, we played back to the affiliates' board all of our coverage, showing that while we had indeed showed, and reported, the violent police reactions, we also reported, and showed to the extent that it was possible for our cameras to catch it, the provocative conduct of the demonstrators.

I replayed portions of the tape; I read transcripts back to them; I argued that we had fairly and accurately reported what really happened. But the affiliates were unconvinced, and they spent days arguing with me, certain that CBS News had reported in error and with bias. They did not give an inch; nor did I. It was, for me, a lacerating experience.

Another affiliate demand on CBS News, which I learned later was directly orchestrated by the Nixon White House, occurred in 1970. Members of the CBS Television affiliates' advisory board came to my office to express their dissatisfaction with our Vietnam coverage. The group proposed that a delegation of affiliates go to Vietnam to talk directly to our staff in Saigon to tell them how displeased they were with our coverage.

---

[2]It was not until the 1980s that CBS recognized that most of the original programming which a local affiliate broadcasts, and [which is] its most profitable activity, is locally originated news, and so CBS appointed a number of newspeople as the managers of its stations.

I told the group that it was an atrocious idea and that it was an intrusion into my responsibility for news coverage. I told them that when any CBS News Vietnam report seemed to them inaccurate or unfair, they should get in touch with me directly, citing chapter and verse, and I would look into the complaints—the responsibility was mine, and affiliates could not, and should not, try to function as a super-editing board. They finally agreed not to go forward with their plan to go to Saigon.

After the meeting, a member of the group told me that the proposal was not the idea of the affiliates' board but that it had been proposed to him by another affiliate after the latter had been to a meeting at the White House. There, an administration official had asked him whether he was happy about CBS News's Vietnam coverage. When the affiliate assured the official that indeed he was not, the official said, "Why don't you do something about it. Why don't you go to Saigon and tell them so?"[3]

•   •   •

No affiliate was more persistent, articulate, and given to writing letters to me than Charles Crutchfield, then the manager of WBTV in Charlotte and a powerful member of the CBS Television Board of Affiliates. He wrote long letters; he wrote short letters; even on occasion, he wrote letters in praise of what we had done. Our exchanges became something of a legend in our shop, and among other affiliates. Some of my CBS News colleagues were exasperated by his letters. On occasion, so was I, just as Charles was with mine.

But I admired and had great affection for Charles. He was up-front. He wrote good letters, and not seldom, there was validity to the principles of objectivity and fairness which he espoused—as did I—and some-

---

[3]Fred Powledge, a freelance journalist, was commissioned by the American Civil Liberties Union to prepare a report on the Nixon administration and the press (published under the title "The Engineering of Restraint"). I told him of this episode, which he included in his report. At the next affiliates' advisory board meeting in Puerto Rico, just before dinner, a group of the members asked to talk to me.

They took me aside, backed me against a stone seawall at the Dorado Beach Hotel, and criticized me for having told Powledge the story. They insisted that dealings between the affiliates' board and me were between us and had to be kept confidential. I had never heard of any such policy, which I thought was unwise, since I felt that the affiliates had no right to black out their representations to me.

If it was a policy, it was one-way: Members of the board did not hesitate to send multiple copies of their complaining letters addressed to me to the trade press and to outsiders. In one case, an affiliates' board member had sent out 2,000 copies of a report, of which I had not even been aware, by an organization critical of CBS News reporting.

times even a germ of validity to his charges that in particular cases, we departed from those principles. And Charles was a fair man: Although he had been particularly critical of our Watergate coverage and he was vociferous in his defense of President Nixon, when finally all the evidence came in, Charles told me he had been wrong about Nixon. On another occasion, as the two of us were walking and talking during an affiliates' board meeting, he told me, with typical frankness, that he was often unhappy with the reporting of his own news staff, but he recognized that he should not interfere—and so some of his letters to me simply gave vent to his frustration with his own shop.

On August 19, 1969, Charles wrote me, opening his letter with "It's me again . . . this time with what I believe you will agree is a legitimate gripe." His "gripe" concerned the *Evening News* coverage the night before of President Nixon's nomination of Judge Clement Haynsworth to the Supreme Court. Crutchfield felt that the coverage was biased and unbalanced, and should not have included an "interview" with Haynsworth because Haynsworth had a speech impediment. He charged that inclusion of a statement by Haynsworth was deliberately designed to show the nominee "in the worst possible light."

Charles also stated as evidence of our bias:

Incidentally, I don't recall that CBS placed two or three conservatives or Southerners or white people or whatever on the air to give their reasons for opposing Lyndon Johnson's nomination of Thurgood Marshall to the Supreme Court. Maybe you did have this anti-Marshall trio on at the time. I just don't recall it.

Crutchfield concluded, "I do feel that CBS News's prejudices showed through mighty clearly last night."

My reply:

Since you don't spare words with me, I'm not going to spare words with you on this one. There is nothing more precious to me than maintaining balance and fairness and not being biased in our reporting. And so you will have to excuse me if I answer your rather sharp charge sharply. Because the fact is that your description of how we handled the Haynsworth announcement is 160 degrees, if not 180 degrees, away from the way it actually was.

First, it was Haynsworth's own press conference which he called, inviting all the media in. If he stutters or has a speech impediment (and I was not aware of that), it is not our job to protect him. . . .

This seems to me to be totally justified news handling. We made precisely clear what we were doing—and why. We did not represent this as a sampling of all opinion and reaction. The news was that there would be a Senate confirmation fight.[4] . . . And certainly we balanced that aspect of it by including Senator Brooke's statement that he was not familiar with Judge Haynsworth's record, and so he had not made up his mind.

I should also note that we were the first to broadcast the Haynsworth story—a month before it was announced. And at those times, we included statements of those who are supporting him.

Finally, why speculate on what you don't remember? The fact is that we did include adverse reaction to the nomination of Thurgood Marshall.

News cannot be handled by stopwatch or by measure of ruler. On any given news broadcast dealing with a breaking story, it would be a distortion as well as an impossibility to give exactly the same number of words to all sides. If and when there is a newsworthy issue that arises out of Judge Haynsworth's confirmation hearings, you can be sure we will handle it with balance.

I can learn to live with loose charges of bias when they are made by know-nothings and strangers. But I do find it hard to live with loose charges, unsupported by facts, from intelligent people who are my friends.

Now I've gotten that off my chest.

As ever (anyhow) . . .

In the fall of 1969, Crutchfield and I had an exchange of letters dealing with bias, Vice President Agnew's attacks on CBS News and the networks, and broadcast news's status under the First Amendment. After an initial exchange in which I had told him that I felt "total hopelessness and helplessness" concerning the attacks on CBS News, Charles wrote me on November 25. He replied that my feeling was "evident throughout" my letter. "Believe me," he wrote,

I can imagine how frustrated you must feel after having been hit with so much heavy artillery. From personal knowledge, I know that you have operated CBS News and are continuing to operate it conscientiously and intelligently. I know, too, that you honestly feel that your newspeople are reporting with complete fairness and objectivity. Hopefully, Dick, you know that I have never questioned your integrity, your sincerity, or your motives—this despite the fact that on many occasions I have questioned the objectivity of some of the people in your shop. Our differences over the years have arisen, I think, from a basic disagreement in news and editorial philosophy.

---

[4]There was a confirmation fight and the nomination was eventually rejected by the Senate.

In his letter, Crutchfield then dealt with issues relating to Agnew, speech and press freedom, and the role of networks. He disagreed with my view that broadcast news should have the same constitutional protection as print; he did not agree that government regulation was a serious problem.

He concluded that "I'll quit [writing]—probably forever" because he felt that neither of us was persuading the other.

I answered:

> Let's just get one thing straight: I simply am not going to read any more of your letters if you persist in suggesting that this might be your last letter and you won't write any more. Who would be my conscience and who would keep me on my toes and who would provide me with the enjoyment and stimulus of good, honest disagreement and thoughtful dialogue. So keep them coming . . .
>
> What all this raises in my mind is the imperative need of finding some way of disentangling licensing from news content once and for all. I confess I don't know how it can be done . . .
>
> And you didn't persuade me, I am sure you will not be surprised to know, in arguing for the vice president's freedom of speech. Perhaps you miss the extremely significant point that the vice president is a member of, and is speaking for, the same government that has the licensing power over us. That is the difference between a government attack on the print media and on the broadcast media.
>
> The former can take it and shrug it off because there is no licensing and no leverage for pervasive regulation. It brings me back to what I just said—I would support 100 percent the vice president's right to criticize if somehow this whole thing could be disentangled from licensing.
>
> I am absolutely aware of, and deeply disturbed by, the unavoidable fact that we must all recognize that the vice president's criticisms do indeed reflect the views of a great many Americans. How we can deal with that overriding fact without compromising basic journalistic principles and reporting only what a majority of the people want to hear in the way they want to hear it—turning journalism into a sort of editing by popular opinion poll—is the toughest and most important problem we in news have to solve. Here again, I have no ready answers, but perhaps the important thing is that I agree that it is a vital problem.
>
> I don't regret, Charles, that we can't agree. Think of all the fun you and I would be missing if we agreed on everything. . . .

When we repeated "The Selling of the Pentagon" one month after it was broadcast in 1971, with so much public comment—pro and con—we added at the end some of the criticism by government officials and a brief rebuttal by me. Crutchfield did not think that this was enough.

He felt that "The Selling of the Pentagon" was unfair and unbalanced. He sent a telegram to Herbert Klein, the White House director of communications, offering the administration an hour on WBTV to reply.[5]

When I learned about this, Charles, at my request, sent me a copy of his telegram to Klein. I wired him back:

> I have your telegram setting out your message to Herbert Klein. Let's get the facts straight—although Agnew three times said that the Pentagon had requested time to reply, and we had refused, we never got any such request, and Jerry Friedheim, speaking for Assistant Secretary of Defense Henkin, explicitly told us that they had made no such request. I would also point out that in addition to the period following "The Selling of the Pentagon" broadcast, we also had [Congressman] Hebert on the *Morning News* for nine and a half minutes; excerpts from Agnew's New Orleans press conference on the *Morning News* for three minutes and ten seconds; Secretary Laird's comments for about a minute and a half on the *Morning News*; seven and a half minutes from Agnew's Boston speech on the *Morning News*; and additional comments of Agnew and [Senator] Dole for about three minutes on last Friday's *Evening News.*
>
> All of these appearances involved criticism of "The Selling of the Pentagon." Since you and I both agree that the public should be fully informed, I trust that you will release these facts—which you could have ascertained by checking with us or the Defense Department or reading Dr. Stanton's statement last Friday. When you are condemning us with telegrams to government officials, doesn't our relationship impel you to check and state the full facts?

But Charles was as elusive as he was unrepentant and unconvinced. He telegraphed me that, as I had requested, he was releasing my wire to the press. In respect of my insistence that there never had been a request to us for time to reply, Charles stated that "technically, you are perhaps correct" but that Henkin had issued a statement before the rebroadcast of "The Selling of the Pentagon" that he "would hope that the factual errors would be corrected." Charles also stated that Agnew had "challenged the accuracy" of the documentary and had "challenged CBS News, in the interest of real and not simulated fairness, to permit the critics themselves to participate in the selection of whatever film footage of their (the critics') remarks will be shown" in connection with the rebroadcast. Crutchfield asked whether it was not

---

[5]Crutchfield and his newspeople represented different philosophies and approaches: One of his newspeople called me to inform me of Charlie's offer and to ask for my comment. The newsperson assured me that he hoped that I realized that the WBTV news department was not in agreement with WBTV management.

correct that we had refused to "accept this challenge" and had instead edited the rebuttal ourselves.

Nor did Charles accept my account of the critics' appearances on other CBS News broadcasts. He noted that only Dole's three minutes had been on the *Evening News;* the others had been on the *Morning News,* which was viewed by only one-tenth the number of homes which viewed the *Evening News.* Therefore, Charles argued in his telegram, the critics of "The Selling of the Pentagon" did not have "fair and ample time" to correct the claimed inaccuracies.

After another series of exchanges along these lines, and perhaps because Charles was tired of it all and because his own news department never did give further balancing coverage to "The Selling of the Pentagon" critics, we soon went on to other issues.

There were dozens and dozens of Crutchfield-Salant letters back and forth—about broad philosophical issues of proper journalism or about specific instances in which Charles thought we had erred, often based on his own general impressions and without checking the facts concerning just what we had said and what our coverage really was.

But not all my correspondence with Charles was that comprehensive or heavy. Once, when he wrote me a letter praising something CBS News had done, I wrote him that my secretary was lying on the floor taking my dictation because she had fainted on hearing that he had written an approving letter. Sometimes, when we had had a particularly virulent exchange and he and I both threatened never to write any more letters to each other, we had our respective secretaries (the real victims of our exchanges) sign our letters—pretending that we had nothing to do with them.

Even though I usually felt that Charles was wrong and was sometimes excessive, he was good for CBS and for me: As I told him, he was an effective one-man monitor who kept us on our toes and made me stop and think, examine, and explain why we had done what we had done or had not done what we had not done. When Charles retired in 1978, his colleagues in Charlotte, recognizing our warm relationship, asked me to speak at his retirement dinner. I presented him with two leather-bound volumes of all our correspondence.

In my remarks at the dinner, I said—and meant—that our relationship over the years should serve as a model for nations around the world, and groups within the United States, because the correspondence demonstrated that Charles and I, often disagreeing, with vastly different angles of vision—he as a conservative Southern member of the business community, I as a journalist—still were (usually) civil, had learned how to agree, to disagree, and still retain our respect and affection for each other, and although the ingredients were there, we never resorted to war.

Part Three
Inside Pressure: CBS, Inc.

CBS Memorandum
To: Senior Vice President, Hard News
From: Richard Salant
Date: December 30, 1975
Re: Fairness and Balance

Perhaps I should not be, but I am deeply bothered morally, ethically and logically, if not journalistically, about the implications of Dan Schorr's interview with a man, kept in the shadows and who was identified as an ex-employee of the CIA, who "left the agency on bad terms and plans to publish a new and extensive list of CIA employees with more than 7,500 names. The man didn't want his name used."

How in the name of justice, equitable dealing, and logic can we put a man on the air who is ready to risk the employment, if not the lives, of 7,500 CIA employees, and who at the same time insists on his own anonymity and we give it to him?

14

"Us Against Them"

*I dislike the increasing practice of using news broadcast seg-
ments to promote other company activities [synergy]. How often are other networks' stars, and other networks' shows, the
subjects of the morning news shows? And what does all that
do to the credibility of a news organization whose North Star
should always be (but demonstrably is not) nothing but honest
news judgments and never intramural back scratching? Con-
glomeratization is a serious issue for all of journalism.... It's a
potentially dangerous business.*

—*Society of Professional Journalists, New Haven, June 14, 1990*

THE PEOPLE IN CBS NEWS were, in their way, a tight and prickly
extended family which circled the wagons at any signal that News
was, in its view, being threatened. With my immediate bosses—and
with others in the rest of CBS—I had earned the reputation of a porcupine who shot stinging quills when provoked by what I thought was
an intrusion on the independence of CBS News.

After Frank Stanton retired as president in 1973 to become vice
chairman, he was followed by three other CBS presidents while I was
head of News.[1] With of each of them I had, in general, a more remote
and formal relationship, and there was never the almost daily personal
give-and-take that I had with Frank Stanton. I rarely met with or heard
from Bill Paley as time went along.

A number of reasons made a loosening of the ties between me and
the president of CBS inevitable. One was that CBS had become so
large and complex that Paley decided that the president should be a

---

[1]Charles Ireland, Arthur Taylor, and John Backe.

businessman. So CBS no longer had a broadcaster at the top—a measure of the transition CBS had made from broadcasting as a special business to broadcasting as a part of any other large business. None of the presidents who followed Stanton (including Tom Wyman, the man who became president after I retired from CBS and ultimately became chairman and chief executive officer, replacing Paley himself) had ever been broadcasters. None, of course, had had any news experience (with the exception of John Backe).

Second, because the new presidents had no broadcasting experience, they were much less involved in that strange and unfamiliar business of news than Stanton or Paley had been. Instead, they delegated decisions to the new layer of executives which had been created in 1966, so the News Division president was once removed from the CBS president.

Third, the new presidents were not quite sure what to do with me or how to handle me. By 1971, I had already set a record for longevity—or survival—in the network broadcast business. I had, by several years, lasted longer as a division president than any of the presidents of other divisions, and it soon became apparent, as CBS presidents came and went, that I was outlasting CBS presidents, too.

As time passed with the new presidents, I found it useful not to discourage my reputation as a porcupine, and, on what I deemed appropriate occasions, I shot out a few quills to keep the reputation alive. Intimidation, I had discovered, is a two-way street. While I despised it when it emanated from above (including from me to CBS News colleagues who worked for me), I found it a useful strategy, if used sparingly, when aimed at higher organizational levels.

• • •

The wall of separation between CBS News and the rest of CBS, including senior management—while not impenetrable (it could not and should not be)—was also given unexpected assistance by an accident of geography, which emphasized CBS News's independence and its psychological separation from the rest of the company.

In the very early years when the Columbia Broadcasting System was at 485 Madison Avenue, senior management was located on the twentieth floor, and most of the CBS News offices, including the offices of CBS News officers, were on the seventeenth floor. In the collegial days of the young Columbia Broadcasting System, there was a good deal of visiting between the seventeenth and twentieth floors. News and senior management were close—both by inclination and by proximity.

When CBS outgrew 485 Madison Avenue, where it had leased space, and built in 1964 the magnificent Black Rock at 51 West 52nd Street as headquarters, the plan was to include CBS News in the building.

The ground floor was to serve as CBS News studios and offices. We were to broadcast our morning and evening news from those studios, which were to have glass walls on the sidewalk sides so that the passing public could watch the live broadcasts. This was an arrangement which NBC's *Today* show in its Dave Garroway–J. Fred Muggs days used with some public relations success in Rockefeller Plaza.

But Black Rock sat over the Sixth Avenue subway, and tests showed that live cameras on the ground floor of the building were subject to serious electrical interference and power surges caused by the subway system. A new home had to be found for CBS News offices and studios. They were—at 524 West 57th Street, five average blocks north and six very long blocks west into the prevailing blustery winds and hard by the Hudson River, adjoining the area which used to be known as Hell's Kitchen.

It is hard to find two more contrasting buildings—the handsome, vertical, contemporary, granite-and-glass Black Rock on Sixth Avenue, and the faded, horizontal, four-story red-brick former milk-processing plant on West 57th. There were many pedestrians and many nice shops—even hotels—in the Black Rock neighborhood. But the pedestrians at West 57th Street were mostly those who were going to, or coming from, our building—and they had to watch where they were going to be sure to step over various types of street people. The contrast alone made CBS News something different, and the geography underscored that difference.

Senior management, and the rest of the CBS people, never just dropped by our offices at West 57th Street; they had to make a special effort. They had to move over into a different world—into our West Side ghetto by the rotting river piers. And they could not pick up the phone and just ask us to drop by their offices—we were too far away and it took too long to get there.

So Black Rock was East, and 524 West 57th was West, and while it was not true that East was East and West was West and the twain never met, they met much more rarely than they otherwise would have. It was a useful arrangement which added to our psychology of autonomy, independence, and separation. At the least, I suspect that there were times when Black Rock denizens were angry at us at CBS News for something or other, summoned us over, and by the time we got there, had either cooled off or had their attention distracted by a different crisis.

It was a lucky break for me and for CBS News that the subways were under Black Rock.

•   •   •

The first CBS president succeeding Frank Stanton in 1971 was Charles Ireland. Ireland died of a heart attack the following year and was succeeded by Arthur R. Taylor, a former executive vice president at International Paper, where he had been in charge of finance. He was interested in news operations, and he liked to be with our news correspondents. My CBS News colleagues and I liked him, but my first piece of business with him was hardly amiable and seemed to get Arthur and me off to a very bad start.

In the fall of 1972, we were working on a *CBS Reports* documentary titled "You and the Commercial." It dealt with the techniques of persuasion—particularly those aimed at children—used by television commercials. After the television network people heard about it, Taylor asked Bill Leonard, the vice president in charge of documentaries, and me to come over to Black Rock to meet with him as soon as possible to discuss an urgent matter. Bill and I went across town with no inkling of what the meeting was about.

When we arrived, Taylor angrily told us that the television network salespeople had complained to him that "You and the Commercial" would be very critical of advertisers, advertising agencies, and their television commercials. They were afraid that advertisers and agencies would be so angry that it could cost CBS as much as $50 million in advertising revenues. Taylor wanted our assurance that the documentary would not cost the network that, or any other, amount.

Nothing like this had ever happened before. Nobody—not senior management, not our peers at the network—had ever suggested shaping CBS News broadcasts to suit advertisers. It was time for the porcupine to engage in a crash course by shooting its quills. So it did: We told Taylor we could not, and would not, give him any such assurance. The effect on advertisers, we sternly lectured him, was something we never had, and never would, take into account. Assurances that advertising would not be withdrawn or withheld from the network because of a controversial program were beyond our capability.

Taylor seemed surprised that CBS nurtured such unbusinesslike characters in its organization. He came from a world which regarded it a cardinal sin to offend one's major customers. He ushered us to the door, emphasizing again that he did not want "You and the Commercial" to have any adverse effect on CBS Television Network sales.

Of course, Bill and I did not report our meeting with Taylor to any of our associates working on the documentary. They proceeded normally with their work on "You and the Commercial." In due course, it was broadcast.

"You and the Commercial" was tough and uncompromising—but accurate and fair. Some advertising officials wrote me extremely critical, but unpersuasive, letters about it, but as far as I know, there was no loss of advertising revenues. My guess is that there was none, for had there been, I am sure I would have heard a few "I-told-you-so's" from my friends across town.

A few months after the meeting with Taylor—which neither of us had talked about in the meantime—he called me again. Would I come over right away—by myself? Oh, no, I worried, what has gotten him angry this time? I expected another onslaught on our dignity and integrity.

When I got there, he went right to the point: He recalled our earlier meeting and told me that that was a terrible thing for him to have done and assured me that he would never do anything like it again. He kept his promise. Taylor was an intelligent person and a quick study. His voluntary apology was, I believe, an extraordinary gesture in a society where admission of error is too often regarded as a grave weakness of character and the more wrong one is, the more stubborn one is about digging in.

•   •   •

Taylor was so generous in his readiness to publicly support CBS News that on another occasion, I had to hold him back. In 1976, the League of Women Voters was in charge of arranging the presidential election "debates" between Gerald Ford and Jimmy Carter.[2]

On the eve of the first debate, the person arranging participants on behalf of the league told me that lists of potential panelists had been submitted to the Ford and Carter camps and that some names had been vetoed. According to CBS News standards, interview subjects were not permitted to have any control over their interviewer—our News standards forbade such a practice. If we were to broadcast the debates, at the very least, we would feel compelled to disclose the fact that the panelists had been subject to approval of the candidates. To get to the root of the matter, I asked for a meeting with league officials and their advisory group.

We met in Washington, and I pressed for the facts. One of the advisers told me that how the panel of news reporters was selected was confidential and the league would not disclose it to me, but I kept pressing. Finally, another league adviser—Mark Walker—as angry and impatient as I was, told me to "shut up." It was a tradition in my family that vigorous discussions at the dinner table were encouraged, but "shut up" was strictly forbidden.

---

[2]They were not, in fact, debates in the classical sense: They were joint appearances by the presidential candidates answering questions put to them by a panel of journalists.

And so, at the league meeting, I lost my temper and stomped from the room—first into a closet, before I found the exit. Once I left, I then had to pop back in because I had left all my papers. I went downstairs in the office building where reporters and television crews were waiting for me, and as I stomped down the street, out of breath, being interviewed as I stomped—I said some very ill-tempered things about the League of Women Voters and their advisers.

It didn't take me long to realize that the incident would be on that evening's news, so as soon as I could, I called Taylor to tell him what had happened. Then I hurried to catch the plane to New York City. When the plane landed in New York, I called Taylor again. He had prepared a statement, to be released in his own name: It was an eloquent expression of support for me and the principles I was trying to vindicate with the league.

But by then I had caught my breath, and some of my temper. On the flight to New York, I decided that I had hardly acted with aplomb and that I had made a fool of myself. So I told Taylor that while I was most grateful for his statement, I had not handled the situation well and, after all, when it came to a showdown between the big, bad, meretricious networks and the indomitable, public-spirited women of the league, we could not win this one. Reluctantly, Taylor agreed and issued no statement.

This episode, too, I believe, was an indication that Taylor was moving from the mendacity of his former business: I doubt very much that a high executive of a large company like International Paper would, except in extremis, be so quick to voluntarily wade into a fight with the good people of the League of Women Voters.

Shortly thereafter, a viewer from Los Angeles wrote me, addressing me as "Dear Mr. Slant—oops, Salant." Questioning my statement that the league's policies were inconsistent with "journalistic ethics," the letter writer wrote, "You were doing pretty good until you added that last word. It comes as a complete surprise to me that anyone at CBS is even familiar with the word ethics." He approved of the league's rule against showing audience reaction because of "past performances with visual manipulation and out-of-context electronic wizardry. How well I remember how you people distorted truth in your infamous 60 Minutes program on mobile homes[3] and also on the experience of Mr. Elmer Fike of Fike Chemicals."

I replied:

---

[3]Some months earlier, 60 Minutes had done a piece on the hazards, including the fire dangers, of mobile homes.

What does a lynching victim say to the mob that has hanged him before trial? I don't know, so all I can say to your gracious letter of September 27 is that the "Dear Mr. Slant—oops, Salant" line is pretty old hat.

Give me one guess—you are in the mobile home business.[4] Second guess: Mr. Fike is your brother-in-law. Third guess: You believe that two wrongs make a right—far, far right.

• • •

The question of my obligations as head of CBS News to the rest of the company came up in perhaps its barest form in the summer of 1973. At the time, we at CBS News were working on the documentary "The Trouble with Rock," about what appeared to be drug use and payola in the record industry.[5] Concurrently, the president of the Columbia Records Division, an important part of CBS, had been dismissed and sued for embezzlement by CBS. He was accused of charging CBS for large personal outlays, including his son's bar mitzvah. There were ugly rumors that other serious matters relating to the record industry might be involved.

CBS routinely held quarterly advisory committee meetings between senior officers of the corporation and of each of its divisions. Just before the advisory meeting on July 17, 1973, I sought out Goddard Lieberson, the president of the CBS Records Division. I wanted to tell him that if he planned to say anything about the record business which I should not know in my journalistic capacity, he should either let me know in advance so that I could leave the meeting or, alternatively, he should not disclose matters which CBS News should not know. Lieberson, an admirable, unbureaucratic, talented man of great integrity, and one of my dearest friends at CBS, apparently told Arthur Taylor and Jack Schneider of my request.

I was immediately summoned to meet Schneider outside the meeting room. Schneider was angry. He told me that it was about time that I realized that I was part of CBS management and that I could not ei-

---

[4]The letter writer had the last word. He answered, telling me that he "really enjoyed my letter. Too bad CBS News can't do as well in the field of journalism." [Concerning the fact] that others before him had called me "Slant," he wrote, that "where there is smoke there is fire." He was indeed in the mobile home business, but he was "no kin of Elmer Fike's." He was not, he wrote, far right, although my last paragraph was "pretty neat."

[5]Payola was a payment made to radio disk jockeys to persuade them to play particular records on the air; it had been rumored that sometimes the payola took the form of gifts of drugs to disk jockeys.

ther withdraw from the meeting or refuse to keep confidential whatever might be said at the meeting about the record scandal. I replied that I thought Jack and I were diametrically opposed in our viewpoints on the issue of my obligations. I told him that it was impossible for me to take off my CBS News hat and substitute a CBS management hat, and that while I was indeed a part of CBS, my job was head of CBS News and that had to come first. I could not, I told him, play a dual role. Therefore, I insisted, I either had to be excused from the meeting or I had to excuse myself from any screening of, or responsibility for, whatever CBS News might develop from our work toward a documentary on the record industry.

I told him that if I were to have any responsibility for the broadcast, I could not withhold from my associates working on the broadcast any relevant information I might learn at the meeting. Jack and I were at an impasse. We disagreed. It was an episode which, I am sure, strengthened Schneider's conviction, which he expressed to me on other occasions, that the trouble with CBS News—and me—was our attitude that it was "us against them."

In fact, nothing happened at the advisory meeting. Goddard Lieberson made no reference to the litigation or the rumors—perhaps because of my warning. In his remarks at lunch, however, Arthur Taylor said that there was nothing more to the suit against the former head of the Records Division than what appeared on its face—that CBS had brought the suit against him because he had embezzled substantial amounts of money. He also said that CBS was determined to get to the bottom of the rumors about drugs and payola and that CBS would clean house if it found anything wrong. He said that the investigation by CBS had not yet been completed but that thus far, there was no evidence to support the rumors of drug and payola involvement.

I could not escape the suspicion that Taylor's remarks were partly for my benefit. At the same time, as I told my CBS News colleagues after the meeting, I came away with the clear impression that Taylor was not putting on an act for me but rather that he was genuinely convinced that on the basis of whatever information he had so far, and whatever the practices elsewhere in the record industry, Columbia Records was clean.

Some months later, we completed and broadcast "The Trouble with Rock."[6] Much of it focused on Columbia Records. The broadcast in-

---

[6]Somehow or other, the CBS News investigation of Columbia Records and the record industry became entangled with our Watergate coverage in the summer of 1973. Conservative columnists accused CBS News of covering up the records scandal at the same time we were reporting Watergate. A conservative congressman even threatened to hold

cluded statements by present or former Columbia Records employees about drug use and drugs for payola. The evening it was broadcast, I was watching it at home. (Of course, I had also screened the broadcast before it aired.) The moment it ended, my phone rang: It was Goddard Lieberson, for whom I had so much admiration and affection. He told me that the broadcast was outrageous, that I had done a terrible thing to him, and that he would never speak to me again. Then he hung up.

In fact, he did not speak to me again until almost three years later. He visited me at my office, and we had a cordial and affectionate reunion. He did not mention "The Trouble with Rock," nor did I. But I had missed him during the years that he did not speak to me.

• • •

There were other instances where we at CBS News went forward despite the potentially negative impact on other CBS business activities. Even before it was broadcast in 1975, a *CBS Reports* called "The Guns of Autumn" infuriated hunting organizations, hunting entrepreneurs, and individual hunters. That documentary was an uncompromising look at some of the less sportsmanlike activities of hunters, and I was deluged with letters and threats of reprisal—legislative actions, boycotts, and lawsuits—if we broadcast it. (Some lawsuits were brought, unsuccessfully.) The great outcry scared all the advertisers away. They all dropped out—except for Block Drug, which stayed in for one commercial.

One of CBS Publishing's most successful magazines was *Field and Stream*, a magazine devoted to hunting and fishing. Much of its advertising came from hunting-equipment and hunting-lodge entrepreneurs. Some advertisers threatened to cancel their advertising in *Field and Stream*, and some did.

But *Field and Stream* was just as angry about "Guns of Autumn" as the hunters were. It published an enraged editorial condemning the broadcast; the editorial's title was "Cheap Shot Heard Around the World." Its publisher wrote an angry memorandum to John Backe (then the president and chief executive officer of CBS), attacking the documentary and attacking CBS News for having been so unmindful of the well-being of *Field and Stream*, a sister CBS enterprise. The publisher noted that the magazine had lost advertising as a result of our broadcast. Backe forwarded the memorandum to me.

---

hearings and subpoena all our notes and work on the documentary. I thus managed to make Schneider and my colleagues angry for going forward, while I made the Nixon supporters angry for not going forward—proving once again that if you want everybody to love you, stay out of the network news business.

I replied, noting that I thought that "Guns of Autumn" was fair and accurate, that its effect on *Field and Stream* or any other CBS enterprise was something we could not properly take into account. I added that it was one of the superb traditions of CBS that each journalistic organization which was a part of CBS was free to go its own way.

I made the same point to an angry hunter, who had written me condemning the broadcast, applauding the *Field and Stream* editorial but threatening to cancel his subscription to the magazine:

> I know that it is contrary to the ethics and practices of all hunters to hit innocent bystanders. But if you cancel your subscription to *Field and Stream*, that is exactly what you will be doing—hitting an innocent bystander. One of the great things about CBS is that it understands, and respects, the great American journalistic tradition of allowing those who are engaged in various forms of journalism the maximum freedom to call the shots as each journalistic organization within CBS sees them. And so we at CBS News did "Guns of Autumn," as the excellent system here at CBS permits us to do, and *Field and Stream* was perfectly free to condemn and criticize us, because that's the way *Field and Stream* saw it. I submit that this is the best way for these things to be worked out in the long run and that this kind of freedom and independence—even the freedom and independence to be wrong—best serves the traditions for which American journalism (of which both CBS News and *Field and Stream* are a part) stands.

The letter was intended less for the hunter who wrote me than it was for the CBS Publishing Group: I sent a copy to the head of CBS Publications, who had complained to Backe.

•   •   •

One of my most troubling instances where corporate considerations were involved was a *60 Minutes* piece prepared in 1968 on the Smothers brothers. The Smothers, comedians and satirists, had a popular variety program on the CBS Television Network. They used their comedy dialogue and songs to make strong political statements about the Vietnam War and other current issues. When the *60 Minutes* piece was screened for me before broadcast, I felt that it was not balanced or fair, especially because it involved a CBS Television Network program.

However, I was uncertain whether more damage would be done—the Smothers brothers would have given great publicity to the issue—if I killed the piece, or whether I let it go on the air. I finally decided had a CBS program not been involved, I would not have permitted it to air. And so I wrote this troubled memorandum to Bill Leonard, the vice president who was in charge of documentaries and *60 Minutes*:

> I have mulled and re-mulled in an attempt to find the right answer to an extremely difficult and delicate problem. And I have come to the conclusion that we shouldn't run the sequence this coming Tuesday because it needs a lot more investigative reporting and a lot more work.
>
> Of course, the problem is complicated by the fact that we are reporting on our own company. This is always a difficult thing to do and the tendency, on my part at least, has always been to lean over backwards to stay out of any supervision of that kind of reporting. But I have come to the conclusion that it is just as wrong to bend over backwards to demonstrate our independence when, in fact, the story is not treated adequately. So in this case, I am persuaded that it is not treated adequately.

My memorandum then set out the problems I had with the proposed piece, and some of the basic questions of broadcaster responsibility, on the one hand, and the creative freedom of writers and performers, on the other. The central issue was whether entertainment programs should give their artists greater freedom to expound on current issues than we gave our reporters. My memorandum concluded:

> In the light of all the circumstances, my every instinct when I screened this yesterday was to go ahead, but on sober second, third, and fourth reflections, I regretfully come to the conclusion that I let my desire to look courageous and independent get the better of my journalistic judgment. When a difficult and complicated issue is handled badly, it ought to be repaired before it is run, even though such a decision may cause all hell to break loose. In the last analysis, letting it run is far more cowardly than not letting it run—and so I think we ought to plan on something else for next Tuesday.

The *60 Minutes* piece was revised. Don Hewitt ingeniously gave it a frame of the letters which CBS had received about the Smothers brothers—pro and con—and it was broadcast a week later. Nobody at Black Rock—neither senior management nor the executives of the CBS Television Network—was informed of the considerations which had been involved.

I believe that I accurately summed up the question of how free a news organization can be when it is part of a company engaged in many other newsworthy activities, in reply to a thoughtful letter I received in 1976: "The rest of CBS's activities are in another world, and they do not affect the topics we choose or the way we handle those topics. It may be hard to believe, but that's the way it is."

15

News as a Business

Ed Murrow put the question which confronts today's propri-
etors and managers of the press. Biting the hand that fed him,
he said that if [television] did not elucidate, educate, or illumi-
nate, that the new kid on the block . . . was nothing but lights
and wires in a box. He recognized that if it failed to reach the
potential he saw for it, it would be because of the harsh reali-
ties of the business. And so he put the $64 billion question
which needs far more urgently to be asked today: What is it
that says each year's profits must be greater than the year be-
fore?

—*Haas Foundation lecture, Seattle, May 5, 1986*

NEWS IS A SPECIAL KIND OF BUSINESS, but it is a business—a
part of the free enterprise system this nation has chosen. It has to
make money in order to spend money. The *New York Times* boasts
"All the News That's Fit to Print," while the former Aspen *Flier*, a
small newspaper more modestly—and accurately—announced, "As
Independent as Revenues Permit." Like it or not—and most newspeople do not like it a bit—the news side cannot decide, all by itself, how
much money it would like to spend to cover the news.

One of my central problems with CBS president Arthur Taylor involved the fundamental issue of budgeting. In the Taylor years, there
was an effort by senior management, and particularly by Taylor, to establish how CBS News spent the money allocated to it each year. It
was an effort to bring to news the notions of "efficiency," which, I assume, are perfectly sensible in other lines of business; but I had great
difficulty when Taylor and his associates decided that they could be
applied to news gathering, editing, and broadcasting.

In considering the question of money available to news, there are a few abiding truisms. One is that the availability of generous amounts of money does not always assure good—complete—news operations. It all depends on how wisely the news organization allocates its financial (and the concomitant, its personnel) resources. On the other hand, insufficient money can often assure inadequate news coverage, both competitively and standing alone on its own merits. For want of a nail—an extra camera, a means of getting the story back to headquarters, or one more reporter or researcher—a story can be lost or inadequately reported.

Second, by ordinary business standards of productivity and efficiency, news is a wasteful enterprise. As a matter of fact, so, in general, is any content-driven creative enterprise. Intense market research—program analysis, testing of programs with representative groups of the public, and all the rest of the costly apparatus to determine what will succeed with the public and what will not—still fails to assure that more than about one in ten new entertainment programs will survive beyond a season or two (and sometimes beyond a week or two), just as the mortality rate of motion pictures and Broadway plays is devastatingly high.

In different circumstances, the same is true of news. Assignments are made and stories are covered which do not pan out or must be shunted aside because of the sudden emergence of other more important stories which cannot be predicted—such as an assassination, a natural disaster, a hijacking. One of the most difficult things for editors to do is to scrap a major story—a documentary, a magazine segment, a special report for hard news—which looked promising but turns out to be a dry hole. A bad editor goes forward, impelled by all the investment in time, money, and reportorial resources. A good editor has the guts to scrap the story, no matter how bad that may look on the financial books to the auditors or to a senior management team which has been brought up in other lines of business.

It has often been recounted that back in the early days of retail advertising in newspapers, John Wanamaker shocked his business community with the lavish purchase of full-page advertisements in the daily New York City newspapers. When his friends and competitors told him he was wasting his money, Wanamaker agreed that, indeed, he was wasting half of it. He said that his problem was that he did not know which half.

So it is with news: We must operate with foresight; hindsight is not available to us. All the news side can do is make the best and most prudent judgments it can in advance, through its editors, and particularly its assignment editors. We cannot assign only those stories which will ripen into pieces for the final broadcast (or newspaper story). If the success of the editors and the news organization is to be measured by the fact that every story assigned will indeed see the light of day, then that newspaper or that broadcast will be pathetically inadequate—there will be too much of what is not worth publishing or broadcasting, and too little of what is.

The third truism is that news budgeting for a forthcoming year—let alone for the next five years, as the CBS planners came to insist in the latter half of the 1970s—is not, and cannot be, an exact science. Much cannot be predicted at budget time, whether it be an earthquake in Mexico or Alaska, an act of terrorism, or the explosion of a spaceship. Even the costs of a presidential election campaign are hard to predict without complete advance information on the number and identity of the candidates, where the conventions are to be held, and what primaries will be most important.

Fourth, since CBS News, when I was there, was not regarded as, or expected to be, a profit center, our budget stood naked. For budgeting purposes, our bottom line was our expenditures—how much we asked for and were permitted to spend. In contrast, for all the other operating divisions of the CBS Broadcast Group, and the rest of CBS as well, the test was not how much they spent but what their estimated profits would be. Since senior management's focus was on profits, the expenditures of the other divisions were somewhat less important, particularly if their estimates of revenues increased more than their expenditures, thus yielding higher profits.

But news had no such protection. We could not justify higher expenditures by still higher revenues, since our books showed no revenues. At least on the surface, therefore, our proposed budgets appeared to be—and often in fact were—direct subtractions from the company's bottom-line profits. It was tempting, therefore, for senior management, or at least its financial staff, to try to cut our requests. If our budget was cut by $1 million, for example, it would show up on the bottom line of other parts of CBS as a $1 million increase in profits. Our budgets became an attractive target.

Fifth, as I have described, some of the senior managers, over the years, were certain that we at CBS News were not very cost conscious, that we spent extravagantly. Some believed—wrongly—that we could be cut by 20 or 30 percent, with no visible diminution in the quantity or quality of our news broadcasts.

Sixth, the conviction that we spent extravagantly was compounded by the gruesome fact of the enormous costs of television. Covering and preparing a simple story for radio might cost a couple of hundred dollars. In television, that cost was several thousand dollars. The unwieldy requirements of television meant a reporter, a field producer, a camera person, a lighting person, a sound person, and the costs of transporting all of these people and their apparatus to the scene of a story, and then getting it back to the point from which it could be broadcast had to be paid for. As a sign in the television offices of the British Broadcasting Company used to say, "The medium gets in the way of the message."

With these several factors at work, our annual budget meetings were, for me, tense and traumatic. Before each meeting, I spent days with my associates, crawling through their requests line by line, sending the requests back for revision, trying again. I had to prepare myself on all the details—yet somehow or other, senior management and its financial staff (which sometimes seemed to have more people than we had reporters) usually managed to ask me questions which I had not anticipated.

One year, Jack Schneider, then the Broadcast Group president, scheduled a lunch for all the heads of the broadcast divisions to be held immediately after the CBS News budget meeting with senior management. This was early in the game—back in 1967, when Bill Paley and Frank Stanton were still running senior management and everybody was more relaxed about their budgets.[1] The era of trying to make us fit into a more normal business was yet to come. Nevertheless, when I received notice that Schneider's lunch would follow our budget meeting, I sent him a note, "We can start saving money right now; don't order any food for me because I doubt whether I will be able to eat." I was not kidding.

• • •

Late in 1972, Taylor took direct action in his push for the News Division's financial accountability. He appointed a committee to examine the News Division's operations with Sheldon Wool (CBS corporate vice chairman of profit evaluation) as chairman. Taylor had brought Wool over with him from International Paper. Wool had no news experience and was totally unfamiliar with the News Division.

My original understanding was that the Wool committee, as it came to be known, was to be an effort on the part of Taylor and other senior managers to acquaint themselves with how news is gathered and processed so they could better understand and judge our annual budget requests. I thought at the outset that the Wool committee could be a

---

[1] In the early 1960s, the annual CBS News budget was about $20 million. By 1973, it was about $63 million. By the time I left in 1979, it was $90 million. In 1985, the CBS News budget was generally reported to be $300 million dollars.

sensible way for strangers to broadcasting and broadcast news to educate themselves on just how news operates.

But almost immediately, the Wool project took a turn I found ominous, and my alarm bells began to ring. Taylor wrote a memorandum characterizing the project as an "operations study" of CBS News as related to costs. I feared this might be an opening wedge to second-guessing our news judgments about what stories to cover, what documentaries to produce, and how.

But what alarmed me most was that Taylor's memorandum defined the committee's "goal" as being

> to find ways to continue the existing level and quality of activities and responsibilities of CND [CBS News Division] at a reduced expense to the corporation. It is further my hope that the study will involve vigorous questioning on the part of the task force and a willingness to probe deeply into CND operations.

It seemed to me that Wool's instructions were not to help Taylor's understanding of news operations but to "probe deeply" into them, making judgments about how sensibly, as well as how economically, we went about our business. I was also alarmed that the Taylor charter reached the conclusion at the threshold as to the very issue which I thought was the subject of the study—whether the CBS News Division could in fact reduce its costs without adversely affecting the "level and the quality of its activities."

Taylor's establishing memorandum did not put that as a question—it simply assumed that we could do less expensively what we were doing, with no loss of quality. The instructions to Wool were to find how to do that, not whether it could be done. Once again, the assumption—not an uncommon or unnatural one among those who know little about news and who are familiar only with factory productivity and factory efficiency—was that we were inefficient spendthrifts who obviously could get a bigger bang for the company's bucks.

I protested that the committee thus was starting with the conclusion—that we could spend less and the quality of our "product" would nevertheless be maintained. Wool soothed me—a little: He assured me that the sentence was only a "hypothesis," still to be tested, and not a conclusion.

In February 1973, Wool prepared a table projecting news losses over the forthcoming five years. According to his calculations, the losses for the past five years had totaled $62 million, and the projected losses for the next five years would almost double—to $115 million. That was bad enough, but Wool wanted the alarms to sound more loudly. He wrote in a memo that he thought the projected sales of the News

Division's broadcasts were based "largely on planning optimism," and since sales were more likely to be flat, the losses over the next five-year period could total $150 million.

Wool sent copies of his memorandum to the members of his committee, which included two CBS News representatives. Word of it spread quickly throughout the News Division. As I wrote Taylor a few days later, the Wool memorandum "created shock waves" among my associates in the division.

Concurrently, Wool and his staff had fanned out within the CBS News Division, observing operations and asking detailed questions about what was being done and why. At my monthly luncheon meeting with hard news producers and executives, they described what was happening and were deeply concerned. I tried to explain what I believed to be the Wool committee's functions; I told them that the committee represented nothing more than a good faith effort by Taylor to learn about our operations so that he could more intelligently judge our annual budget requests.

But at the lunch, my colleagues pressed me for a more specific definition of the committee's functions, since they could not reconcile the nature of the questions which were being put to them by Wool's people with my attempted assurances. The uncertainty about the committee and the concern that it was examining our operations in terms of second-guessing my people's daily operating news judgments were clearly affecting morale.

In June 1973, Wool presented his final report to Taylor at a meeting attended by Jack Schneider, Wool, the committee members, and me. It was a tense two-and-a-quarter-hour meeting. In a memorandum which I prepared for my own files immediately after the meeting, I wrote that after I had once again stated that one of the difficulties with the project was that there never had been any specific term of reference or definition of the mission of the committee, "Mr. Taylor blew up at this—totally and completely—saying that he couldn't make it any clearer than he already had—that the purpose of the committee was to determine whether we could not achieve the same results at a lower cost." I pointed to Wool's report, which, on the contrary, stated that there had been no terms of reference.

After this head-on collision between Taylor and me, the meeting went further downhill. I asked why, with the other broadcast divisions spending so much more money than the CBS News Division and constructing their expenditures budget much the same way as we did, the News Division had been singled out for the study. In a memorandum for my files, I reconstructed what happened next at the meeting. I stated:

I was sick and tired of the constant suspicion that we were extravagant, careless, and imprudent. He [Taylor] then stated that he would make a "blunt statement"—"blunter than he had ever made to [me] before" and "he did not want any comment on that statement from me." The statement was that CND was special and presented special problems because we regarded ourselves as so "separate" from the rest of CBS.

Since I was forbidden to do so, I made no comment on this, but I am certain that Mr. Taylor is raising the same fundamental issue that he and Mr. Schneider had raised before—the "we" and "they" syndrome; the alleged fact that we do not regard ourselves as being part of the CBS team; that we regard ourselves as the elite etc., etc. (Sooner or later there must be a showdown on this issue, since I feel strongly that at least as far as our news judgments are concerned, we must maintain absolute separateness and independence if we are to be a viable news organization.)

On the other hand, if Mr. Taylor means nothing more than that we should not regard corporate intervention or policies with cynicism and all corporate people as the enemy, the point has validity, although it might also be pointed out that it is a two-way street and that many other people in other divisions and at corporate level treat us as the enemy, just as we may treat them as the enemy. This is not the last we have heard of the issue.

Suddenly, as the meeting was concluding, Taylor announced that the Wool committee had finished its work and that it was, at that point, dissolved. The issues and any possible changes were to be left to further discussions among Taylor, Schneider, and me. There would be no study by any outside management consultant company unless I wanted and requested it.

Of course, I never did want it or request it.

There the episode—or as I regarded it then, the crisis—ended. There were no changes imposed on the News Division as a result of the Wool committee project; there were no changes in policies governing the relationships between the News Division and the corporation. And our annual budget requests were treated with no less generosity than they had been before.

Underreaction and understatement are not among my notable characteristics. We in the News Division, and most certainly I, tended to fire shots across the bow of passing CBS corporate ships even if they were not headed our way to try to board us. It was during a period of great transition for CBS and hence, I thought, for the News Division and for me. We were passing from the Paley-Stanton era to a new era in which nonbroadcasting businesspeople, experienced as executives in very large, and very different, lines of business, were now at the top. The Wool committee and its repercussions could reasonably be interpreted—at the time—as a watershed for the place of CBS News in the CBS organization. What I saw, therefore, in the Wool committee episode in 1973 was an attempt to make a basic change at CBS, fundamentally affecting CBS News Division's autonomy and how it went about its business.

Perhaps. And perhaps not. The episode may well have been nothing more than what I tried at first to assure my alarmed CBS News colleagues that it was—an effort by a newcomer, so unfamiliar with broadcasting in general, and news in particular, to try to understand us. And, as I conceded to myself in my memorandum for the files, summarizing the anticlimactic meeting with Taylor and Schneider, we in News did regard ourselves as very special—elitists removed from the commercial considerations which impelled our colleagues at Black Rock to earn their comfortable keep by such entertainment programs as *The Beverly Hillbillies.*

Except on payday or when we were negotiating our own contracts, we scorned the commercial considerations which were the driving force of the rest of the company. We did tend to hold our noses high— and look down on the rest of CBS broadcast activities, even though it was the huge success of those mostly entertainment activities which made it possible for us at News to operate the way we did. As Jim Aubrey, an earlier president of the CBS Television Network, is reputed to have told Fred Friendly when Fred was CBS News president, "The entertainment end of the network business did its worst so that CBS News could do its best."

Given our elitism, our separatism, our strange and—to a businessman accustomed to careful cost controls—inefficient way of creating our "product," it is, then, entirely understandable that an intelligent man like Arthur Taylor should have had serious questions about the News Division and that he should have sought to find some solutions to the problems he quite reasonably perceived.

I was then, however, an ardent believer in the thesis, expressed in a very different context, that the only time to defend and fight for one's liberty was while one still enjoyed it.[2] The clouds may have been no

---

[2]While I was in charge, CBS senior management always dealt with the news budget with a scalpel, not a meat axe. Unfortunately, that was not true by the mid-1980s, after I had left CBS, and after the economics of network television changed. Under owner Lawrence Tisch, CBS senior management did cut deeply into the CBS News budget, firing more than three hundred news employees. Although there was an expectation that quality would not suffer, it did. Both NBC and ABC also reduced their news budgets during this period.

bigger than a man's hand, but in the Wool project, I saw the threat of a cyclone. It may well not have been looming after all.

It is also possible that by the summer of 1973, Taylor had something more serious, as far as he was concerned, to occupy his attention. By then, Mr. Paley had become disenchanted with Taylor and had decided he had made a mistake in anointing him. Perhaps the whole affair petered out, then, because Taylor, not long after, and for reasons which had nothing to do with the episode, was fired by Paley.

16

Fighting for Airtime

I regret the widely noted disappearance at CBS of serious-issue documentaries. Less widely noted, and at least as deplorable, is the disappearance of prime-time instant specials dealing with suddenly emerging news events or issues. CBS used to average two of these a month. Has anybody here seen a prime-time special on a commercial television network ... examining or explaining the savings and loan crisis, or an analysis of the Panama invasion, or the budget deficit? Instead, the commercial networks give us such escape hatches as "Life in the Fat Lane," and "Bad Girls," and "Satanism."

—Society of Professional Journalists, New Haven, June 14, 1990

THE MIX OF A NETWORK SCHEDULE—how much shall be entertainment and how much shall be news and information—defines the basic character of a broadcast company and its management. Yet no single issue in my sixteen years at CBS was as difficult and as amorphous as trying to get time on the air for news programs. The budgeting process may have been nerve-wracking and tense, but at least the decisions were made by a systematic and orderly process. That was not the way it was with scheduling time on the air.

I got an OK to my requests for airtime too often for me to believe that the sole criteria were ratings and profits. And in cases of transcendent importance which occurred suddenly—the assassination of President Kennedy, for example—the News Division had the authority to take over the network and preempt the regular schedule.[1] But in all other

---

[1] In the case of President Kennedy's assassination, we preempted the schedule for four days. It was, however, Frank Stanton who made the decision to eliminate all commercials for the four days. One affiliate—the only one, to my knowledge—complained bitterly about the loss of commercials. His complaints were ignored.

cases, whether it was a news special with a day or two of lead time, a documentary, a special limited series, or a regular news series, the News Division could not unilaterally make the decision to acquire time on the air. CBS News could only propose; it was for others to dispose. And for most of my years at CBS, there were, so far as I could see, no clear standards, criteria, goals, or underlying philosophy in the decision-making process. It was a constant source of irritation—and bewilder-ment—to me that the process was as inchoate as it often seemed to be.

• • •

One problem was finding who made scheduling decisions: It was just "they," and often I was not sure who "they" were. But an even more difficult problem was figuring out how the decisions were made. In the earliest days of the Columbia Broadcasting System, when Bill Paley was the head of our collegial family, it was simple enough—he made the scheduling decisions. Later, as he delegated more and more, Frank Stanton stepped in, and he, with Paley's consent, made the deci-sions. They did what senior management is there for: They set the tone, broadly defined the policy, and scheduling in the final analysis was the result of their decisions.

It was Frank Stanton who correctly defined a broadcaster's public ser-vice obligations: He recognized that under the commercial broadcasting system this nation has chosen, it is necessary to appeal to most of the people most of the time, in order for broadcasting to be a viable busi-ness. But because of broadcasting's responsibility for making informa-tion available to people so they can make their decisions in a democracy on an informed basis, it was just as important to appeal to less than most of the people some of the time. As early as the mid-1950s, when much less was at stake than was the case in succeeding decades, Wall Street's demand for constant growth and increasing profits already posed excruciating dilemmas for CBS's senior management.[2] Because of

---

[2]In 1958, Ed Murrow made a now-famous speech in Chicago to a meeting of the Ra-dio and Television News Directors Association. He publicly went to the heart of the is-sue. "This instrument [television] can teach; it can illuminate, yes; and it can even in-spire. But it can do so only to the extent that humans are determined to use it to those ends. Otherwise it is merely a collection of wires and lights in a box."

And he asked what required a broadcasting company to make 10 or 15 percent higher profits each year, suggesting the networks could earn slightly less and invest somewhat more in news and information programming. I was present—I was still a corporate vice president—when copies of Ed's speech reached the twentieth floor of 485 Madison Av-enue, then the corporate floor of the Columbia Broadcasting System. It hit them—Mr. Paley especially—where it hurts. He felt that his friend Ed, whose patron Bill had been, was fouling his own nest and, simultaneously, biting the hand that was generously feed-ing him. Ed, he believed, did not understand the business imperatives and the obliga-tions to the company's stockholders.

the economics of the business, the two imperative objectives—doing good and doing well—often collided head-on.[3]

I would like to underscore that, if left to their own consciences, their own character, and their own personal desires, every CBS senior manager, I am certain, would have been delighted to accede to my pleas for an hour of evening network news, for weekly prime-time documentaries, for more news specials, for more daytime and prime-time News Division series. But only if these had been economically possible, only if they had not carried such an enormous price in loss of revenues, ratings, and profits.[4] Each was a prisoner of the system, however—the business system, which demands increasing profits and which must take into account the expectations and desires of its stockholder-owners as well as its affiliates.

Indeed, if it were not for the economics of it, I would not have had to plead at all—my colleagues would have come to the News Division. The problem then would have been whether our supply of news could have met their demand. But that was not the way it was.

• • •

It is apparent that the forces of the marketplace and Wall Street are stronger now than ever. For some time now, CBS senior management has not only demanded that the News Division overall be a profit center but that even a proposed series or group of broadcasts must have promise of being profitable as a condition of their eligibility for the

---

I have always felt that it was Ed Murrow's speech which really underlay the most unfortunate breach between those two good friends, Bill Paley and Ed Murrow, neither of whom would have had the brilliant career that each did, and neither of whom would have made the enormous contributions to society, which each in his own way did, without the other. The towering irony is that both were right. After Murrow left CBS for the USIA [U.S. Information Agency], and after Murrow became terminally ill, the breach between them was healed.

[3]*Editors' note:* All news cable networks have made many of these critical scheduling decisions less critical, since an all-news channel can preempt scheduled news programming more easily with less loss of revenue.

[4]News broadcasts generally have lower ratings, and they yield lower revenues and lower profits (if any) than entertainment programs. Yet I cannot in good conscience reject ratings as a criterion for what gets, and then stays, on the schedule. I wish I could—generally, ratings were a principal obstacle to our news programs' entry into the television network schedule, and so I grew to hate them. But it is both quixotic and mistaken to contend that ratings should be ignored in the scheduling process. This is because commercial television is an advertising medium, just as newspapers and magazines are, and advertisers must know, in deciding where and how to spend their money, what the circulation of the advertising medium is. Ratings are simply broadcasting's measure of circulation. If ratings were abolished tomorrow, broadcasting would shrivel as an advertiser-supported medium.

schedule. The genre of News Division broadcasts which has suffered more than any other as a result of practical economic criteria is the documentary. Fairly early on while I was president of CBS News, the battle over documentaries began. It was one of the results of *60 Minutes*, which had contributed to my reservations about scheduling that series in the first place because I knew that it would lead to a reduced number of documentaries.

When, in 1969, I had proposed that *60 Minutes* be scheduled on a weekly basis, I coupled that with a request for at least twelve other preemptive prime-time hours elsewhere in the schedule for documentaries. Not surprisingly, the question was raised whether a weekly *60 Minutes* would not take care of all our needs, so that one-hour documentaries would become superfluous. I replied that "we have been wrestling with this problem, and we have concluded that it would be extremely unwise to cut down significantly on the number of full-hour documentaries." Eager as I was to have *60 Minutes* on a weekly basis, I was not willing to pay the price of eliminating documentaries.

I asked Bill Leonard, the CBS News vice president in charge of documentaries, who had not only produced but also reported some distinguished *CBS Reports*, to prepare a memorandum setting out the reasons for my conclusion that documentaries should not be abandoned. Bill wrote:

> It is impossible to do justice to a really important subject within the magazine format without destroying the qualities of that format which make it attractive. In other words, it has been our experience that a subject like "Hunger in America," if treated fully, takes the time, effort and money which require 50 to 100 minutes of broadcast time. . . . The important thing is that to make an impact, to effect a change, to arouse public opinion, to be taken seriously (the most frequent and frequently justified criticism of broadcast journalism is that we are superficial) requires the complete treatment, or as nearly complete as we can make it. Not only does that require, with some frequency, the special hour but more and more often time in excess of an hour. . . .
>
> Although it is true that NBC does few and ABC almost no prime-time documentaries, the fact that we have been doing so is surely one of the reasons for the preeminence of CBS News. If we were to pour it all into something like *60 Minutes*, abandoning the one-hour format, we would reap the whirlwind from our own correspondents, our own producers, and our best and most thoughtful supporters in the press and in Washington.

And then Bill Leonard concluded his memorandum, with the most persuasive argument of all: "As a footnote, you would lose me."

Our arguments saved documentaries for a few more years. But the difficulties of scheduling documentaries on any sort of regular periodic basis, and at a reasonable time in the schedule, persisted. We thought documentaries were very important; the Television Network and the Broadcast Group presidents thought they were a bloody nuisance.

This is ironic because more than any other genre, it is the documentary which has produced the most memorable landmark broadcasts of historical significance and more clearly established the honorable reputation of CBS News. From the great Edward R. Murrow and Fred Friendly *See It Now* broadcasts to the *CBS Reports* and other such documentary specials as the Joseph McCarthy broadcasts, "Harvest of Shame," "Hunger in America," the examination of the assassination of President Kennedy, "The Italians," "Smoking and Cancer," "1945," "The Search for a Safer Car," "Black America," "The Fire Next Door," "The Selling of the Pentagon," "The Boat People," "The Vanishing American Family"— these are documentaries which have for many thoughtful observers defined what CBS and CBS News are all about. And yet documentaries have, over the years, progressively become a dying breed, fighting a losing battle against the laws of commercial broadcasting.

After half of ABC News's documentary staff was let go in 1983, one "high-level source" at ABC was quoted in *Variety* as saying, "They [documentaries] don't make money, and they certainly don't generate any ratings to speak of. And when each weekly Nielsen separates the networks by one point or so, the programming department would be crazy to give up valuable air time for documentaries."

Yet a documentary today will attract 12 to 15 million viewers. When one compares those figures to the number of subscribers to magazines like the *Atlantic Monthly* or *Harper's* or the *Nation* or the *National Review*, or to buyers of serious nonfiction books, the audience for documentaries is large indeed. It is a demonstrated appetite to which attention should be paid. Less than most of the people is still an enormous number of people who are not being served, nor is our society, by the gradual disappearance of documentaries.

If demonstration be needed that the one-hour documentary is still a useful form, one need only look at the Public Broadcasting System which, in addition to its many special documentaries and its *Nature* and *Nova* series, also broadcasts on a weekly basis, on the same day, at the same prime time, *Frontline*.[5] *Frontline* establishes that there are many subjects of importance to which the documentary form lends it-

---

[5] I should note that I was on a small advisory board of *Frontline* during its first year.

self very nicely indeed, and for which a magazine format with fifteen-minute segments is inadequate.

And that is the nub of it. The great variety of documentaries and informational specials that flourish on noncommercial television can only barely exist in today's climate at the commercial television networks. But the issue is not whether CBS, NBC, or ABC ought to be as nutritious as PBS. They cannot be. And that is why noncommercial broadcasting was created—to do what the market forces pressing on commercial television prevent it from doing.

However, public broadcasting is subject to its own market forces: It must be attractive enough to generate individual contributions of money from its supporters; it must shape a program schedule which is appealing—and, unfortunately, often noncontroversial—enough to generate corporate grants and "sponsorship"; and it must look to Congress and the president for a major source of money. That is why I would suggest that commercial broadcasters seriously consider grants to public broadcasting, earmarked for the news broadcasts and series which they ought to broadcast but for which they can find no room.

This idea, bolstering PBS and generating important documentaries for the public, would, I believe, be a fitting contribution for commercial broadcasters as part of their corporate responsibility, without subjecting them to the pressures of ratings and network competition. Charity should begin at home—and home is broadcasting. Especially in the light of the shrinking federal appropriations to public broadcasting, voluntary and substantial grants consistent with the average percentage of revenues or profits of the commercial networks would be appropriate.[6] In some significant measure, this would allow conscientious broadcasters to do what they would like to do but cannot do in the light of the perceived business imperatives—to the direct benefit of the viewing and listening public to which broadcasters owe their existence.[7]

---

[6]The contributions would have to be more than nominal. They would represent a significant fraction of what the broadcasters would have spent for the broadcasts on their own networks. While I believe the commercial broadcaster should be able to designate the general purpose of each individual grant—that is, for example, a series on the press or a specified number of documentaries—there could be no other strings attached insofar as content is concerned. That would be the sole responsibility of the public broadcaster. The customary credit which public broadcasting now permits the grantor would be permitted for the commercial broadcast grantor. And each grant must be for a specified period—at least a year or two—so as to minimize content control.

[7]Volunteerism is an essential condition of my suggestion. An enforced contribution, through a special tax of a percentage of broadcaster revenues or profits, not only unfairly discriminates against broadcasters, among all free competitive business enterprises, but also involves the government too deeply in the process.

• • •

By August 1977, my time at CBS was running out and I had resolved, during the months which remained, to abandon my attempts to persuade senior management to set scheduling policies—a decade of futility discouraged me from further efforts. It seemed sensible for me to leave the issue to whoever might be my successor. But in January 1978, scheduling problems came to a head and I made one more try—this time a furious one.

In mid-January, we broadcast Hubert Humphrey's funeral live from Minneapolis. But before the ceremonies were complete and before ABC and NBC went off the air with their coverage, I was instructed by the head of the CBS Television Network to return to the network's regular schedule at 5:00 P.M. This meant that I had to leave the funeral ceremonies so that CBS could carry a one-hour tape of the postponed conclusion of a golf tournament which had been rained out on the day before. By the time we broadcast the taped conclusion of the tournament, the winner was, if one listened to the radio, already known.

There was more. On the following weekend, the television network scheduled, and broadcast, a tennis match—on a clay court, where long rallies are the norm—between Bjorn Borg, a notoriously long rallier, and Jimmy Connors. The network and the Sports Division scheduled the Borg-Connors match to begin at 4:00 P.M., when they must have realized the unlikelihood of its being completed in time for our news—our first feed of the regular weekend evening news was scheduled at its usual time of 6:00, the second feed at 6:30. Of course, the match wasn't finished until 6:50, wiping out our evening news altogether.

But the worst was yet to come on Super Bowl Sunday. The kickoff wasn't until 6:15 P.M., the halftime lasted twenty-five minutes instead of the customary fifteen, and the postgame coverage lasted twenty-eight minutes. And instead of broadcasting *60 Minutes*, which by then had moved to 7:00 and which normally would have followed the Super Bowl, the network had decided, the month before, to insert *All in the Family*. The result was that *60 Minutes* did not begin until 10:50 that night.

I was so outraged that I had to wait eight days before I wrote an angry memorandum—and then I wrote it only for the files, as a kind of therapy.

"I deliberately refrained," I wrote to myself,

from writing this memorandum on the Monday following this sequence of events because I wanted to give myself time to cool down. But in the intervening week, my anger refused to subside. Indeed, my juices started to run all over again.

What all this means to me, to my associates, is that CBS News broadcasts are at the bottom of the totem pole. In appearance, as well as actual practice, in these cases we are the tail end of priorities. And it is mighty hard to maintain a going organization and a precious reputation in all these circumstances, each of which piles up on the other.

Coming back to my oft-sung theme, I continued:

The first instinct—ours as well as others' within CBS—was to point fingers and to find a scapegoat. But I think that this is a mistake. . . . This is not ultimately [the] fault [of the president of the CBS Sports Division], or [the president of the CBS Television Network], or [the president of the CBS Broadcast Group]. Each is able and intelligent; each carries out the mission which he believes to have been assigned to him. And the ultimate mission which they believe has been assigned to them is to do the best they can for their respective operations. They define "the best" as it is generally defined—to maximize their performance and their profits. . . . What I believe to be the basic malady is that the point beyond which this mission should not be carried has never been defined by the only people who can define it—the senior managers. The emphasis has been, as it generally must be, the bottom line—plus reasonable autonomy. But the flaw is that there never has been an underlying philosophy or guidance to govern where and what the limitations are.

And in my gloomy ruminations, I concluded:

If CBS is to recapture its old reputation for class, statesmanship, and leadership, affirmative steps have to be taken at the top level to make it clear what we stand for and to make it clear that those principles must play a role in the day-to-day scheduling . . . clear not only to those immediately below senior management but to middle management as well. We take our orders, and it is one of the strengths of CBS that the orders, or what are perceived to be orders, are executed well. It is up to senior management to set the tone for the nature of the orders.

Having thus relieved myself of my inner turmoil, I spared senior management another passionate lecture on what it ought to be doing—and, in my mind, was failing to do. But simultaneously, I wrote a brief memorandum and discussed the scheduling issue with CBS president John Backe. I do not know what, if anything, he did in later discussions with other Broadcast Group and division heads. I only know that, once again, so far as I was aware, no articulation of principle and policy resulted. That was my last try. After over a decade of pushing, writing interminable memos, and delivering speeches to my bosses, I was no further along than I was when I first started.

17

News and Advertisers

CBS News management seems to ignore the written standards issued after we spent four years developing and writing them . . . based on forty years of CBS's experience pioneering broadcast journalism. . . . [One] standard catastrophically ignored is the one which forbids, without special permission, live interviews in edited news broadcasts. Mobil Oil used to refuse any interviews for our news broadcasts unless its representatives could appear live and unedited—so Mobil could control the news process. That's why we wrote the prohibition into our news standards.

—*Society of Professional Journalists, New Haven, June 14, 1990*

MAINTAINING AN IMPENETRABLE WALL of separation between CBS News and its advertisers had been a basic policy from the earliest days of CBS News. As Bill Paley said in "The Road to Responsibility" in 1954, "An advertiser who sponsors any type of information produced by us does not thereby purchase, or in any way gain, any rights to control the contents of the program." Despite this policy, however, the question of advertiser control over what stories CBS News covered and how it covered them was an issue I persistently confronted.

• • •

When I was at CBS, basic company policy required that the News Division make its own decisions on what broadcasts to produce and how they were to be produced. Advertisers had no control and no influence over the stories we chose, their subject matter, or their treatment. The sales department dealt with advertisers and their agencies. We described to the salesmen, in general terms, what our documentaries, or specials, or news series would be. Then it was up to the network salespeople to sell the commercial availabilities—we in the News Division did not participate further in the sales process. News was news, sales were sales, and never did the twain meet.

Nor, at least in the case of CBS News, and, I believe, other network news organizations, were special broadcasts devised for advertisers with a direct interest in specific subject matter. That practice is not uncommon among newspapers, however, which add special sections (sometimes not even prepared by the newspapers' staff) in order to attract such advertisers. The real estate section is an example of a newspaper practice in which network news did not engage.

With few exceptions, neither were advertisers or advertising agencies ever in my office or in the newsrooms. I can recall only three meetings with advertisers. One was with the officers of Philip Morris, who met with me and a number of my associates in the early 1960s, when CBS News was broadcasting several documentaries on smoking and health. The Philip Morris people were unhappy—they insisted we had not been accurate or balanced and that there was no linkage between smoking and cancer.

A second meeting was with officials of Lever at a time when there was considerable media coverage—including CBS News coverage—of the effects of detergent use on water supply. The Lever people made an elaborate presentation on their side of the issue.

The third was a lunch given by Exxon officials to which my associates and I were invited. The Exxon people talked about their business and its economics.

In none of these three cases were there any CBS Television Network people or salesmen present. The meetings were arranged directly with me. While there was some criticism of our coverage, there was never the slightest hint of any connection with their advertising expenditures. I met with them just as I met, from time to time, with other groups, although in general, I learned it was better to avoid such meetings. Thus, for example, when the public relations people of Citicorp invited me to lunch with Citicorp's chief executive officer, I declined.

It became my policy to decline when I felt that a business, or any other individual or group, wanted to meet with me in order to discuss our coverage. I explained that such meetings were a waste of their time, as well as mine, and that if they wanted to present their side of an issue, they should follow the normal route of communicating with the assignment editors. And even more important, they should make their decisionmaking officers available to whatever reporter was covering a story affecting them. I tried to explain to officials who sought meetings with me that it was no use trying to sell me on their facts and views, since I was not about to pass them along secondhand to our reporters and editors covering the story or to order in advance how they should report. I also explained that I would, of course, consider and check out any specific complaints about coverage which they thought was inaccurate and unfair if they wrote me the specifics.

Unless I was prepared to spend an inordinate amount of my time in meetings whose premise was that I would intrude in advance on my associates' news judgments, it was a sensible policy, even though it caused some chief executive officers and their public relations people to conclude that I was arrogant and unfriendly. All I was doing was trying to educate them about how a news organization works and to save them from wasting their time. If, however, I had any suspicion—as I did not in any of the previously mentioned cases—that any company officer or other critic of CBS News was using his muscle as an advertiser to influence our news content, I assumed the porcupine mode and shot out my quills.

For example, in 1978, the vice president in charge of public relations for a major CBS advertiser (in which, coincidentally, I own a small amount of stock) mistakenly wrote me a letter complaining that WCBS-TV in New York City (over which CBS News had no authority) had failed to cover the announcement of the construction of his company's large new plant. He pointed out that the *New York Times* had reported the announcement on its front page and at the bottom of his letter appended a handwritten note complaining, "The people around here feel that as one of CBS's top advertisers . . . we deserve better treatment."

I replied, saying,

> I am sorry you wrote that. News judgments here at CBS News, and I am certain at WCBS-TV and all other responsible news organizations, do not and cannot turn on whether or not the subject, the event, or organization is related to, or is of special interest to, an advertiser. This is a fundamental axiom of good journalism. The "treatment," if any, that a potential story deserves has, and can have, no relation to the presence or absence of advertising consideration.

A few days later, I received a memorandum from a CBS corporate vice president who was a personal friend of the public relations official. The CBS officer wrote me that his friend

> had done very little business with us up until two years ago and at that time decided to put all his money in CBS. Now, due to some strong feelings regarding news in general, he has withdrawn from CBS. He would

appreciate the opportunity to chat with you and if you have a free luncheon . . . I would like to set it up.

Out shot my quills. I wrote back to the CBS vice president that my reply to the company official "exhausts my quota of being polite to him. . . . I will have lunch with a gentleman no matter what his views. I won't have lunch with a boor no matter what the dollars he has to offer us—when I joined this business, there was nothing that said I had to be a whore."

To further emphasize the separation of news from advertisers, CBS—and particularly Frank Stanton—developed policies to assure no crossover and to make it clear that the News Division, not advertisers or their agencies, was in control of news content.

One such policy, unique to CBS News, forbade the News Division to state that the broadcast is "brought to you by" a particular advertiser. ABC still introduces its network evening news, *The World News Tonight*, as being "brought to you by" an advertiser, and even informational broadcasts on the Public Broadcasting System are introduced at the top of the broadcast as being "made possible by" a corporate grantor, whose line of business is identified. The CBS prohibition of the phrase "brought to you by" was simply designed to underscore what is the fact: that the broadcast is there because CBS decided it should be there and CBS News produced it, and neither its presence on the schedule nor the content was by the grace of advertisers.[1]

A second policy sharply limited the circumstances in which advertisers or their agencies could prescreen a CBS News broadcast. In the earliest days of my tenure, such prescreening was flatly prohibited for any broadcast unless the subject, and its treatment, were entirely noncontroversial, as, for example, a historical or cultural documentary. Even for such noncontroversial subjects, however, CBS policy forbade advertiser viewing (or in the case of radio, advertiser listening) until the production had been completed; no changes suggested by the advertiser would be made in the content.

It was formerly the rule that all other CBS News productions could not be prescreened before actual broadcast. But in the 1960s, it be-

---

[1] It is one of the ironies—and misfortunes arising out of inadequate funding—that, in contrast to the way CBS News was able to operate, even documentary and other public affairs series on the Public Broadcasting System are stated to be, and are in fact, made possible by the granting company. Thus the important and useful PBS series *Inside Story*, a weekly examination of the performance of the press, was made possible by a generous and public-spirited grant from General Electric. When GE ended its grant, unfortunately, *Inside Story* ended, too.

came necessary, whenever time permitted, to preview our documentaries and other specials for our affiliates, who, as licensees, had the responsibility for what was transmitted by their stations—no matter what the source of the programs. In a few instances, we learned that special interest groups, concerned about a scheduled documentary, prevailed on an affiliate to allow representatives of these special interests to attend the closed-circuit screening. We had no way of stopping that.

I believed it was hardly fair for those with a special interest in the subject matter to find a way to screen the documentary before broadcast and yet forbid advertisers to do so. We revised the policy accordingly. The new policy provided that if a broadcast dealt with a controversial subject, advertisers could view it or hear it but not prior to the date on which it was previewed for the CBS affiliates.

"CBS News Standards," which I issued in 1976, also reaffirmed and assured the independence of CBS News. At the very beginning of the standards booklet is the provision that the News Division "retains sole control over the content of its broadcasts. They are not tailored in any way to the desires or requirements of advertisers. Requests by advertisers for script approval or any other form of content control have been, and must be, rejected."

"CBS News Standards" included other advertising regulations; for example:

- It was prohibited to identify an advertiser or its products during a broadcast, except for time devoted to billboards or commercial messages. For example, it was forbidden to place an advertising logo on the desk of a broadcaster so that it could be seen during a broadcast. NBC, for example, had an oil company which sponsored all of its special news coverage, including the political conventions. Throughout these broadcasts, the name of the company was conspicuous on the anchor's desk.

  So, too, in the earlier days of television news, NBC's evening news was sponsored by Camel cigarettes and was called the *Camel Caravan*. It was also common for Esso to sponsor local news under the title *Esso Reports*. CBS-owned stations rejected that identification and never carried any *Esso Reports*. The CBS Television Network lost important sponsorship because of this policy.

- CBS correspondents were forbidden to participate in billboards or lead-ins to commercial messages on television broadcasts.

- Political advertisements were unacceptable in commercials within hard news broadcasts. They were also barred from public affairs broadcasts if they were incompatible with the content of the particular broadcast.

These policies governing our relationship to advertisers were basic. For us at CBS News, they were a way of life.

• • •

This is not to say that ultimately and indirectly, advertisers do not affect what appears on the network. Of course they do—that is in the nature of our free-enterprise system. For most of its broadcasting history, this nation has thought the risks that go with advertising are preferable to the risks of government ownership or reliance on government funding.[2] Instead of a government-owned, tax-supported broadcasting system, we have chosen a free-enterprise, advertiser-supported system, just as American newspapers are free enterprise and advertiser supported.

To the extent that advertisers decide where to put their money and also to the considerable extent that most advertisers look, especially in network television, for maximum possible circulation, advertisers do play a major role in what the American people read, hear, or see. But beyond this, advertisers have relatively little control over program content. While in earlier days single sponsorship of network television entertainment programs was the rule, now it is the exception. This is because network entertainment programs can be so costly. A single sponsor cannot afford a whole program, nor does [a sponsor] want to put all its eggs in one expensive basket. Also, advertisers want to spread their risks and reach different audiences at different times. With these changes has come a loss of advertiser control even over entertainment programs, since each advertiser is one of many within the program. The result is that today advertisers rarely buy programs; they

---

[2]As the history of the British Broadcasting Corporation shows—during the Suez Crisis and more recently, during the time of the troubles in Ireland—even if a government-supported system is theoretically insulated by dedicated taxes—so formidable a system as BBC is not immune from government pressure and control. And, depending on the pleasure of Parliament, the amount of moneys available can and does vary. The American alternative of noncommercial television, too, trades one set of potential controls for another: It relies in part on federal appropriations, which, as Nixon demonstrated, may contract, or even disappear, if the government is not pleased with its programming.

Indeed, apart from the creeping commercials which are beginning to pockmark American "noncommercial" television, the noncommercial system of grants by commercial companies plays a direct role—greater than advertisers' commercials in commercial broadcasting—in what particular programs do, or do not, get on the noncommercial system.

buy a schedule of commercials within programs, just as advertisers buy space within a newspaper or a magazine.

Undoubtedly, if advertisers decided to use their unquestioned economic clout, they could control the print and broadcast press, which cannot exist, under our system, without them. And there have been periodic efforts to encourage, or even to coerce, advertisers to bring the press to heel. But to the great good fortune of our free and independent broadcast press, in my own experience the following three cases are rare exceptions to the general conduct of advertisers.

One was Pat Buchanan, who urged advertisers to boycott that part of the press which he regarded as too liberal. This idea was proposed in an address delivered to the students at the University of Pennsylvania's Wharton School, when Buchanan was an official of the Nixon White House.

It is the same message which Reed Irvine and his Accuracy in Media (AIM), a private, conservative self-appointed press watchdog organization, regularly urge on advertisers. AIM lists the advertisers who place their commercials on programs and broadcasts which Irvine finds offensive and urges that their products be boycotted. Irvine's plain purpose is to encourage the readers of his reports to coerce advertisers, by threat of boycotting their products, into withdrawing their advertising from the news organizations which displease him.

That, too, was the purpose of the campaign by the Reverend Jerry Falwell and his organizations, the Moral Majority and the Coalition for Better Television. While Falwell's focus was less on news than entertainment programs which he and his groups found to be inconsistent with their notions of "decency," he called for consumer boycotts of advertisers which advertised on the programs which did not meet his standards.

Theoretically, it would not be surprising if advertisers responded to these threats of boycott. Advertisers are not ideological or moral crusaders. Their business is to attract, not repel, customers. If advertisers lose customers by advertising with a particular newspaper or a particular broadcast program or a particular network, and they can place their advertisements elsewhere just as effectively and without offending any customers, that is sensible business.

At first glance, then, it would seem that the press is exceedingly vulnerable and that in normal and expectable course, advertisers could, with their life and death power over the press, control it. The wonder—the miracle—is that it just has not happened that way. Many of the nation's most successful newspapers—and news broadcasts—no doubt fail to report the news in a way that most members of the advertising community would like. Yet at least those advertisers with which I am familiar have refrained from imposing ideological criteria in their decisions on where to place their advertisements. They place them where they can reach the most of the particular type of people which they want to reach. All they want is that the advertisement does the job they want it to do. They—or most of them—superimpose no other societal or political requirements.

I like to think—indeed, I believe—that something more than hard-nosed business considerations—including a recognition that with very few exceptions, boycotts have not been successful—has kept advertisers' swords sheathed. The general effectiveness of their advertising message depends on the public's confidence in, and the credibility of, the press which carries their ads and commercials.

A 1986 study of public attitudes toward the press by the Gallup Organization for the Times Mirror Company shows that the public insists on press independence—independence from, among others, advertisers. Public confidence in the press, and hence the effectiveness of advertisements in the press, would be threatened by advertiser influence on the press. In the long run, then, it is to the advertisers' own self-interest to stay out of newsrooms.

But I believe that ultimately, advertiser self-restraint stems from their recognition of the dangers to a free and independent press, and hence to our democratic society, which would be presented if they sought to use their advertising dollars to coerce the press. Those who hand out black hats and white hats have failed to recognize that advertisers, in general, should be awarded white hats, ahead of the senators, congressmen, White House officials, and others in the government whose self-restraint, as we have seen in earlier chapters, is considerably less than that of the advertising community.

•   •   •

A special problem involving advertisers and news content did pop up from time to time—and that was the problem of propinquity. Our attention on the news side was focused on content of the news story; as far as commercials were concerned, we just decided on the best places for the commercial breaks. Sometimes, we forgot to be conscious of the content of the commercial and its relationship to the nature of the neighboring news story. The consequences were occasionally embarrassing.

For example, in 1961 in New York City, a derelict had been arrested and charged with having committed a murder in his room. The police allowed reporters and cameramen to inspect and film the room. It was littered with clearly legible cans of Rheingold beer—the sponsor of the news broadcast.

A member of our production staff realized that the film and the commercial were incompatible: The Rheingold beer cans were not in a suitable setting for the sale of the beer. The Rheingold people were notified and were permitted to withdraw their commercials from that broadcast. They did.

But we were not always so alert. At the end of an interview with the Russian dissident Anatoly Kuznetsov—a special broadcast which seemed unlikely to present a problem of its relationship to the scheduled commercial—the closing commercial was for Visine. Its first words, immediately following the interview with Kuznetsov, were "Get the red out of your eyes!"

All of us, including the sponsor, missed it. A friend wrote me to call it to my shamed attention.

More serious was a story on the *CBS Evening News* during the famine in Ethiopia, which was immediately followed by a commercial for food products. While we had examined the list of commercials and it showed that a battery commercial was scheduled, it turned out that we had looked at the list for the wrong day. An outraged viewer wrote me that "it was the ultimate in bad taste and careless indifference to immediately follow these terribly sad scenes with a commercial advertising food products such as sausages, hamburgers, etc."

I wrote back to tell the viewer he was absolutely right, and I apologized.

Sometimes a news story was in direct conflict with the product advertised in the contiguous commercial. For example, an airline commercial might be scheduled after a story on a plane crash; or (before they were banned altogether) a cigarette commercial might be scheduled near a report on the dangers of smoking. I felt that it was unfair to insist that the advertiser stay next to a story which collided with its message, and so I developed a policy of notifying the network sales department, whose representative called the advertiser's agency to give the agency a chance to withdraw the commercial and put it somewhere else, or, if time was too short for this procedure, we pulled the commercial on our own.

Some of my CBS News colleagues were uncomfortable with this policy. The vice president in charge of hard news wrote me that the practice "demeans us as journalists and gives agencies and advertisers too strong a whip hand." The executive producer of the *CBS Evening News* also questioned the policy, stating that its "very real danger" was that "we would seem to be compromised" because "some ad man may very well think that he has some form, however small, of veto power over us when indeed he has nothing of the kind."

I found it a close question. The basic issue, I believed, was whether the practice of allowing advertisers to withdraw in these special circumstances did or did not affect our news judgments in any way. I was certain that it did not. I could not see how we could be compromised, or our news judgments could be affected, when we went ahead with the story, as we always did.

As I wrote, "I simply do not believe that anybody on our staff is so lily-livered that the danger of a sponsor's pulling out will affect his judgment in including or excluding a news item. If we have any such people, they ought to be fired." I had raised the question with our hard news producers. Each of them was emphatic that the practice did not affect his news judgments in any way. And so it seemed to me to be a matter of simple courtesy to allow an advertiser to move away from a story which cast adverse reflection on his product. The policy, therefore, was retained.[3]

• • •

Despite CBS News's strict advertising policies and our efforts to comply with them, the belief persisted that the press, and particularly network news, censored itself to avoid offending advertisers. A classic statement of this thesis appeared in *TV Guide* (July 1969) in an article entitled "The Silent Screen," written by FCC commissioner Nicholas Johnson. Johnson insisted that broadcasters were withholding vital information from the American public for economic reasons. And, therefore, broadcasters' concern about government content regulation was hypocritical since the real evil was self-censorship arising out of broadcaster timidity and economic self-protection.

To support his thesis, Johnson alleged:

- That "the broadcast industry has been less than eager to tell [the viewer] about the health hazards of cigarette smoking," since cigarette advertising "provides the largest single source of television's revenue";
- That the networks had not dealt with the belief of auto-safety engineers that American automobiles were not designed properly to safeguard lives;
- That we had "underplayed or ignored events and statements unfavorable to food processors and soap manufacturers";

---

[3]The CBS News policy is precisely contrary to what appears to have been the policy of *Time* magazine in 1969. It was reported that for one of its issues *Time* had scheduled the cover piece to be on Ralph Nader, then General Motors' harshest critic; that *Time* had also scheduled a gatefold advertisement for Chevrolet in the same issue; and that, accordingly, *Time* pulled the Nader cover piece and substituted one about Golda Meir. And so it would appear that where *Time* pulled the story and saved the ad, CBS News policy was to pull the ad and save the story.

- That we had withheld information about potentially harmful over-the-counter drugs;
- That we had kept the public in ignorance of black lung disease as well as the dangers of emissions of X-ray radiation from color television receivers;
- That we "avoid stories of human death, disease, dismemberment, or degradation."

All this, Johnson alleged, was the result of self-censorship to avoid offense to advertisers or to our own company managers. To support his thesis, he invoked a statement by Eric Sevareid that Eric "has said of the pressures involved in putting together a network news show: 'The ultimate sensation is that of being bitten to death by ducks.'"

I wrote an article in reply, which I entitled "Commissioner Johnson Has a Right to Be Wrong—and He Is," published in a later issue of *TV Guide*.[4] In my reply, I cited chapter and verse showing that CBS News had in fact done documentaries or major news stories on every one of the items he had cited as our having ignored.

On the health dangers of cigarette smoking, I pointed out that although at the time cigarette advertising was the largest single source of network television advertising, accounting for more than 10 percent of advertising revenues, CBS News, since the late 1950s with an Ed Murrow documentary, had intensively focused on the issue before it had become a common news subject. Even before the surgeon general issued his first report warning of the dangers of smoking, CBS News had, in addition to the Murrow documentary, broadcast *CBS Reports'* "The Teenage Smoker," in September 1962. In January 1964, on the day the surgeon general issued his report, we did a prime-time news special on smoking and health, based on the surgeon general's report.

Three months later, we broadcast another *CBS Reports*, "A Collision of Interests," which was a detailed review of the health, economic, and public policy issues raised by cigarette smoking. Early in 1968, we broadcast a one-hour special, "National Smoking Test," of which *Newsday*'s television critic wrote: "It took courage on CBS's part to show the way. Especially since as the program mentioned that

---

[4]Eric Sevareid also wrote a letter, published in *TV Guide*, pointing out that when he had talked about being nibbled to death by ducks, he was referring not to advertisers and management pressures but rather to the cumbersome apparatus of television journalism, with its cameras, lights, technicians, and layers of personnel which are inherent in the complex nature of television—which Eric was contrasting with the simplicity of a print writer or reporter who can sit in a corner by himself, type out his story, and send it in.

cigarette manufacturers are TV's largest advertisers. Viewers are in the network's debt."

In the CBS News *21st Century* series, in a broadcast entitled "The Wild Cell," we also dealt with the carcinogenic properties of cigarettes. And, of course, we had included scores of stories in our daytime series *Calendar* and in our regular hard news broadcasts: In the six years between June 1963 and June 1969, there were almost 100 special stories on cigarettes, including the showing of the American Cancer Society's antismoking film and E. William Henry's attack (at the time he was the chairman of the FCC) on television cigarette advertising.

On the question of automobile design safety, CBS News had broadcast a one-hour prime-time special, "Crash Project—the Search for a Safer Car"—prominently including Ralph Nader. *Variety*, reviewing that broadcast, commented:

> Of more significance . . . than the arguments pro and con on car design was CBS's lack of inhibition in confronting one of the giants of advertising and letting the chips fall where they may. Thus, a direct comparison of two competitive makes was shown with a tester from Consumers' Union detailing the faults in one car and extolling the virtues of another while identifying both by name. This is indeed strong stuff and certainly more than most newspapers would do under similar circumstances.

Further, CBS News dealt with the subject in its "National Driver's Test" and between 1965 and 1969, there were forty-four reports on the *CBS Morning News* and the *CBS Evening News*, dealing with the charges against the automobile industry on auto safety and with callbacks, including a demonstration of just what some of the defects leading to callbacks were.

Johnson maintained his unbroken record of error on his charges concerning the absence of stories concerning food processors and soap manufacturers. His particular charge that Senate subcommittee hearings on "truth in packaging" bills and on the high cost of food processing were not covered was also erroneous. CBS News did cover the hearings and included statements of consumer representatives and witnesses in support of the bill.

Among other stories relating to food processors, the *CBS Evening News* reported that the Campbell Soup Company had put clear glass marbles in bowls to make its soup look thicker on television. (Campbell insisted that the marbles made the soup look the way it actually looked off television.) We also reported on the dangers of pesticide contamination of cranberry sauce; the dangers of botulism in canned tuna fish; the story of the processing and sale of unfit meat; Ralph Nader's testimony attacking the standards of intrastate meat packers;

and the FTC's [Federal Trade Commission] action against the manufacturer who used a commercial to demonstrate its shaving cream by purporting to shave sandpaper.

In fact, I often reminded my CBS News colleagues that since our audience was, of course, television viewers, we had a special obligation to inform the viewers of matters concerning such commercials and their possible abuse. This led, some years later, to our *CBS Reports'* "You and the Commercial."

Contrary to Johnson's charge that we failed to include information on potentially harmful over-the-counter drugs, CBS News reported the thalidomide story, the FTC allegations concerning Bufferin and aspirin, the government action against drug price-fixing, the congressional hearings on the excessive cost of drugs, including American profiteering in Latin America, the charges of dangerous side effects of certain birth control pills, and the FTC action against Geritol and Tums—widely advertised on CBS Television. We twice included stories on the reports of the National Academy of Sciences on ineffective drugs and pharmaceuticals.

We not only covered the black lung story in our regular news broadcasts, we did a special entitled "Danger, Mines." We also reported the allegations of dangerous X-ray radiation from color televisions, including a report from the surgeon general calling for action to minimize the dangers.

As for Johnson's broad charge that we avoided stories of "human death, disease, degradation, and dismemberment," of course we had broadcast extensively stories of the war in Vietnam. And we had broadcast such documentaries as "Harvest of Shame," "Hunger in America," "The Silent Spring of Rachel Carson," "The Tenement," "Christmas in El Barrio," "The Poisoned Air," and "Men in Cages."

On the *CBS Morning News*, we had broadcast a continuing series depicting life on a single street in a Washington, D.C., ghetto. Johnson had evidently forgotten—or was ignorant—of what we had broadcast (and about which there was a constant cascade of angry mail from the public criticizing us for emphasizing the negative and failing to accentuate the positive in American life). I admit, though, except for our reporting during the war in Vietnam that American and South Vietnamese troops had cut off the enemy's ears as souvenirs—and sometimes their fingers—I could not recall CBS News stories on "dismemberment."

Apart from Johnson's mistaken specifics, his general implication that, in deference to advertisers, CBS News avoided or suppressed stories unfavorable to consumer products was also just plain wrong. We did many consumer stories, in areas in addition to those which he specified, which involved industry and network advertisers. For example, CBS broadcast stories on the housewives' boycott of supermarkets, protesting high prices; the dangers of flammable toys and clothing; the advertising and sale of toy guns and other warlike toys; the trading stamp industry; lumber industry activities in the forests, concerning which CBS News also broadcast a documentary, "Bulldozed America"; the dangers of pesticides, including the documentary "What Are We Doing to Our World?"; automobile insurance rates involving racial discrimination and arbitrary cancellation of policies; retail credit abuses, concerning which we also broadcast a one-hour documentary, "IOU $315,000,000,000" (IBM dropped its sponsorship because banks were customers of its computers); automobile warranty abuses; and the dangers of cholesterol caused by meat and butter fats, margarine, and other shortenings and vegetable spreads, which were examined in a *CBS Reports'* "The Fat American."

I did not include in my reply to Johnson the instances where, because of our policies assuring separation of news content from advertisers, CBS lost or rejected business. We turned away one major advertiser who wanted to advertise on a series of special bicentennial broadcasts when the advertiser's agency made it clear that the advertiser wished to discuss with us what the series should contain and wanted to participate in the development and production of the series. I told the agency that it was useless for the advertiser's officer to come in to talk to me, since we were not in the business of creating or tailoring our broadcasts for the advertiser, nor did we share decisions about the content of our broadcasts with advertisers. The call from the advertiser's agency representative ended with his saying, "OK, let's leave it at that." We never heard from them again.

In another instance, the sales vice president of the CBS Radio Network told us that a food company—and the network—were interested in our devising a radio series about matters of interest to consumers, but the series was to include "no negative stuff" and exclude "tough investigative" reporting. I instructed the CBS News vice president in charge of radio news, "Let's get it clear and let's get it straight now: We will do no such series [with those] specifications. . . . We are not in that line of work. . . . [L]et's not give an inch here." We did not, and the advertiser went elsewhere.

The short answer for all the years I was at CBS News is that there was no self-censorship. Neither I nor, I am confident, any of my associates at CBS News ever avoided a topic, or altered treatment to protect, or to avoid displeasing, corporate management or any advertiser. As I stated to my colleagues on a number of occasions, anybody in

CBS News who avoided a topic or distorted his or her normal news judgments in the treatment of a topic in order to avoid offending the economic interests of any advertiser or in order to please CBS management would thereby betray his or her professional heritage and would disqualify himself or herself from working for CBS News.

Perhaps even Nick Johnson was ultimately converted. Several years after he wrote his article, and after he had retired from the FCC, he and I were both among the participants in an Edward R. Murrow Symposium at Washington State University. At a Sunday evening reception, I found a television set in another room, where I could watch *60 Minutes*. Nick Johnson heard what I was doing, and he joined me. He obviously enjoyed the broadcast. At its end, he said to me that *60 Minutes* had become the nation's ombudsman.

18

Journalists and Lawyers

I hung on my office wall for every visiting lawyer to see, a framed quotation from Shakespeare's Henry the Sixth, "The first thing we do, let's kill all the lawyers." I was delighted to learn from a visiting Shakespeare buff that the speaker of that call to violence against lawyers was a minor character named, by happy coincidence, Dick the Butcher.

—Salant Papers

IT WAS NOT EASY TO MAKE the transition from law to journalism. During my years as head of CBS News, I was often asked whether my background as a lawyer was an advantage. The answer I gave was yes—a little; and no—a lot. Most of the yes came simply from the fact that had I not been a lawyer, CBS and I would not have met and I would not have ultimately wound up at CBS News.[1]

But most of the no comes from the fact that my colleagues at CBS News were suspicious of their boss, the lawyer, and those outside CBS News never let my past as a lawyer be forgotten. Sid Eiges, who was

---

[1]In the mid-1960s, a young radio sports announcer in Topeka, Kansas, who was charting his career path, asked me whether he should aim to be a lawyer (he was attending night law school) or get into news. I urged the latter, which he chose. He became a successful reporter for a local television station, then joined CBS News as a correspondent; then he went to Chicago to become a successful anchor at WBBM-TV. From there, he returned to CBS News to anchor the *CBS Morning News*. He then went back to WBBM. He is one of the best in the business. His name is Bill Kurtis. (*Editors' note:* Bill Kurtis in now with the Arts and Entertainment Cable Channel.)

NBC's skillful and effective public relations person, somehow managed to persuade the trade press to attach "lawyer" to my name whenever it appeared, as though "lawyer" was my first name—as in "Lawyer Salant." Sometimes, it even came out "corporate lawyer Salant."[2]

I went to excessive lengths to erase the scarlet letter of having been a lawyer—some would say a scarlet letter writ ineradicably on the forehead and in the soul. Just as the most militant crusaders against cigarette smoking are those who have kicked the habit, I held myself out as an unyielding antilawyer. At the slightest opportunity, I insisted on quoting the Dickens character Bumble, who said, "The law is a ass"—even when it was not.

• • •

Lawyer bashing is a popular pastime among journalists. One of the masters is the articulate Reuven Frank, twice president of NBC News. At a convention of lawyers, Reuven described the war between the two estates of law and journalism thus:

Lawyers hate our guts, and lawyers matter ... [T]hey have us outnumbered, outdollared, and outgunned. .... The three-part separation of powers ... which is central to our system, gives one branch to lawyers by definition.[3] They have seized the other two long ago by naked aggression, and have held them ever since as zones of occupation. .... All restrictions on how news is gathered and presented are imposed by lawyers, and when we want relief we must go to other lawyers to fight them. Whatever happens, happens their way. And whenever we decide to do something, we must do it their way. And their way is the adversary system. Everything is lawyer versus lawyer. .... Do unto others before they do

---

[2]*Editor's note:* In his notes, Salant writes, "Even in 1990, I'm still referred to as a CBS corporate lawyer. Sally Bedell Smith notes in her book about Bill Paley that in a conversation Paley had with Stanton, Paley couldn't remember my name but identified me as, 'You know, your lawyer.'"

[3]I assume that Frank referred to the judiciary as the branch which belongs to lawyers "by definition." But in many areas—including the United States Supreme Court—there is no explicit requirement that judges be lawyers. Once, in the mid-1960s, I was on a panel of lawyers and journalists at a bar association meeting. A lawyer suggested that journalism needed more lawyers to serve as reporters. (He was right as far as reporters covering law matters are concerned. Today many law correspondents have been lawyers—as was CBS law correspondent Fred Graham, whom I stole from his Supreme Court beat on the *New York Times*.) I responded by offering the assembled lawyers a deal: more legally trained general reporters in return for one journalist on the bench for every eight lawyers on the bench. None of the assembled lawyers at the convention thought that was a good idea.

unto you. . . . Clarification is not the aim. For every winner there must be a loser. It is not a system of laws but of lawyers. . . .

Lawyers do not understand what we do, because they do not think as we do. Their thinking is organized, ritualized, and bipolar. Ours is disorganized, individual, and multipolar. . . . When a reporter goes forth on a story, he has no idea of what he will find, and only a general idea of what he is looking for. He does not—or at least he should not—seek only such information as buttresses a conclusion he has already reached. Within limitations of reason and budget, he will go anywhere and talk to anyone for information of any kind. . . .

Professionally, they [journalists] and lawyers use different methods of thinking and have diametrically different habits of thought. That is why we cannot understand each other. . . . [It is] a conflict between two methods of thinking.

Perhaps it is the basic similarities, however, that make the differences between lawyers and journalists particularly annoying to one another. My theory finds support in an examination of just what a journalist's and a lawyer's work really is. It should be (and in most cases, it is) the Holy Grail of both lawyers and journalists to get at, and reveal, the truth, as nearly as they can come to it. The difficulty is that the methods each uses to achieve that goal are very different.

What a journalist accepts as truth is dredged from talking around, from digging into obscure records, from piecing together illegible notes on scraps of paper, and having a gut feeling of who is telling the truth and who is not. It is a synthesis of elbow grease, hearsay, professional hunch, and an ability to know a good, reliable source from a bad and unreliable one. If journalists are good professionals, they include all significant sides, facts, and views—whether or not they fit their preconceptions or go against the grain of their personal feelings. They are adversaries only to the extent that they are watchdogs of the power center and try to elicit the truth from those who would shade it.

On the other hand, objectivity (and sometimes fairness) is not a lawyer's goal. The lawyer is a prosecutor or a defender, serving the client, obliged to present only those facts which help the client. The lawyer leaves it to the opposing counsel to present the other side. The lawyer's truth is advanced—or entangled—in what seem to laymen arcane rules of evidence, which ordinary people in their day-to-day lives do not observe or even understand. A lawyer can make a witness sit still and, unless the Fifth Amendment is involved, answer the most embarrassing questions—under oath. If a witness lies, he can be prosecuted for perjury. But if somebody lies to a reporter, the legal process does not intervene.

The lawyer is sure that the journalist's pursuit of truth is sloppy, uncertain, undisciplined, unprofessional, amateur, and juvenile. The journalist believes that the lawyer's way is obfuscatory, pedantic, glacial, unintelligible, and obsolete. Journalists know that if they had to do it the lawyers' way, under what seems to journalists to be strange and illogical rules of evidence, today's news could not be reported until the day after next. And journalists know that even worse, many stories—Watergate, for example—would not get told at all if journalists were bound by lawyers' rules.

Therefore, when it comes to advising that ornery bunch who call themselves journalists, broadcast attorneys—whether in-house or outside counsel—have a tough and unenviable job. It is the attorney's job to keep the company out of trouble; a journalist can't worry too much about potential trouble without inducing self-paralysis. A corporate lawyer's every instinct, understandably and properly, is to play it safe. A journalist who plays it safe may wind up as a successful and highly paid public relations person. He will never win a Pulitzer Prize.

I insisted that CBS lawyers stay out of the newsroom. I barred them as totally as I barred CBS senior management from across town (or from anywhere else) and advertisers or advertising agency people. Whether with literary quotations on the wall or by constant arguments with the lawyers, eternal diligence, I decided, was the price of the newsroom not being plagued by lawyers. The danger was not only of distraction but, even more serious, of a chilling effect on the newspeople.

•　•　•

One of my more difficult confrontations with CBS's Law Department occurred in the late 1960s and resulted from the FCC's concern about an allegedly staged pot party filmed by the news department of WBBM-TV, the CBS-owned Chicago station. WBBM-TV had reported on the prevalent use of marijuana at universities in the Chicago area and during their investigations learned of a group of students who frequently met to hold pot parties. The station's reporters decided to film a typical party.

Although CBS denied that the station's reporters had suggested that a party be held for purposes of filming, the FCC found that the particular party which was filmed would not have been held at that particular time or place had it not been for the WBBM-TV reporters' encouragement. Accordingly, the FCC held that, contrary to the public interest, WBBM-TV had staged the party. That the party was typical in character or in time or place was not questioned by the FCC.

The FCC invoked no sanction against the CBS Network. (While the CBS News Division and I had no responsibility for, or authority over, the news departments of CBS-owned stations, the FCC could have revoked WBBM-TV's, and all other CBS-owned stations', licenses.)[4] Instead, it warned CBS that it must adopt clear written policies and strict internal procedures to prevent a recurrence of the WBBM-TV episode. The clear signal was that if CBS did not do so, its licenses would be in jeopardy.

Understandably, that was enough to thoroughly frighten the Law Department (and, no doubt, CBS management). The Law Department necessarily had to play the lead role in assuring that CBS took steps to comply with the FCC decision. In consultation with a distinguished outside lawyer, Newton Minow, who had represented CBS in the case and who himself was a former FCC chairman, proposed guidelines were drafted that were designed to satisfy the FCC. They provided, among other requirements, that the Law Department "should be consulted prior to the commencement of any investigative project and should be kept advised as the investigation proceeds." Since the proposed rules were to govern CBS News as well as the stations' news departments, they were sent to me for comment.

I worried that the wall between lawyers and journalists would come tumbling down and our newsroom would be flooded by lawyers peering over our shoulders. Unsympathetic to the position in which the FCC had put CBS lawyers (who were only trying to do what they were supposed to do—protect billions of dollars of CBS's investments, as well as its very existence), out came my twenty-foot pole. I pointed out to the Law Department that I hoped CBS News would broadcast nothing (except live presidential press conferences and other live events) without first checking and digging, since all our reporting involved "investigative projects."

In any event, I huffed, the requirement of the Law Department's prior and concurrent participation in our reporting was

> onerous and impractical. . . . I am sure you know that there would exist here [in the CBS News Division] a widespread distaste for any such formal requirement for the Law Department's participation in the coverage of an unfolding story. I recognize, of course, that there are circumstances in which we ought to consult the Law Department. But I believe that the requirement is too broad. . . . I would hope . . . that we can comply with the FCC requirement without raising more questions and turmoil than necessary.

---

[4]Networks are not subject to licensing, but their owned stations, integral to network operations and a major source of a network company's profits, are.

In 1969, after extended and rigorous discussion with the Law Department, the guidelines were issued in somewhat less peremptory
form and the red flag proposed to be waved in our faces lost some of its
color. By way of appeasement and in the hope of minimizing any chilling effect, the department added a statement that the guidelines

> must be understood in the context of CBS's long-standing commitment
> to investigative journalism, which may often cut deep and arouse sharp
> reaction. . . . The issuance of these guidelines is not intended to mark a
> departure from our preexisting policies and standards which made possi-
> ble such documentaries as "Abortion and the Law," "Ku Klux Klan,"
> "The Invisible Empire," "The Business of Heroin," and "Biography of a
> Bookie Joint."[5] . . .
> This does not imply any changes from past practice. *Our lawyers will
> continue to be lawyers, not participants in the coverage of news.* (Italics
> are mine.)

In fact, despite the Law Department's ominous initial draft and the
great flexibility which the department gave itself in the final version, I
never had difficulty in respect of their participation—nonparticipa-
tion, really—in the News Division's investigative reporting. It turned
out that the department meant what it said in the guidelines. There
was no change from past practice, and happily for the News Division
and, I am sure, for the Law Department, the lawyers did indeed continue to be lawyers and not participants in our reporting.

• • •

It is important to note that despite the built-in abrasions between
lawyers and journalists; despite my macho efforts to dissociate myself
from my prior servitude in the law; despite my often impatient, rude,
and probably oversensitive communications with the CBS lawyers,
those with whom I dealt in the Law Department were good men and
women who understood our problems. They were patient, tolerant,
and as a rule good-humored. Above all, they were constructive, dedicated to helping, not interfering with, us. Far more often than not, the
Law Department succeeded, finding sensible ways to permit us to proceed as we proposed while minimizing the risks.

I learned that, after all, journalists and good lawyers can live, most
of the time, in uneasy but reasonable peace. Détente and containment
rather than confrontation seemed to work best.

---

[5]These were all *CBS Reports.*

Part Four
Management Philosophy

CBS Memorandum
To: Senior Vice President, Hard News
From: Richard Salant
Date: May 24, 1976
Re: Political Coverage

I am attaching a transcript of the piece we did on yesterday's *Evening News* . . . on the Oregon Democratic primary. I listened to it and wept and now I have read it and I weep even harder. All we reported was strategy, tactics, and who's ahead and who's behind.

The only word about issues was: "Then the senator took to the issues. He says the other Democrats are not giving straight answers on those issues"—then utter silence from us on what was said about what issues. And all this was accompanied by the customary picture opportunities—the tossing of frisbees; the high-school band; crowds milling around, etc.

We have just got to shift gears—fast. This is shameful and indefensible. I know that it is harder and less "interesting" to dig out what the candidates are saying about the issues, either for film bites or for paraphrasing. But that's what we are [here] for and we have to fulfill our responsibilities better than we are now fulfilling them. . . . [Our plans for focusing on the issues] should be dusted off at once and all hands should be forcefully reminded of them.

19

Loose Reins

My theory was to pick the best guys, let them pick the best guys in their areas, and except for broad issues and tone, leave them alone. It was a completely loose-reins philosophy, and only when you get to basic issues do you tighten the reins a little bit. . . . The guy works best in our field, which is journalism, who is the freest to do his work and not have someone sitting over his shoulder all the time.

—*Taped interview with Peter J. Boyer, October 1986*

A NEWS DIVISION PRESIDENT is something of a hybrid—not quite a traditional editor in chief and not quite a publisher. Since I could not clearly define what the "publisher" at CBS was supposed to do, and in later years, just who, if anybody, was the publisher, I could not define my job by the process of elimination—leaving as my functions all those left over from the publisher's functions. I had to feel my way along, working out as best I could what I felt I ought to be doing and what I felt I was equipped to do—two quite different things.

One of the great—and most uncompromising—editors, Norman E. Isaacs, wrote an angry and stimulating book about the press called *Untended Gates: The Mismanaged Press*. It is Isaacs's basic thesis that the reins have to be held very tight, and the good editor has to be a son of a bitch. Thus, he writes that "democracy in the newsroom is the refuge of the weak."[1] Since I believed strongly in a collegial atmosphere in the newsroom—sometimes a democracy, sometimes, some

---

[1]Norman Isaacs, *Untended Gates: The Mismanaged Press* (New York: Columbia University Press, 1986), p. 137.

thought, an anarchy[2]—I did not fit Isaacs's qualifications. He approvingly quotes the late John Fischer, the great editor of *Harper's* magazine, who, commenting on the business of editing, wrote, "Happy is he who is born cruel, for if not, he will have to school himself in cruelty. Without it, he is unfit for his job, because the kindly editor soon finds his columns filled with junk."[3]

Isaacs also agrees with Malcolm Mallette, former director of the American Press Institute, who criticizes editors for having become, in recent years, "too genteel . . . wanting to be too popular with their staffs."[4] And Isaacs writes admiringly of Carl Van Anda's disapproving look—"the Van Anda death ray"—a look well known to Van Anda's staff on the *New York Times*, where at the turn of the century he was managing editor for nearly thirty years.

Norm Isaacs may have it right. But not for me. I just was not the autocratic type. And no one who is an on-the-job trainee, as I was, can get away with that kind of behavior, ruling by fright rather than by more or less friendly persuasion—especially in the case of a creative enterprise. The tough discipline appropriate in some kinds of corporate enterprises may be self-defeating in a news organization. Reporters and editors are, more than most workers, separate, different, and proud individuals whose stock in trade is using their own eyes, their own ears, their own hearts, and then—the last and most difficult task—translating what they see, hear, and feel into words through which they can share their impressions.

They are, after all, individuals who work best as individuals. Although they can be difficult and a mite egocentric, they must be nurtured. I remain convinced that a boss who is consistent, compassionate, respected, and liked and whose judgments are accepted because they are understood and trusted is more likely to inspire better work from his or her employees than one who is feared.

This is not to say that I ever really believed in anarchy. And even collegiality and democracy have their outer limits. When a matter of basic policy is involved or a reporter is lazy or demonstrably incompetent or just not up to the job, the reins must be tightened. And I could not duck the fact that the reins were in my hands for the tightening.

• • •

---

[2]*Editors' note:* In his 1986 interview with Peter Boyer, Salant said this about the CBS newsroom: "The place was almost like a dormitory at school, with people wandering around, dropping in and holding bull sessions. Very rarely were there any orders of any kind."

[3]Isaacs, *Untended Gates*, p. 84.

[4]Ibid., p. 86.

When Fred Friendly was CBS News president from 1964 to 1966, his management style was different because his background, experience, and nature were different. He was a journalist from the beginning, and a superb documentary producer. He had left his own mark on all the broadcasts which he produced, and so a hands-on style of management suited him where it would have been impossible for me. He knew what he was doing in the editing room and in the control room. I did not. I could not have managed CBS News the way Fred did, nor could he have managed it the way I did.

In fact, his hands-on method made it possible for me to manage better than I otherwise would have when I came back to News in 1966. Many of the News people were restive under Fred, and when he left, there was a sigh of relief that his restless and dynamic hands were off their typewriters and buttons in the control room. They were uncomfortable with a News Division president who carried on as executive producer of all broadcasts. They—some of them—felt they could not stretch their own muscles and use their own discretion.

If Fred had not departed after such a short tenure, the News staff probably would have become used to him, and he to them. But Fred certainly made it easier for me when I came back. My impression was that they became determined to work a little harder, a little better, to prove that it was more satisfactory to work as freer people—without the looming omnipresence of their boss over their shoulders—for their own sakes and, incidentally, to make me look good so that senior management would let me stick around for a while. I do not believe it was a coincidence that Walter Cronkite and Eric Sevareid were the ones who went across town to Black Rock to urge Frank Stanton to send me back to the News Division or that it was Charles Kuralt who was a leader of those who welcomed me back: These were all men who did their superb best when they were left alone to do their best.

•   •   •

My methods of management were derived from the fundamental facts. First, the CBS News Division was, in 1961, a superb news organization which had become a little complacent, a little fat and flabby, but all the elements for greatness were still there. And second, I was not experienced enough journalistically and not tough enough by nature—even if I had had the experience and the self-confidence—to run a tighter ship. As Popeye used to say, "I yam what I yam"—and I had to build around that. From this was born my rather oversimplified principle that the news organization which is managed least is managed best.

My definition of management functions and duties was simple to state but sometimes difficult to execute. Basically, I sought to define new policies, where new ones were needed, and to embrace existing policies, so that all hands knew that CBS News stands for:

- Accuracy
- Fairness
- The honest and unrelenting pursuit of objectivity even if it is not always attainable
- Integrity, which includes strict rules against conflicts of interest, total insistence on every element of our reporting being what it purports to be (no staging, no actors, no directing of people whom we are covering to say, or do, anything)
- Reporting only what is newsworthy and giving major priority to stories that are important rather than merely interesting or entertaining, and, except in clear cases of national security or threat to human safety, reporting stories which meet the criteria of newsworthiness and importance
- Accountability to everybody except the government, by all mechanisms available
- Autonomy and independence—from internal corporate interests, from advertisers, from government, from all external interests
- A deep respect for the craft of journalism and its importance to our society

I also sought to hire, and retain, the best journalists, and in the process of hiring and retention (and promotion):

- Make sure that the policies are known, and embraced, by the organization
- Assure that special efforts be made to hire, and promote, women and minorities

Since I believed in an open, collegial, and friendly climate in our newsrooms, I did feel that it was important that I be accessible and available. Except in unusual circumstances—a meeting with outsiders, for example—my door was literally always open.[5]

---

[5]When I returned to CBS News in 1966, I discovered that Fred Friendly had had a doorway cut into the wall of his inner office. This enabled him to escape from his office directly into the hall in order to avoid people who might be waiting to see him and whom he wanted to duck. I had the new exit blocked up on the assumption that those who wanted to see me so badly as to drop in without an appointment and whom I might be anxious to avoid were often the very people whom I ought to see.

My practice of keeping the door open and wandering through the halls and the newsrooms—all in the name of accessibility and to persuade people that the boss did not wear horns—was not always successful. Recently, a friend who is still at CBS News told me that a technician had complained to him that the trouble with the heads of the News Division was that they were so remote. This was after I left and during a period when a CBS News Division president closed his office door and apparently rarely emerged.

My old friend told the technician that this had not been the case when I was president of the division and that I had made daily trips down the halls, through the newsrooms, and even used the communal men's room, despite the fact that my office included its own washroom. "Oh," said the technician, "is that what he was doing, always walking around. I just thought he had nothing else to do or his toilet was not working."

All sorts of problems and issues were vacuumed up as a result of my policy of accessibility. Sometimes I would be asked about what was going on at Black Rock (usually I did not know) or in Washington (usually I did not understand). Sometimes I was asked about policy—why I disliked music on CBS News broadcasts so intensely or other similar questions.

•   •   •

Andy Rooney tells a story which helps to illustrate my management style.[6] He told this story at the International Radio and Television Society [IRTS] banquet in 1979 where I was given the society's annual Gold Medal Award. I wish Rooney's account were apocryphal. But it is not and will surely set the purists'—and even the semipurists'—teeth on edge. It is typical of my not-infrequent (but not invariable) way of handling associates whom I especially admired and respected.

The incident involved my screening of an hour-long documentary-essay of the kind Andy did so well. Its subject was hotels. The scene I did not like showed a bellboy greeting an incoming male guest and offering to supply a woman.

I felt that the scene was jarring and in bad taste. In addition, though I had been to many hotels over the years, I never had been approached.

---

[6]Like so many great humorists, Andy Rooney was, deep down, a serious man who felt deeply about important issues. My first encounter with him was in the 1960s when he was the chief writer for the excellent daily daytime series *Calendar*. I gave a lunch celebrating its first anniversary on the air. In the midst of the lunch, I became aware that somebody had moved a chair next to mine at the table. It was Andy Rooney. Without further ado, he started: "The trouble with you, Salant," and then he told me of all my flaws. He was mostly right, and a lasting friendship had begun.

That led me to believe it was so uncommon that the incident was dragged in for the sensation of it. I told Andy that I did not like the segment, but it stayed in—and I was furious. I stormed in to see Bill Leonard, Andy's boss, to let him know how displeased I was.

At the IRTS banquet, Andy described what happened next:

> We all have fond memories of Dick. One of my fond ones involves an incident that took place about ten years ago. It's a good example of why people go around saying nice things behind his back. It's a good example, too, of how raging mad he could get if one of us did something wrong, [did] something he didn't like or violated his code of journalistic ethics; but [he] forgave us almost immediately if he trusted us. I suspect one of the hardest things he did so well was defend us when we were wrong.
>
> Anyway, I was doing an hour documentary on hotels . . . "An Essay on Hotels." I finished it with a great friend and film editor, Jules Laventhol, and Dick screened it. He liked everything about it except a scene near the end where "The Star" [Andy] interviewed two bellboys about the availability of prostitutes in Miami hotels.
>
> Two weeks later, the essay was broadcast just as he'd seen it, with those scenes left in. The next morning, Bill Leonard called me and said, "Did Dick tell you to take those scenes out?" I said, "No. He told me he didn't like them." "Well," said Bill, "you better go in and talk to him. He's really sore about it."
>
> I went to Dick's office, trembling a little. He was sitting at his desk looking stern. He said, "What's the use of my looking at these things in advance if no one pays any attention to what I say?"
>
> I said, "Dick, we did pay attention to what you said. We [Laventhol and Rooney] talked it over and decided you were wrong."
>
> Dick looked at me for a minute and then broke out laughing. "You son of a bitch," he said, "get out of here." And that was the end of it.
>
> How many of you have bosses you could do that to? How many of you are bosses that you could do that to?
>
> Incidentally, I never decided he was wrong again.

The Rooney episode illustrates well, I believe, the wisdom of an editor in chief who had just been appointed publisher. He wrote a memorandum to the editor who was about to succeed him.

"Remember," he advised his successor, "that a newsroom is talent-and-content driven, rather than management driven. Good personnel practices are important to getting the best out of people, but what's in the paper makes the ultimate difference. Sometimes you have to pay the price of letting talent flourish as long as the price isn't too high."

20

CBS News Standards

My basic philosophy [about broadcast journalism] is set out in the 1976 "CBS News Standards." I think that most, if not all, of the things that bother me about today's broadcast journalism scene are in fact departures from these principles. I'm stubborn—I believed what I wrote in 1976, and I still do. I'm not sure whether some of my successors at the CBS News Division still believe in them.

—Benton Seminar, Chicago, October 25, 1990

I STRONGLY BELIEVED IN THE development and articulation of basic journalistic policies governing all those who worked for CBS News—policies as clear and precise as possible, so that all CBS News personnel would know what was expected of them. Also, since the standards were made available to the public, the public could measure our performance against our stated policies. And so the "CBS News Standards," as we called them, became a principal mechanism for management control.

I recognize—as I recognized when I embarked on the long and difficult project—that there are journalists who do not believe that codes, guidelines, and standards are wise. They believe that so much depends on the circumstances of each case that codes and standards either must be so general and flexible that they are meaningless and provide no guidance or that they are so specific that they become paralyzing because they have failed to take into account the myriad of unanticipated variations which ultimately occur.

More colorfully than most, Don Hewitt of *60 Minutes* spoke out against codification of journalistic practices at a luncheon in 1985. "I think it's kind of stupid," he said. "I think all newsmen ever have to answer is: 'Have you ever done violence to the truth, and is what you're putting on the air what the audience thinks it is?' If you can answer those two questions, the rest is baloney."

Except for the word "baloney"—in normal conversation, Don wouldn't have been that polysyllabic—the statement is quintessential Hewitt. But Don is very special, and he works superbly from gut feeling. His two questions are fine—for him. But they are only a starting point, and they do not answer the issues and problems for those whose experience and instincts are different from his.

In fact, I do not believe that they answer all the issues even for Don, and I do not believe that he believes that they do. The "CBS News Standards" were in process for several years and were circulated throughout CBS News for criticism and comment before they were finally issued. Yet it was not until his speech six years after I left CBS News and nine years after the standards were issued that I was even aware of Don's skepticism about standards which went beyond his two seemingly simple, but actually very complex, questions.

But others share Don's feelings. There are those that believe codes are a trap, because courts may at some point translate written standards into rigid law. Even some cautious communications lawyers take that position: They say that the danger is that courts will co-opt the standards a news organization sets for itself and, in a libel case, the news organization will be hanged by its own rope. I think the danger is more imagined than real, born of a desire never to be pinned down by any written standard of conduct.

If the issue in a libel or other court case is whether there has been sloppy, or negligent, or reckless journalism—and that usually is the issue—I would think that a defendant news organization is more vulnerable if it says it has no code, no policies, no standards. And if, instead, it says that it does have them but they are only oral, it is likely to be stuck either with an imprecise statement that has not been carefully worked out or one so broad as to be without meaning or help in that particular case. On the other hand, if the oral statement is precise, and honest, the plaintiff's lawyer may persuade the jury to be skeptical about why they were not in writing in the first place—and about the extent to which reporters and editors were aware of them.

Perhaps written standards are unnecessary for a small news organization, where the reporters, the editors, and the publisher are all gathered in one place, in constant contact with each other. In that kind of news organization, the editors and the veteran reporters can be the teachers, orally passing their wisdom and their journalistic ethics on to the newcomers.

But that was not the way CBS News was, or could be, organized. Its reporters and editors were scattered all over the globe. There were more than a thousand of them. Even the possibility of editorial gate-keeping is more limited in broadcasting than it is in print. I became convinced that written standards, no matter how difficult to shape so as to be reasonably specific, on the one hand, and not paralyzing, on the other, were an imperative tool for the management of CBS News.

•   •   •

I began the standards project in 1970. It was a gargantuan undertaking. The task was to gather all the policies and standards which had been established—some in memorandum, some oral traditions—at CBS News from its earliest days. This was when basic policies had been established—policies of fairness, objectivity, and presenting the salient facts and viewpoints of others evenhandedly, free of personal bias, so that listeners or viewers could make up their own mind on an informed basis, without CBS News making up their mind for them.

Those basic policies had been set by Bill Paley (later with Frank Stanton) and his original news deputies, Ed Klauber, Paul White, and Ed Murrow. As the years passed and CBS News grew in size and complexity, there grew up a kind of common law of CBS News policies, principles, standards, traditions, and guidelines which developed on the basis of experience as issues and problems had arisen.

I turned over the immense task of digging out all these common-law statements of policies and putting them together in an initial draft to the only person who I knew could do it and whose principles were the same as mine: David Klinger, the CBS News administrative vice president. A veteran of CBS and CBS News, he was patient, indefatigable, unflappable, meticulously thorough, and gentle. He was the one person to whom I could entrust the job, which required exhaustive, laborious research involving old files and old memories.

His orderly mind could put it all together lucidly and intelligently. He was a master of spotting curves in the road long before I could see them. Thoroughly knowledgeable about the ways of news gathering and news editing, he tested every suggested standard, no matter how seemingly obvious, with a series of what-if's and suppose-that's, which sometimes exasperated me at first, because I was in my customary hurry. He managed always to make me take into account leeway for the unforeseen. Dave Klinger managed the impossible job of drafting meaningful and intelligible standards which said something—finding just the right and narrow channel between the Scylla of empty generalities and the Charybdis of entrapping specificity.

As we developed the "CBS News Standards" and circulated them among the news personnel for their comments, we quickly learned that seemingly obvious principles may not always have sensible results and that flat prohibitions might turn out to be foolish. We learned how dangerous it is to say "never," when, in certain circumstances, "OK" is the right answer. For example, in our first draft of a section on editing, we stipulated that an answer to one question should never be attached to a different question. That seemed elementary.

But occasionally, in the course of an interview, long after the interview subject had answered question A and [was] in the process of answering question Z, the interviewee would say that he would like to add to or modify the answer to question A—and proceed to do so. It then makes good sense to attach the addendum to the earlier question and little sense to insist that question Z be included and the answer relevant to question A be left in the answer to question Z.

So, too, it seems an obvious policy, long established at CBS News, that questions should not be supplied in advance to an interview subject. But it sometimes happens that during a preliminary off-camera interview, interviewees tell a clear and relevant story, but when the cameras are brought in, they freeze and become confused. That serves no useful purpose. It makes sense to stop, and start over again. But a literalist could reasonably argue that since in general the same questions are put the second time, this violates the policy against submission of questions in advance.

The practice of redoing an interview should be permissible provided that it is not abused: Reinterviews should be available whenever it is clear, on the basis of the preliminary off-camera interview, that the interview subject has become confused. But it should not be a privilege granted only to "friendly witnesses" and withheld from unfriendly ones whose statements are in conflict with what the producer or correspondent wants to establish.

There are many more examples. A flat prohibition against CBS News staff violating the law or misrepresenting themselves at first blush seems an important and obvious principle. But if the story is to show how easy it is to obtain false passports, or to buy tax-free cigarettes in one state and resell them in a state where they are subject to heavy taxes, or how easy it is to buy an unregistered gun—the issues are a matter of public concern and may establish either lax law enforcement or legal loopholes which need new laws. Sometimes, they can best be told by violating the law or misrepresenting one's identity. But misrepresentation and law violation must be the exceptional cases and must be used only sparingly where the nature of the story, its importance, and the means of exposure clearly justify them.

Accordingly, the "CBS News Standards" provided that misrepresentation and law violation were permissible only with the specific approval of the News Division president or a designated deputy. But in other cases—the editing issues which I have described are examples—we thought it best to leave the flat prohibition and rely on our associates, when special circumstances were present, to come to me or to my chief deputies to ask whether we really intended the prohibition to apply in those special circumstances.

Delicate judgments had to be made in preparing the "CBS News Standards," and we made them. They were, at the time, unique in the broadcasting industry[1] and, I believe, unique in any branch of the press in their comprehensiveness.

• • •

When the "CBS News Standards" were finally issued on April 14, 1976, I included a preface stating:

Every answer to every contingency cannot be provided by any written statement of ethics, policies, and guidelines covering one's professional conduct. And this is especially so in journalism. This is why judgments have to be made by each individual, as conscientiously as is humanly possible, and why neither computers nor the equivalent of the Internal Revenue Code will serve the purpose.[2]

One of the wondrous things about the practice of journalism is that it cannot be practiced by rote, and each new month, if not each new day, presents new, challenging, and difficult issues calling for nice and decent judgments. There will be, as time goes along, refinements, amendments, and, I think, improvements, for daily experience is so much a part of journalism and the changing experiences never end—and hence the learning process never ends.

[I would emphasize] the overriding importance peculiar to our form of journalism of drawing the sharpest possible line—sharp perhaps to the point of eccentricity—between our line of broadcast business, which is dealing with fact, and that in which our associates on the entertainment side of the business are generally engaged, which is dealing in fiction and drama. Because it all comes out sequentially on the same point on the dial and on the same tube, and because, then, there are no pages to be turned or column lines to be drawn in our journalistic matrix, it is particularly important that we recognize that we are not in show business and should not use any of the dramatic licenses, the fiction-which-represents-

---

[1] NBC News and ABC News issued guidelines or standards later.

[2] Nor can federal laws and FCC regulations. There must be flexibility, room for discretion, and quick decision. Therein lies the essential difference between sensibly drafted internal standards and federal laws and rules. As indicated by the examples in the text, the exercise of management discretion is imperative to make the policies workable.

truth rationales, or the underscoring and punctuations which entertainment and fiction may, and do, properly use. This may make us a little less interesting to some—but that is the price we pay for dealing with fact and truth, which may often be duller—and with more loose ends—than fiction and drama.

Second, it is my strong feeling that our news judgments must turn on the best professional judgments that we can come to on what is important rather than what is merely interesting. Again, our function, then, contrasts sharply with the broadcast schedule which surrounds us and, indeed, supports us. In general, to the extent that radio and television are mass media of entertainment, it's entirely proper to give most of the people what most of them want most of the time. But we in broadcast journalism cannot, should not, and will not base our judgments and our news treatment on our guesses (or somebody else's surveys) as to what news the people want to hear or see, and in what form. The judgments must be professional news judgments, nothing more, nothing less.

A corollary of this basic principle is that if we are to provide what it is important for people to know, we must not shrink from reporting what is newsworthy, even though there are no pretty or dramatic pictures to go with it. There is nothing wrong with a talking head—provided the head has something to say and says it well. . . . The most exciting thing in the field of information is an idea.

And finally, this is as good a place as any to remind ourselves that our paramount responsibility at CBS News is to present all significant facts, all significant viewpoints, so that this democracy will work in the way it should work—by the individual citizen's making up his own mind on an informed basis. Our job is to contribute to that process and not to make up for them the minds of those who listen to and watch us. We must always remember that a significant viewpoint does not become less significant just because we personally disagree with it, nor does a significant and relevant fact become less relevant or significant just because we find it unpalatable and wish it weren't so.

By this preface to the "CBS News Standards," I set out my own credo which had guided me. Through the preface, I sought to let everybody know what I stood for and what I wanted them to stand for. I do not know whether the preface (which I was careful to include in the loose-leaf book of standards immediately after the index) still remains a part of the standards book—and if it does, who, if anybody, reads it and believes in it.[3]

---

[3]*Editors' note:* Salant's preface is still part of "CBS News Standards."

The original "CBS News Standards" covered more than sixty single-spaced pages. They included subjects such as these:

- Policies and procedures governing analysis and commentary, including prohibition against editorializing except in defined limited circumstances
- Requirements that errors be corrected
- Standards for coverage of demonstrations, riots, and other civil disturbances and of terrorists
- Restrictions governing electronic eavesdropping, including limitations on the use of hidden cameras and on recording telephone conversations
- Limitations on the use of handouts, including filmed and taped handouts
- Restrictions on interviews with victims of accidents or other tragedies, or their relatives
- Standards governing investigative reporting, including the definition of circumstances in which authorities should be notified, and prohibition, except in limited circumstances, against a newsperson's misrepresenting his or her identity or engaging in law violations
- Standards governing the use of "objectionable" (i.e., possibly obscene or profane) material
- Prohibition against accepting outside contributions for production costs, including policies governing acceptability of outside-produced broadcasts
- Policies governing requests by the president for live coverage of speeches, addresses, and talks
- Policies defining the circumstances and procedures for reply to such presidential broadcast appearances and providing for analyses of such appearances
- Prohibition against the use of music and sound effects
- Policies governing on-air identification of sources and protection of confidential sources
- Prohibition against acceptance of free transportation, accommodations, meals, services, or other gifts, and a limitation on outside activities of CBS News personnel

Of course, making standards and policies effective requires enforcement. And I acknowledge that the judgments required to enforce these standards are often difficult. For example, in using the rule against personal editorializing, there is a fine line between permissible analysis, on the one hand, and editorialization, on the other. Where there are issues involving questions of judgment, enforcement must at least in the first instance be left to the editing gatekeepers, prodded by insistent reminders or even orders from me by memoranda in particular cases.

Without enforcement, standards—no matter how carefully and soundly devised—are simply used as informational guides for the news organization or public relations ploys intended largely for outsiders.

21
Management by Memo

*Just to make assurance doubly sure, I want all of you to do
nothing more and nothing less than exercise your normal news
judgments in seeking out, interviewing, and including or excluding [anti-Nixon-Agnew demonstrators]. . . . Normal news
judgments must prevail. We must neither lean over backward
nor forward but simply stand up straight.*

—Memo to the News staff, December 23, 1968

ROBERT MCNAMARA ONCE SAID to Lee Iacocca, "The discipline
of writing things down is important. . . . Go home tonight and put
your great ideas on paper. If you can't do that, then you haven't really
thought it out."[1]

Long before I read that account of McNamara's advice, I utilized
memoranda as a central management mechanism, although I cannot
claim that I reserved my memos only for great ideas. I extended them
to passing thoughts as well. Nor did I wait until I came home at night.
I cascaded them out the first thing in the morning when I arrived at
the office before anybody else was in, and I did not stop the flow until
the day ended.

On relatively minor matters, usually relating to what I had seen on
our news or the competitors' the night before, I used to scribble my
thoughts, observations, criticisms, questions, and praise by hand.

---

[1]Quoted by Robert Townsend in his review of Lee Iacocca's autobiography in the
New York Times Book Review, November 4, 1984.

Many of these went to Gordon Manning. Gordon came in one day and said, "You write these things faster than I can read 'em, but for Christ's sake, I can't read 'em. Why don't you get a typewriter?"

I dutifully brought in a portable typewriter—and typed my memos. But I am the world's worst typist, and my typing was even more illegible than my handwriting. (My colleagues should give thanks that word processors were not around in those good old days.) Gordon came back three months later and said, "Go back to handwriting."

Whenever my patience permitted, then, I waited for a secretary to arrive. Even before she took off her coat, she knew that she would hear me shout into the outer office, "Bring in your book," to take my dictation. My words tumbled out so fast that it normally took my secretaries—and all of them were incredibly skilled—several months to get used to me. Even then, they had to tell me—gently—to slow up.

In considerable part, I am sure, it was because I had a compulsion to put on paper whatever I had on my mind. Also, my way of management normally precluded prebroadcast intervention. This left me with postmortems.[2]

A memo has the large advantage, it seemed to me, of being less confrontational. It gives the addressee more time to collect his or her thoughts before responding. Memos of criticism, for example, are a little less likely to result in reactive defenses. Policies have more permanence—are more likely to become embedded in daily practice—if written down. And if my idea—a story suggestion, for example—was a lousy one, as many of them most certainly were, the recipient felt more comfortable composing a response less blunt than "It stinks."

Also, I found that memos were a means of letting my associates know that I was there and that I was not ignoring or being indifferent to what they had sweated over to produce. There was the danger of my memos turning into nit-picking or of me acting the role of big brother, and so I tried, wherever appropriate, to keep it light, although there were some memos that were insistent or even angry. But memos were an important way of informing my colleagues of my policies and letting them know that I was an interested listener and viewer, and not

---

[2]How this is done depends on the manager. Some later presidents of the CBS News Division, such as Van Gordon Sauter, visited the "fishbowl"—the offices on the perimeter of the *Evening News* newsroom from which the broadcast is aired—four or five times in the course of the day, and held postmortems or critiques with the staff immediately following the *Evening News*. I visited just twice a day, to keep myself informed on how the broadcast was taking shape—and to learn, rather than to instruct. My approach was that subject to compliance with basic policies, the *Evening News* (and all other CBS News broadcasts) should, in general, reflect the concepts and judgments of the executive producer and the managing editor/anchor.

an absentee landlord. (Since radio is so often given short shift by management, I also made it a point to listen to radio broadcasts and comment on them—the radio newspeople appreciated it, since television is such an overshadowing presence.)

* * *

A number of my memos over the years sought to keep a steady eye on the problem of editorializing. As I have noted, one of the earliest and most fundamental policies established by Bill Paley was that, with certain specified exceptions, correspondents were encouraged to provide analysis, but editorializing—the presentation of ultimate evaluative conclusions and calls for action—was forbidden.

I felt I had to tread easy: There are fine judgments and close calls involved. In some cases, it is particularly difficult to distinguish between what is factual reporting or analysis, on the one hand, and editorializing—the expression of the correspondent's opinion—on the other hand. I have described later on how enforcement of this policy led to the departure of Howard K. Smith. But such a drastic and unhappy action was exceptional and only occurred where violations were persistent, frequent, inarguable, and without contrition.

These are some examples of editorializing misdemeanors:

Memo to the deputy director, news (copies to vice president, news, and to executive producer, *CBS Evening News* (June 11, 1968):

In his piece included on the Cronkite *News* on June 6 reporting the British reaction [to the U.S. congressional position opposed to gun control], [Morley] Safer closed with this sentence: "The main reaction by Englishmen is anger—anger born of frustration of watching a close friend destroy himself by a stupid gun law, created by pioneers and, it seems, enforced by fools." Perhaps Morley was trying to say that this was British reaction . . . but he certainly didn't make it clear, and it comes out as a very strong condemnation by Morley of the gun law and its enforcement. This is simply not our function, in a hard news broadcast at least. We have not let the bars down to the extent that in hard news our correspondents can take an editorial position on gun laws or anything else.

Let's not move too far, too fast; we still must maintain a distinction between reporting and editorializing and not mix the two.

Memo to Gordon Manning (with copies to other news executives, January 29, 1974):

[I] remind all concerned that our policies relating to analysis and prohibiting personal editorializing are precisely the same for radio as they are for television. . . . And I also suggest that whatever the difficulties of drawing the line, we should stay even more safely on the side of the analysis line and be even more wary of straying toward the editorializing side [when the correspondents involved] are also engaged in hard news reporting.

Few journalistic principles are more important to me than keeping a separation between reporting and editorializing—between the first page and editorial and op-ed pages, and so I think that it is particularly vital for [the hard news reporters]—and their editors—to follow the policy of not doing a piece under the guise of analysis when they are doubtful whether it is within the rules. Here again is an ideal situation to adopt the rule "when in doubt, don't." If it is close enough to be doubtful, it is close enough to cast shadow on their main business of being hard news reporters.

•   •   •

No issue was a more frequent subject of my memos than fairness and balance. No other policy was more firmly embedded in the CBS News tradition than the mission of news to present all relevant facts and significant viewpoints on issues with which our reports dealt.

Monitoring broadcasts as they appeared on the air, examining transcripts, and then utilizing my memos was my principal mechanism for assuring such fairness and balance insofar as humanly possible. At the same time, I did not think that our journalistic function was always fulfilled merely by reporting that one side said "Katy did" and the other side answered "Katy didn't" where our own journalistic inquiry might fairly throw further light on the issue.

For example:

Memo to director of news (October 16, 1969):

Maybe I'm just tired . . . but I find it necessary to point out that the *Morning News* is no less obligated to observe the CBS News policy of overall balance than are our other broadcasts. In general, that means that a particular broadcast series must maintain balance within itself and not go its merry way and rely on different series to make up the difference.

What precipitates this is this morning's broadcast, particularly the double-length [live] interview with Barbara Tuchman. Maybe she got away from us and we didn't expect her to abandon her role as historian and turn into a super-dove advocate opposed to the war in Vietnam. When it became apparent that that was what she was doing, perhaps it was too late not to come back for a further interview in the second half hour. Certainly the teeny-weeny, itsy-bitsy, peripheral smidgen of interview with [Herbert] Klein and the South Vietnamese ambassador hardly righted the balance. . . .

What it comes down to is that I think we are obligated, at the very first time possible—and it ought to be tomorrow—to have a major interview on the *Morning News* with a dedicated hawk—Goldwater, [John] Tower, [William F.] Buckley, somebody.

Please get this in the works immediately.

The following day, the major interview guest on the *Morning News* was Congressman Lukens, a strong supporter of the administration's Vietnam policy.

I was persistent. Concerning our coverage of black lung disease, in a series of memos, I didn't give up.

(1) Memo to news director (March 5, 1976):

I have checked the transcript of our March 1 *Evening News* black lung story to see whether my impression, on watching the story, that it was an unbalanced piece was correct. The transcript . . . confirms my impression. I do not believe that the fleeting reference to the opponents of the bill calling it "a costly, unreasonable, welfare plan for the miners" provides the kind of balance that I think good journalism requires.

With the emotional appeal inherent in including the victims of black lung, plus statements by a doctor and an official of the Bureau of Mines supporting the bill, this reference to the other side was quite inadequate. Could we get no one from the mining companies or from the congressmen who oppose the bill to say anything?

I am afraid that unless there is something here that I missed, our principles of fairness and balance compel us to go back to this story to include the missing elements.

(2) Follow-up memo to news director (March 30, 1976):

I am attaching copies of . . . memoranda I wrote you on March 5 in which I raised questions about balance in stories we did on . . . black lung. To the best of my knowledge, I have had no response.[3]

Along with accuracy, balance is the imperative of our way of journalism. When serious questions of balance are raised—and naturally I believe my questions are serious—we need self-analysis, and where warranted, correction. Yet twenty-five days have elapsed without any response.

We are going to have to do better than this, and I insist that we do so.

(3) Further follow-up memo to news director (June 8, 1976):

---

[3]The original March 5 memo went into my f/u [follow-up] file. This March 30 memo represents how the file worked, so that I could assure response and action.

I am a persistent fellow—on March 5 I sent you two memos relating to our two pieces we had done on black lung—noting that they were not . . . balanced. I stated that we were compelled to go back to the story to include the missing elements. Have we—when I wasn't looking?

———————

Memo to Bill Small (February 24, 1975):

I am concerned that the piece on the Edelin case [a conviction of a doctor for performing an abortion] which we had on the *Saturday Evening News* lacked the kind of balance that so important, sensitive, and controversial an issue warrants.

I think I know what happened: Our intent was to do a piece on what effect the verdict had on abortions in general and second-trimester abortions in particular. That would have been perfectly legitimate (although I would have liked to have some indication of how large a proportion of all abortions are represented by second-trimester abortions). But we slipped into a discussion of the merits of the verdict, partly through the interview with the doctor at Vanderbilt, but more specifically and importantly, through the interview with the woman at the end. The resultant impression, it seems to me, was that the piece was an argument in favor of the Edelin position and critical of the verdict. Since this is so, it seems to me that we ought to have had somebody on to defend the verdict.

Will you have a careful look at this, and if you agree, I believe we ought to have a follow-up somewhere and soon.

•   •   •

I believed strongly that news, dealing as it does with reality, must be kept separate from the fiction of entertainment. I felt there should be a strong wall between them. Therefore, as a general rule, I prohibited music and sound effects in news broadcasts. But the producers and others sometimes found music, and, more rarely, sound effects, tempting, either to attract the audience or to make a point. From time to time, therefore, I had to remind my associates about the use of music and sound effects.

To hard news and election units vice presidents: (February 25, 1976):

Have you all decided that we must introduce our campaign 1976 specials with that goddam music? I hate it. And I will call to your attention that our policy states that no music is to be used in any of our broadcasts unless I specifically approve. I did not specifically approve.

Concerning a news story on the fad among West Coast young people to restructure their cars so that they became "low riders," I wrote this memo to the news vice president (December 13, 1978). Rock music was used throughout the story:

> What I am saying is that we can't use music this way (even though at some point the car cassettes may be playing rock) unless it happens naturally and the piece of music we use is in fact the piece of music which is playing at some point while we are shooting. My basic difficulty in this story is that as I watched it I kept on thinking that I was watching ABC News or NBC News.

But in special circumstances where the question of using sound effects was a close one, I deferred to my colleagues when they felt strongly about using an effect which could not possibly mislead because it was immediately recognizable as a sound effect. In 1969, when the producers of the *CBS Evening News* was prepared "The Selling of the Pentagon" (exposing Pentagon waste and boondoggles), they included at the end of each example the sound of a rubber stamp—to represent the fact that Pentagon officials had approved each expenditure which was filmed. I objected.

One of the two producers came to my office to argue the case; the other wrote a memo to me which began, "At the risk of seeming dumb or rebellious, or both, let me insert my two cents' worth" on the issue. His memo pointed out that a recent *60 Minutes* piece reporting the ways in which Joe Namath was capitalizing on his fame used the sound of a cash register each time Namath was shown throwing a forward pass. The *Evening News* producer asked in his memorandum to me, "Are we the victims of a double standard?" Good and fair question.

I was pleased that the two producers felt free to argue the issue with me. I thought that they were entitled to a full statement of my views, instead of a curt order that they do it my way. It also gave me the opportunity to explain what my loose-reins philosophy was all about— that is, of relying on the good faith of my skilled professional associates.

And so I replied by memorandum with copies to the *Evening News* executive producer and the vice president in charge of hard news. I wrote that the visit and the memorandum "do not quite persuade me but they certainly shake me."

> Briefly, my rationale is that we in broadcast news are so surrounded by entertainment and fiction that we must err on the side of excessive purity and avoid playing anything that looks like games. I do not think that the sole criterion is whether we mislead or are dishonest.
>
> If that were the criterion, the use of music in hard news or hard news documentaries would be permissible, since nobody believes that swelling orchestras or choirs are performing for the camera while the events we

are showing occur. It is simply my deep desire not to engage in any dramatic sound devices to jazz up our reports.

[Your] point about the use of the cash register in the Joe Namath piece is a good one—thank God, [you] decided to go into broadcast news instead of law. I can only say that I was bothered by the cash register, but it was a light piece and I let it go.

Having said all that, let me add that the most important principle of all which guides me in my attempts to properly assume responsibility for the greatest news division that ever existed is that the people who have the immediate responsibility for reporting and producing should, if we are to go forward with spirit, be given the greatest leeway and, in general, must be left free from being controlled by my own notions. I have long since discovered that the most important part of a news division is the people in the direct line of fire. My primary job is to pick the right people. And then to fight for them, protect them, get time for them, and get money for them. They are the ones, then, who have to step up to the plate, on their own.

And so if you . . . feel so strongly about the importance of a stamp audio, after taking my views into account, go ahead.

And one more point: For heaven's sake, don't worry about appearing either "dumb" or "rebellious" when you undertake to disagree with my ukases. In the first place, as Oliver Cromwell once said, "By the bowels of Christ, consider the possibility that I am wrong." In the second place, your strong disagreements with my conclusion indicate not stupidity or rebellion but only that you give a damn about what you are doing. And that's great.

They went ahead and used the sound of the rubber stamp. That may have been democracy in the newsroom. But I felt comfortable with it, and it was my way.

• • •

Staging an event—causing or directing anything to occur which does not of its own accord occur when and in the manner in which it actually occurs—breaches the wall of separation between the facts, with which news deals, and fiction, with which entertainment, including drama, deals. I insisted that the wall be maintained.

For example, in June 1977, the hard news director told me that the weekend television news was planning to do a piece on the widespread use of cocaine. He asked for my approval. I replied:

I think that we can film this under our news standards, but before I approve, I must know exactly how the *Weekend News* people intend to proceed. The critical point is that the people involved not engage in the use of cocaine for our benefit and that it not be perceived as being done for our benefit. That means that it must not be arranged by us—either the event itself or the time or place. We can only film it as it happens, and we must make sure that it would have happened at the time or place even if we weren't there.

The issue of how to avoid misleading the audience concerning what we say or how our broadcasts are prepared arises in a variety of ways in addition to the act of staging. Thus, in 1974, the *CBS Evening News* broadcast an informative story about Vietnam veterans returning to civilian life who could not make the adjustment and engaged in acts of violence as a result of their traumas. One such case involved a Vietnam veteran who terrorized the area in Griffiths Park in Los Angeles in 1974.

In reporting the tragic episode from the area where it occurred, the producer interspersed scenes of bloody battles which had taken place in Vietnam. It was intended to illustrate what was presumed to have flashed in the veteran's mind during the Griffiths Park episode. When I saw it on the air, by memorandum to the director of hard news, I questioned the intercutting device:

Do me a favor and have a hard look at last night's flashback piece. Perhaps—or rather indubitably—I am oversensitive, but I couldn't escape the feeling that we resorted to a kind of fictional recreation ... creating the impression, as I suspect was intended, that these were in fact the mental images which the veteran had during the ... episode. ... It is something like some of the new journalism that Tom Wolfe and Norman Mailer—as well as a new breed of biographers—engage in: Reporting on conversations that might have happened but never did or things that the writer imagines went on in the subject's head. It seems to me that it might be a special form of staging and fiction that blurs the line between news and fact, on the one hand, and show business and drama, on the other hand, and it makes me uncomfortable.

The device was not used again in news broadcasts during my tenure.

Another device which I forbade had been commonly used on CBS News radio features. An example was "Wallace at Large," in which Mike Wallace narrated pieces about people in the news and included interviews with the newsworthy subject.

The CBS Radio Network was eager to have leading correspondents, otherwise identified with CBS News on the television side, to contribute on radio as well.

Wallace himself, however, rarely interviewed the subject of the broadcast. Instead, the interviews were conducted by a newsperson on the staff whose questions were eliminated for broadcast, leaving only the statements made by the subject. Mike did the lead-ins, the lead-outs, and the bridging material.

It was a natural and understandable process: Leading correspondents like Wallace had full-time jobs on the television side and did not have the time to engage in much original reporting and interviewing for radio. But the "Wallace at Large" pieces did not make it clear that Wallace was not the interviewer. By memorandum of December 31, 1975, to the vice president of our news broadcasts for radio, I put a stop to the practice:

> I realize there is nothing we say in these broadcasts that indicates Wallace is the interviewer, but the juxtaposition of Wallace's lead-ins and transitions, without hearing the actual questions in the interview, does, apparently, reasonably create the impression that Wallace was involved, since he used the statement "We interviewed . . ."
>
> The integrity of news is too important to create such an impression, which can reasonably mislead a reasonable listener. Therefore, from here on in, when the subject is not actually interviewed by Wallace, I want it clearly stated somewhere in the course of the broadcast—preferably at the top—that so-and-so—whoever he or she is—talked to the interview subject. Our labeling should be just as clear, designed to avoid misleading impressions, as we insist drug and food labeling should be. This question has come up too often to fool around with any more.

• • •

Although CBS News included some superb writers among its correspondents, the misuse of language troubled me. So over the years, I niggled over many questions of style, language, and grammar. I tried to monitor usage and to persuade our people to use greater care.

For example, I found the proper use of the word "like" an intractable issue. I hate "like" as a conjunction. I tried to instruct my colleagues that "like" was fine as a verb or as a preposition, but it was verboten as a conjunction. Some examples of my attempts at correction:

> May 21, 1968: Perhaps I was bitten by an old prep-school teacher of English and repelled by Winston cigarettes,[4] but hearing "like" used as a conjunction, instead of exclusively as a preposition, affects me worse than scratching nails against a blackboard. One of our most senior, most

---

[4]The advertising slogan for Winston cigarettes was "Winston tastes good like a cigarette should." As a result, I never smoked a Winston.

able, most respected correspondents, who has an enormous influence over the speaking habits of tens of millions of Americans, said on the air last Friday that somebody "acted like he missed it." Good God, that sounds lousy, like a grammarian shouldn't.

June 8, 1977: Isn't it about time to remind all our reporters, writers, editors, and producers that we are not in Winstonland and that "like" may be a verb or it may be a preposition, but it never, never, never—at CBS News at least—[is] a conjunction. In recent days, I have noticed an increasing use of it as a conjunction.
1. OK as a verb: "I don't like using like as a conjunction."
2. OK as a preposition: "It is just like him to do a thing like that."
3. Not OK as a conjunction: "It looks like the consumer protection bill is in serious trouble."
   When anybody is tempted to use "like" as a conjunction, just have him or her substitute the words "as if," which is as correct as using "like" is wrong.

But I had to withdraw that last suggestion in a hurry:

June 10, 1977: After extensive post-midnight contemplation, it has occurred to me that my June 8 memo—last paragraph—dealing with the question of the proper use of "like" oversimplified the solution. The phrase "as if" as a substitute for "like" as a conjunction does not work in all cases. It wouldn't do to say, "Tell it as if it is." Nor would it do to say, "Winstons taste good as if it should." More often than not, the proper substitute would be just plain "as." No ifs and, in fact, no ands or buts.

Memo (January 20, 1969) to Manning, Ralph Paskman, Emerson Stone:

Do you think that we have a chance, ultimately, of persuading our correspondents and writers that "presently" does not mean "now" or "currently" but rather means "shortly" or "in the immediate future." I know that the erroneous meaning has come to be accepted—but not by me.

Memo (September 24, 1973) to Emerson Stone:

Listening to [the] . . . 6 P.M. hourly yesterday . . . reminds me that one small part of the English language that has buffaloed too many people is the difference between "rebut" and "refute." While the dictionary fuzzes it up (*Webster's Seventh New Collegiate Dictionary* makes them synonyms), the fact is that rebut means to answer back and refute means to answer back successfully. In other words, "refute" has much more of a connotation of disproving—or proving that something is false—while "rebut" is not nearly so positive and is much more of an attempt. So when we say that Congressman Albert "refuted" the president's miniature State of the Union Address, we really meant that he was responding to it. We should avoid "refute" because it is in fact an editorial evaluation.

All clear?

Memo (October 27, 1975) to Emerson Stone:

Something I noted listening to the radio over the weekend—not serious, but enough to indicate that greater care is necessary: On our Saturday 6 P.M. hourly, [our correspondent] referred to Franco's death as "eminent." Of course, he meant "imminent."

Memo (August 29, 1975) to Don Richardson:

Some of our correspondents . . . persist in using the word "hopefully." The word means "full of hope." This has become such a common error that I think it would be worthwhile to get an expert to define what the word means and when it is properly used and improperly used, and send out some guidance to our people.

Memo (February 14, 1978):

In yesterday's evening news, in leading in to the story of the Brazilian girl who strapped herself to a wooden cross for three days, we referred to the crowds that had gathered and stated that "some even set up fast-food stands, charging, it is alleged, usurious prices."

I think we mean exorbitant. "Usurious" is defined by the dictionary as "practicing usury." And "usury" has a limited meaning—it is defined as "a lending of money with an interest charge for its use" or, more commonly today, as "an unconscionable or exorbitant rate of interest." In other words, usurious has to do with interest charges in the lending of money—not high prices in general for products or services.

• • •

I also found time to write memos about miscellaneous irritations.

Memo to the deputy director of hard news (April 14, 1969):

[Bob] Schakne's piece on the Friday *Evening News* about the businesses that have run away to Mexico was excellent. But he did make one error which an awful lot of people make and which annoys me no end because of its chauvinism: He confused the United States with America and treated them as synonymous. For example, over pictures of Mexico, Schakne said, "This isn't America"; in fact, it was America—Latin America. America is

North America, Latin America, and South America, and if I belonged to any of those [areas], I would be annoyed to be excluded from "America."

We ought to watch out and make sure that if we are talking only about this country, we say the "United States" in cases where there may be any confusion.

Memo (June 9, 1975) to Emerson Stone:

[Our correspondent] on the 3 o'clock today referred to Fred Graham as the CBS News "legal correspondent." I like to think that all our correspondents are legal—and none illegal. Fred is our law correspondent.

Memo (August 28, 1975) to executive producer, *CBS Morning News* regarding Fanne Fox, a nightclub performer, who had been widely publicized as a companion of the chairman of the House of Representatives Ways and Means Committee [Wilbur Mills]:

On the August 21 *Morning News* broadcast, the transcript says that Hughes [Rudd], in his closing piece about Fanne Fox and her proposed new book, said . . . "the critics are laying in the weeds for you [Fanne Fox]." Please God, he didn't say "laying," did he?

I refused to accept the possibility that Hughes may not have made a mistake . . . that he indeed meant "laying."

Memo (December 21, 1977) to Emerson Stone:

Hasn't the time come when we should watch very carefully how we phrase the tease for the story after the commercial? On the 2 P.M. hourly today, Douglas Edwards said, "A storm in California after this message." It sounds just as silly as it reads—unless our hourly news is going in for weather forecasting.

Memo (November 9, 1978) to Emerson Stone:

[I]n her 4 P.M. hourly newscast, we had Stephanie Shelton say as the lead-in to the first commercial, "The president's news conference—coming up." That, of course, is inaccurate. It wasn't the news conference that was coming up; it was a report on the news conference. I am afraid that people who may have already heard the news conference or weren't very interested in hearing it in full may have made a quick switch of their dial to see what else was news somewhere else. Our editors should really tighten up a bit.

Memo (November 29, 1978) to Shad Northshield, executive producer, *CBS Morning News*:

[I]n the course of a piece that Hughes Rudd had been doing, he made a reference to Hunter Thompson—without any further identification. While I'm all in favor of talking up, rather than down, to our viewers, how many of them have the slightest idea who Hunter Thompson is— and for that matter, how many of them should? Hughes and all editors might be reminded gently from time to time that we are not talking to ourselves.

On June 3, 1976, I wrote a memo to Bill Small:

For heaven's sake, let us not in any circumstances refer to next Tuesday's primaries as "super Tuesday" (ABC), "big casino" (Reagan) or any other nonsense like that. This is a political campaign—not a card game, not a football game, not any kind of game, but a deadly serious political process.

But the message was lost—perhaps in the wastebaskets of the recipients. Our reporters were back at the old stand four days later, and I was angry.

Memo to Bill Small (June 8, 1976):

One of the things I like least in this world is to blow in the wind. Last night (June 7), in his report on the *Evening News,* Dick Wagner referred to today's primaries as "super Tuesday" and on the *Morning News* today [Ed] Rabel referred to it as "so-called Super Bowl." (I should be, but am not, grateful for the "so-called.")

It is water over the dam, I concede, but in order to prevent future Teton collapses, I would like to know how my June 3 message was passed along—if it was passed along—and why it fell on deaf ears and big mouths.

Our reporters are reporters—not Howard Cosells.

•　　•　　•

Lest I have created the impression through the preceding memos that my written communications were confined to carping and plaguing my associates by pointing out shortcomings, many of my memos were also delighted ones.

For example:

Memo (April 7, 1975) to Bill Small:

On the Friday *Morning News,* Mort Dean reported that General Weyand had stated that the South Vietnamese "government forces still had the capability to defeat the Communists." He didn't stop there but went on to point out that the prior Saturday, Weyand had visited Nha Trang and said "he was 'heartened' by the performance of the South Vietnamese troops there," that the "situation at Nha Trang appeared 'stabilized,' and the troops were not demoralized in any sense."

Dean then pointed out that two days thereafter, Nha Trang was given up without a fight.

This is my idea of what really good reporting should be. Great!

Finally, since I believed passionately that it was essential that when we erred on the air, we should broadcast corrections, I tried to follow the same principle in respect of my memoranda.

Memo (May 19, 1978) to Bob Chandler, vice president of documentaries, and Ellen Ehrlich, director of press information:

My conscience is bothering me: Sometime a week or so ago, I got into a violent disagreement with one of the two of you—about the meaning of the word "pejorative." I took the position that the word does not have a negative or critical implication. One of you took the opposite position. I finally got around to looking it up in the dictionary yesterday. I was just plain 100 percent wrong. You were just plain 100 percent right. What it means is "depreciatory" or "disparaging."

Let that be a reminder to everybody that the more positively I take any position or make any assertion, the more doubtful is the accuracy and validity of my position or assertion.

22
Changing a White Male Bastion

*I guess that some of our reporters and editors (and maybe exec-
utives, too) need a little consciousness-raising to avoid sexist
reporting. . . . Over the weekend, one of our reporters on one of
our hourlies referred to Hurricane Carmen's changing its anticipated course by stating that it was exercising its woman's pre-
rogative to change its mind. Come now—let's have no more of
that. It not only is a demonstration of male chauvinist piggery,
and a cliché, but it also in my experience happens to be untrue.
I change my mind much more often than my wife does.*

—Salant internal CBS memo, September 9, 1974

DURING THE YEARS OF MY SECOND TENURE—from 1966 to
1979—not only were there major changes in broadcast journalism but
also evolutionary changes within the News Division—all had an important impact on CBS policies, practices, and character. Chief among
these was the recognition at CBS of the important role of women and
minorities in our line of work.

In terms of personnel, there was something of a revolution as, belatedly, I became aware of what a white male bastion the News Division
was. It had been negligence, not conscious discrimination. Kay Wight,
who was director of administration when she joined CBS News and
later became a vice president and assistant to the president, was un-
compromisingly dedicated to the feminist movement. She decided—
rightly—that CBS News needed, and needed very badly, a president
who knew something about the women's movement. I give Kay—

along with my wife and four daughters—credit for raising my consciousness from below sea level.

It was not so many years before—in the mid-1960s—that I had told a *TV Guide* reporter who was doing a piece on the absence of women reporters in network television news that the reason was that neither men nor women viewers would accept women reporters as authoritative. I was not misquoted; the writer did not take my statement out of context. Heaven forgive me. I said it, I meant what I said, and I said what I meant. It took me a decade to realize how mistaken I was.

As my consciousness was raised, so were my shame and determination to reform. Early in 1973, Esther Kartiganer, an associate at CBS News, brought me a copy of a manual for company secretaries prepared by CBS, Inc. called "A Good Right Arm." I had glanced through it before—with mind and eyes closed. Esther had me read it with both open—along with my consciousness. After reading the manual, I wrote a memo to the CBS, Inc. labor relations vice president, saying it might have been subtitled "A Woman Secretary's Place Is at the Male Boss's Feet."

May I respectfully suggest that after a suitable period devoted to consciousness-raising, you ... read it and imagine what your reaction would be if you were a female. Better yet, after you have read it, I urge you to have some reasonable, sensible female read it alongside of you to get the benefit of her reaction. I am afraid that entirely inadvertently, and doubtless with the best of intentions, it dramatically and conclusively illustrates why we are regarded as male chauvinist pigs. We are so regarded because that is the way we seem to write, to think—and quite possibly to be.

There is a terrible tone throughout "A Good Right Arm" of chucking our little office woman under the chin. She seems to be reminded throughout that her major functions at the office are equivalent to that of a wife's duty of fetching the slippers and the pipe. Maybe it is a secretary's duty [as stated in the manual] to "play the gracious hostess" and to pay close attention to that very important part of her job which, believe it or not, is fetching coffee for him—but I hope not.

Note, too, that throughout, "bosses" are always he ... Were I a woman, I would find particularly offensive the section ... entitled "Wardrobe," which emphasizes the importance of good taste and good grooming. Have we issued any such written reminder to mail boys, couriers, or even division presidents? Or have we ever found it desirable to issue instructions to males similar to those appearing on page five on the importance of maintaining the confidentiality of confidential information?

I suppose all of these things are small and none of them are intended the way they sound, but quite properly, the company is now focusing on what we have done, and not done, and what we are doing, and not doing, in this area. These little things mount up, and they betray us. Hiring and promotion are important. And were I a woman and the first thing I saw was "A Good Right Arm," I would just wonder how good a place CBS is for a woman with reasonable pride, drive, and ambition to make her career.

The manual was, soon, very considerably revised.

My zeal for reform grew year by year. By 1974, this was a standard memo to all officers in the News Division, suggesting we all could do better in terms of affirmative action in hiring:

This memorandum will reemphasize and reassert my determination to correct the imbalance and inequities in the number and character of positions currently filled by females and minorities in CND. We need to make continuing efforts to raise the overall number of females and minorities within the division and, in particular, the number of females and minorities in the United States in specific positions or cities where there is an especially marked deficiency in the executive, professional, and administrative areas. . . . Accordingly, I urge that new or replacement positions in these categories be filled by women or minorities whenever feasible.

In a memo concerning the replacement of a male associate producer by a female, I wrote:

I am not impressed, and I will not be impressed, by sad tales of feelings by males who are passed over [in favor of women]. While I am sorry about that, just think of the feelings of women passed over since time immemorial. Why all of a sudden should we get so sympathetic when it is males who are involved? Did we ever advance that argument when the shoe was on the other foot?

And in a memo to the head of the CBS Law Department in December 1973, I wrote:

I happened to see . . . the letterhead of [the large and well-known Washington law firm which represented CBS in many legal matters]; I noticed that not one of the thirty partners is a woman, and only two (or possibly as many as five, depending on whether Barry and Noel are girls' names or boys' names) of the forty-eight associates are women. This does not seem to me to be a particularly good record since from my own knowledge, dating all the way back to 1938 when I shared an office with Carolyn Agger (Mrs. Abe Fortas), I know that there are good lawyers who are women.

CBS is indeed doing an outstanding job in this whole area of catching up on women's employment.[1] But don't we also have the obligation not to lend our support—economic or otherwise—to others who at least on their face seem not to have their consciousness raised very high? . . . I am bothered that in this day and age, we should be represented for major work by a firm whose record of women employed seems to be so poor.

The head of the Law Department, who was as argumentative and self-righteous as I was, replied that the law firm in question had nine women. (A senior partner later wrote me that they had used an old letterhead when the firm had written me—they had forgotten to replace it with a new one; and besides, they were about to hire more women and announce some women's promotion to partnership.)

The head of the CBS Law Department also noted—dryly, I suppose, but alas, accurately—"Your division has no women among its officers." I replied in a memo, beginning "I knew you wouldn't let me down."

Touché as to our women officers here at CND, and I am thoroughly ashamed of it. But it all depends on what you mean by "officers." I do have a number of women at management levels, but none of the seven vice presidents is a woman. I have, however, had outstanding for several months now a request to make one woman already on staff a vice president, and I also have an offer of a vice presidency outstanding to another woman. So I'm trying, but presumably so is [the Washington law firm].

Shortly thereafter, in early 1974, my requests were approved, and two women were appointed.

• • •

In the spring of 1974, a very talented woman producer in our documentary unit came to my office to ask why the company did not provide paid maternity leave for pregnant staff people. It was not an issue of which I was even aware. I learned that CBS did not give paid leave

---

[1]Arthur Taylor, then the president of CBS, provided leadership on this issue, which was more than going through the motions. Taylor was active, insistent, and persistent. He hired an outside consultant firm to raise our consciousness: We were required to attend the firm's sessions. Years later, in tracing the history of the women's movement at CBS, Judy Hole, an associate producer, said, "in February [1973], Arthur Taylor . . . issued a policy note on equal opportunity for women at CBS. A policy note that was sincere in its intent . . . incendiary in its effect. That was the match that lit the brushfire . . . and nowhere did the fire of feminism burn as brightly as among the women at CBS News."

for what the company considered "voluntary" disability. The producer prepared a memorandum for the company personnel office, arguing that it should provide paid disability leave; she gave me a copy. I wrote a memo to the corporate official in charge:

> Nobody asked me for my views, but in my customary manner, I express them nevertheless. I completely agree with [the producer's] substantive points, and I most urgently hope that the company adopt a policy of paid maternity leaves. Maternity leaves . . . seem to me a great deal more constructive and fruitful than a double hernia operation, which put me on a paid leave for six weeks a year ago.
>
> Further, I am curious about the rationale which apparently leads to a distinction between "voluntary" and "involuntary" disability. It has not been unknown for employees of various companies—possibly including CBS—to get seriously injured because they have drunk too much and then tried to drive, which seems to be a "voluntary disability." I understand that they have been paid during the period of their recovery, although this seems about as "voluntary" as pregnancy. In any event, as I am sure you all know, there are some pregnancies which are not "voluntary" at all.
>
> If the policy turns on the distinction between "voluntary" and "involuntary," we are getting into the necessity of some extraordinary corporate inquiries!

Shortly thereafter, CBS did adopt a new policy of paid maternity leaves. And CBS also restored seniority for those who were still with CBS but had lost their seniority under the old policy when they left because of pregnancy.

It was not enough, I found, just to say that we must remedy the underrepresentation of women and minorities at staff meetings. Along with memos, I had to find other ways to implement the policy. And so at each staff meeting, I had my associates report on progress, or lack of it, since the last staff meeting. I also used bureaucratic paperwork as my ally: I required monthly written reports; I required that all job availabilities be held open for a fixed time to allow for a search for qualified women or minority candidates and if the opening was proposed to be filled by a white male, I required a written report to me on what efforts had been made to find a woman or a member of a minority and why the search had failed. I bounced back the recommendation if I was not persuaded that sufficient effort had been made.

Perhaps most effective of all my tactics was that in setting the criteria for year-end bonus, profit-sharing, and incentive payments to CBS News officers, I established as the first criterion the progress that had been made hiring and promoting minorities and women. As a result, we did make progress.

When I returned to CBS News in 1966, we had no women vice presidents. When I left thirteen years later, we had ten CBS News vice presidents; four of them were women. The number of women correspondents, producers, writers, and technicians all had multiplied many times over, in addition to our hiring many minority employees.

I had been educated—and heckled—about the importance of full opportunities for women and minorities at CBS News so persistently and successfully that in my final year at CBS News, just before retirement, the CBS Women's Advisory Council gave me the first (and, at this time, only) award it had ever granted—a framed portrait of Susan B. Anthony. Under her picture is a statement handwritten by Ms. Anthony: "Perfect equality of rights for women—civil and political—is the demand of Susan B. Anthony. Rochester, N.Y. March 29, 1885." And under that was a little plaque: "Presented to Richard S. Salant by the Women's Advisory Council in grateful appreciation for his endeavors on behalf of women."

In that last year before my retirement from CBS News, I received a number of awards.[2] I am grateful for them, but I suspect they were primarily for professional longevity rather than for substantive achievement. None meant as much to me as the recognition by the Women's Advisory Council. Women at CBS News—or anywhere else—had not come nearly so long a way as I had.

---

[2]*Editors' note:* Salant received many awards in recognition of his leadership at CBS News, his distinguished contributions to American broadcasting, and his defense of the First Amendment guarantee of a free press in electronic journalism. These awards include an Alfred I. DuPont–Columbia University Silver Baton, a George Polk Award, a Gold Medal Award from the International Radio and Television Society, and a personal George Foster Peabody Award.

23

People Fired,
People Hired

*No good journalist ever reported, edited, or published by wet-
ting his or her finger and holding it up to see which way the
popular winds blow. Journalism diminishes itself and becomes
just merchandising of another product if it marches to the
loudest drums. As William Lloyd Garrison, the great and uncompromising abolitionist editor put it, "The success of any
great moral enterprise does not depend on numbers." And under our constitutional system in a democratic society, the press
is a great moral enterprise.*

— **Washington University lecture, Seattle, May 5, 1986**

I FOUND FIRING THE TOUGHEST and most unpleasant part of my
job. It was playing God with the lives of my associates and their families—and I was not equipped to play God. However, I had to fire three
people during my sixteen years at CBS because of persistent or flagrant
policy violations or intolerable and destructive conduct that threatened the morale of the people at CBS News. Each incident was excruciatingly painful, but in each case, I felt I had to act regardless of my
admiration of, or affection for, the person involved.

Thus it was with the very able and intelligent Howard K. Smith, one
of the original Murrow boys, and our senior Washington correspondent. In the early 1960s, Smith persistently violated the basic CBS policy against editorializing except in clearly specified circumstances and
against mixing news reporting with editorializing. It was an issue I
had discussed with Howard a number of times.

In one 1961 news broadcast, Howard reported on a Senate debate to raise the ceiling on the national debt. The proposed ceiling, as I recall, was in the neighborhood of $360 million (how times have changed). In the broadcast, Howard delivered himself of a clearly editorial pronouncement condemning the proposal.

I summoned him to New York. He did not argue that it was analysis or that it was not an editorial. He defended his editorial on the ground that the nation had been, and continued to be, leaderless—that Eisenhower had been a passive figurehead and Kennedy was a callow fraternity boy. Therefore, Smith argued, somebody had to fill the vacuum of national leadership and Howard felt he had to do it.

I loved Howard. He was a great correspondent. I happened to agree with him on the dangers of the Senate debt limitation proposal. But I fired him.[1]

The two other cases involved David Schoenbrun and Dan Schorr—although in Dan's case it was not really a firing but a resignation.

Schoenbrun's departure in 1962 had its inception in my own mistake. David was a driving, relentless reporter whose abilities were matched by an overpowering ego and ambition for power. For many years, he had been the senior correspondent in Paris. He had been there so long and his relationships with the French government had become so thoroughly developed that sometimes it was hard to tell whether he was the CBS News correspondent or the U.S. ambassador to General de Gaulle and de Gaulle's ambassador to the United States. He was immodest, but he had much to be immodest about.

When, early on, I was in Paris during President Kennedy's first trip to Europe on the way to a summit meeting, Schoenbrun took charge of everything. In those days, we were dependent on commercial airlines to bring our film back to New York for broadcast. David took charge of that, too.

---

[1]*Editors' note:* Most other accounts of Smith's firing, including Smith's own memoirs (Howard K. Smith, *Events Leading Up to My Death: The Life of a Twentieth-Century Reporter* [New York: St. Martin's Press, 1996]), conclude that it was Paley who finally pushed Smith out; he departed in October 1961. Other accounts also say the final breach with CBS occurred because of Smith's editorializing in a commentary and documentary on the civil rights struggle in Birmingham, Alabama. In the spring of 1961, Smith witnessed the brutal beating of Freedom Riders at a Birmingham bus station by Ku Klux Klan–led thugs while City Police Commissioner Eugene "Bull" Connor's police were withdrawn from the area. Smith's conclusion for the documentary *Who Speaks for Birmingham?* was to have included the quotation from Edmund Burke: "The only thing necessary for the triumph of evil is for good men to do nothing." The quotation was deemed "straight editorial."

One day, I was with him when he was trying to arrange for our film to be taken aboard a Pan Am flight to New York. It was doubtful that the film could be delivered to the plane before takeoff. David worked the phone, cajoling, shouting. He wanted the plane to wait. He did not identify himself as David Schoenbrun or as a CBS News correspondent. He identified himself, over and over again, as "Monsieur le directeur" of American television. The plane waited until the film arrived.

When David decided that it was time for him to come back to the United States, Blair Clark and I agreed. But David believed he could not, after his stint in France, come back as just a correspondent. He wanted something more. I agreed that he could come back not only as a senior Washington correspondent but also as head of the Washington Bureau, replacing Howard K. Smith in late 1961.

That was my mistake. The Washington Bureau chief was the head of our largest and most important bureau. He had power over assignments, and hence over airtime—that most precious of commodities to reporters. As other news organizations have learned before and since, management—the bureau chief's job—and reporting should not be combined in a single person, particularly when the person has an insatiable appetite for power, for airtime, and for visibility.

The appointment was a disaster, compounded by the fact that David, who anchored his own weekly Washington program, used that broadcast to cultivate and woo his sources in Washington and to reward his friends. I feared that he was working his way toward becoming President Johnson's ambassador to CBS News as he had become de Gaulle's in Paris.

Blair Clark and I met with David in a New York hotel room to solve the problem. We told him that the functions of bureau chief and on-air reporter were not compatible and had to be disentangled. The meeting went badly. David delivered himself of a diatribe involving a vituperative personal attack on Blair, his old colleague. Although David was a fine reporter with a distinguished track record, I felt that I had to let him go.

David never found a comparable job as a broadcast correspondent. Some years later, after I had been fired in 1964 and then taken back as head of News in 1966, I attended a banquet in New York. I was at the head table; David Schoenbrun was at a table in the back of the room. He walked to the head table to greet me. Just as one of those lulls occurred that always seem to happen at affairs like these, David's voice boomed out, "Dick, they gave you a second chance. Why don't you give me one?" I had no answer.

The most publicized and difficult departure from CBS News on my watch was Dan Schorr's. Dan was a very special reporter—super-aggressive and determined. He fought with everything he had to get a story and get to the bottom of it, and then to get it on the air. He used his shoulders to shove not only competing news organizations' reporters aside but even his colleagues at CBS News. He was not universally beloved. But he was very good.

Over the years, I had staved off Bill Paley's efforts to get rid of Dan. When Fred Friendly was president of CBS News, Dan had reported on a trip Barry Goldwater made to Bonn, Germany, where Dan was our chief correspondent. It was just after Barry Goldwater had been nominated as the Republican candidate for president, and in his story, Dan linked Goldwater's visit to Germany to a neo-Nazi group of Germans. Goldwater was the guest of the U.S. general in charge of American forces in Germany—an old friend.

Schorr's story must have been somewhat long on innuendo and short on nailed-down facts (although the *New York Times* carried a similar story on the episode). Paley was very angry; he pressed Friendly to act.

I was present on an occasion when Fred telephoned Dan in Bonn to get the facts. After the call, Fred turned to me and asked me what to do. As on the occasion of Cronkite's removal from anchoring the 1964 Democratic Convention, I told Fred to make his own decision and weigh it on the merits: If Schorr was so intentionally or carelessly wrong and the error was born of bias, that was one thing. If not, it was another. Fred took no action.

After I came back to CBS News, on many occasions when I met with Paley, he asked me whether Schorr was still working for us. I got the message—but I was not familiar with the details of just what Dan had reported on the Goldwater matter or the facts supporting his report. I did not feel that, two or three years later, it was appropriate for me to investigate the matter and consider firing Dan. I did not act. Paley, as was his custom, was making himself perfectly clear, but he never made a demand. So without an explicit order from Paley, Schorr stayed with us.

Ultimately, Schorr was reassigned to our Washington Bureau, where he did much fine, original reporting on the Nixon administration and, later, on Watergate. When the Nixon administration complained about his reporting, his stories held up and the criticisms turned out to be groundless. He not only was a very good reporter but I felt he was mellowing. After a lifetime of bachelorhood, he had married and had children.

But there was still a lot of mellowing to do: During one broadcast on Watergate, there was a roundtable discussion among our correspondents, including Dan and Lesley Stahl. When the moderator asked Dan a question about some rumor which had surfaced, Dan dismissed the question as involving gossip, which he said was therefore in Lesley's department. The response did not endear him to Lesley, to many women in the audience, or to men.

On another occasion, after our broadcast on the night of Nixon's resignation, Dan, in talking to some college students at a public meeting at Duke University, criticized his CBS News colleagues for their reporting that night, charging that they had gone soft—a remark which did not endear him to his CBS News confreres.[2]

In the mid-1970s, the CIA and the history of its activities had become a major story. Dan was our lead reporter, breaking some important stories. A House of Representatives committee, chaired by Congressman Otis Pike, held hearings and prepared a report critical of the CIA. Before the Pike Report was released, Dan gained access to it and broadcast a number of reports describing its contents for both radio and television. Although the Pike Report had not yet been stamped secret when Schorr obtained a copy of it, it was before he made it public. Then, through me, Schorr offered the Pike Report to Holt, Rinehart, the CBS-owned publishing house. But before I received an answer from Holt, Rinehart, the report was published in full in the *Village Voice*.

When Dan was asked whether he was the source for the *Village Voice*'s copy of the Pike Report, Dan suggested that the source might be Lesley Stahl (who was the fiancée and later the wife of a *Village Voice* writer who, Dan said, had been in our bureau office near the Xerox machine just before the *Voice*'s publication of the report).

A day later, Dan admitted he had been the source of the copy of the report. He felt strongly that the Pike Report should be made public, and he gave the money the *Voice* had paid him for the Pike Report to the Reporters' Committee on Freedom of the Press. A congressional committee announced it would hold hearings to find out how Dan had obtained a copy of the still-secret Pike Report. The hearings promised to be a major story, involving the critical issue of a reporter maintaining the confidentiality of his sources.

Because of all the circumstances, I decided to suspend Dan until the hearings were over—with full pay. There were a number of factors in my decision: the fact that Dan would himself be a person much in the

---

[2]When I asked Dan just what he had said, he denied that he had criticized his colleagues. He sent me a tape of his remarks at the college and the question-and-answer session in which the statements were alleged to have been made. The tape had a gap in it. I asked Dan what inferences he had drawn from the more famous and important eighteen-minute gap in a Nixon tape.

news; the fact that he had at first tried to cast suspicion on a colleague; and the fact that, as it seemed to me then, Dan had turned over the report to the *Village Voice* without our permission.[3] I felt the report was the property of CBS News since it had been obtained by Dan in the regular course of his news-gathering duties at CBS.

Because an important First Amendment issue—the protection of a journalist's confidential sources—was involved, we also offered to supply Dan with a lawyer to represent him or to pay for a lawyer of his own choice. He chose one of Washington's leading lawyers—Joseph Califano, former secretary of health, education, and welfare, whose bill totaling several hundred thousand dollars we paid. We fully and publicly supported Dan's refusals to disclose his confidential source.

At the House Ethics Committee hearings, Dan stood fast in an eloquent and stirring defense of press freedom and the importance of maintaining the confidentiality of a reporter's sources.[4] When Dan completed his testimony, I sent him a telegram in which I stated: "Congratulations. Your appearance today was superb and an immense service to all your fellow journalists, to the Constitution and to the public's right to know. I am grateful."

Dan's testimony before the Ethics Committee was so effective that it voted not to hold him in contempt for refusing to disclose his source. Then I had to face the issue of what to do about Dan and his relationship to CBS News.

In order not to affect the vital issue of source protection, I had postponed reaching any conclusions on the other issues—what Dan had said at Duke about his colleagues in the Washington Bureau; whether Dan had any right to dispose of the Pike Report without CBS News's consent (an issue on which there was disagreement as to whether it

---

[3]Dan later told me that in fact he had informed me of his plan to offer the Pike Report elsewhere for publication. He said he had done so as he was making an early departure from a bureau breakfast meeting I was conducting. He had had to leave because it was Parents' Day at his son's school. I had no recollection of the conversation. I suspect that what happened is that in the distractions of the meeting, I simply missed Dan's message.

[4]*Editors' note:* In his testimony, Schorr said, in part: "We all build our lives around certain principles, and without these principles, our careers simply lose their meaning. . . . Now, for a journalist, the most crucial kind of confidence is the identity of a source of information. To betray a confidential source would mean to dry up many future sources. . . . The reporter and the news organization would be the immediate losers, but I would submit to you that the ultimate losers would be the American people and their free institutions. And if you will permit one last personal word . . . To betray a source would for me be to betray myself, my career, and my life. And to say that I refuse to do it isn't quite saying it right. I cannot do it." Edward Bliss Jr., *Now the News: The Story of Broadcast Journalism* (New York: Columbia University Press, 1991), pp. 430–431.

was Dan's property or ours and whether at some point, if a news organization does not use the fruits of a reporter's work, the reporter can make it public elsewhere[5]); and whether Dan had in fact, as had been reported to me, but as Dan had flatly denied, sought to divert suspicion from himself to Lesley Stahl.

I asked Dan to meet and discuss these issues with me; I wanted to hear his side of the story. While the Ethics Committee hearings were still pending, Dan had told the *Wall Street Journal* that while "there could be problems between" CBS News and himself, "this is not a good time to talk about them. We have so many things to struggle against now that we're putting those things in abeyance." But when the hearings were over and I tried to meet with Dan to discuss "those things," Dan declined, saying that he was resigning, that he did not wish to return to CBS News, and that he had made other commitments. Thus, there never was any discussion or resolution of the "other things" which we had left in abeyance. Dan was gone.

The record as I have described it seems clear: Dan was not fired; he resigned before I had made up my mind concerning what action to take. But I had managed to muddy up the issue and give substance to the insistence of others, including another lawyer who later represented Dan, that, in fact, I had fired him.[6]

I had done so by signing an agreement with Dan in February 1976, at the outset of the episode, when I had decided to suspend him during the period of the Ethics Committee hearings. The agreement had been drawn up by the CBS Law Department, and unquestionably I had committed a major sin: I signed it without reading it carefully. The agreement did indeed provide that when the Ethics Committee hearings were over and the issue before it was finally disposed of, "we [CBS] shall notify you to such effect and upon the giving of such notice you shall notify us of your resignation." Clearly, that provided for an automatic forced "resignation"—a firing.

---

[5]The issue may be a difficult one where the news organization suppresses, for inappropriate reasons, the fruits of a reporter's work. But in this case, Dan had fully reported the substance of the Pike Report on both the radio and television networks.

[6]Dan himself apparently did not contend that he had been fired. In his book *Clearing the Air*, Dan wrote that Bill Small had had dinner with Califano, then Dan's attorney, and had told Califano that "Salant had been 'really ready to take Dan back' after going through a three-point agenda that included the disposition of the Pike Report, the suspicion that fell on Lesley Stahl and my criticisms of CBS at Duke University." In fact, however, if Dan had been able to satisfy me on the points we had left in abeyance, I was ready to put him back to work, but, at least for a considerable cooling-off period, not in the Washington Bureau, where the ill will of his colleagues had made it inadvisable to assign him there.

Nevertheless, when the Ethics Committee hearings ended and it belatedly dawned on me that the agreement had gone beyond what I intended, I tried to back away from it and retain my options. In fact, difficult as Dan was from time to time, he was a great investigative reporter. I wanted to keep him on if I could find a sensible way.

But Dan and his attorney refused to modify the original February agreement. I nevertheless sought to proceed as though it provided what I wanted it to provide—that the agreement left me with the discretion to decide whether Dan would have to "resign." How I would have exercised that discretion I do not know, since our discussions had been aborted because Dan had already made other commitments.

I remain an admirer of Dan's great abilities as an investigative reporter.[7] I will have to leave it to others more objective and less self-defensive than I to decide whether Dan voluntarily resigned or whether I fired him—or whether it was a little bit of both.

It is conventional wisdom that the public writes only to criticize or complain; those who are pleased do not ordinarily write. The conventional wisdom was supported by the mail about Dan Schorr: Before he left CBS News, the mail was universally critical of him—and of me for not terminating his employment. After he left us—in what was mistakenly regarded by his supporters as my having fired him—the Schorr

---

[7]At least until the Pike Report matter, I believe that the admiration was mutual. In the winter of 1975, on the eve of the controversy over the Pike Report, Dan delivered a lecture at Aspen, Colorado, at which I was present. In the course of his lecture, Dan, who knew that I was in the audience (as was former Supreme Court justice Abe Fortas), said, "If you'll permit me a small personal aside. . . . [A]s I find myself being pictured in the public prints as an intrepid investigative reporter [for his reporting on Watergate, and, later, on the intelligence community], I sometimes feel a little guilty that it isn't all earned. And the reason I say this tonight is that there are two people . . . who to me seem to delineate two sides of what makes investigative reporting possible. One is former justice Abe Fortas, who has always seemed to me to be a beacon light on the meaning of liberties, including freedom of the press in this country. . . . The other—[who] may not be known to you, because executives are, on the whole, nameless to large sections of the people—is Richard Salant. And he is my boss. And anyone who knows me, including him, knows that I'm not much of an apple polisher with bosses. But the temple that a Fortas helps to construct in freedom of the press has to be defended, and through the years, Dick Salant has stood at the portals, defending it, sometimes against almost unbelievable pressures. . . . And through the worst and toughest of those times, I have had the feeling that, however controversial what I was doing [was] and however much I was bucking a very powerful government, I felt secure in support of a man who may not have felt all that secure himself at certain times. . . . So, if anybody thinks it is easy to be an investigative reporter, remember that you dwell in a temple that others have built and others have . . . maintained. And if Abe Fortas is here tonight, and Dick Salant is here tonight . . . I would like to make a small bow to them."

loyalists turned to their pens and typewriters and condemned me for having let him go. The only common ground between the two groups of letters was that it was my fault—first for keeping him, then for letting him go.

But those who wrote in 1976 gave me the opportunity to try to explain the complicated circumstances. A friend of the then president of the CBS Television Network wrote him a letter in February 1976, during the period of the congressional contempt proceeding against Dan. The network president turned the letter over to me to answer. The writer stated that

> I consider the matter of Daniel Schorr so basic to the future of our Country that I am writing . . . I have simply become a confused, frustrated, and, I believe, a betrayed Patriot. . . . By what rule of conduct does Dan Schorr usurp the right of Congress to hold certain material confidential, especially when it may involve National Security? Do the political views and values of Schorr take precedence over the National interest? Most important, Schorr has now shown that his loyalties lie not with his country nor its people, but with some obscure moral value that he chooses to call "literary conscience." On this basis alone, so long as Daniel Schorr is functioning as a news source for CBS, the public has the obligation to question the truth of any CBS report and to suspect an ulterior motive behind any CBS release. . . . This is the problem Schorr has laid at your feet, and a lot of the future of CBS in particular, and the television media in general rides on how it is handled.

I made this reply, after first explaining why CBS supported Schorr in his legal battle with Congress:

> I should state, in all candor, that I cannot agree that the Congress, or any government official, should have the ultimate and final right to decide, on the mere blanket claim of "national security," or "executive privilege," or whatever, what news should be published and what should not. If history from the time that we were a colony of Great Britain to the time of the present day establishes anything, it is that government has a tendency to misuse and abuse its powers of press control in order to avoid embarrassment and to suppress news or views which it finds unfavorable. It is a harsh fact, but it is nevertheless the fact, that an independent and free press cannot automatically submit to a government edict on what to print and what not to print. It is the responsibility of the press carefully to weigh any claims of executive privilege or national security. But if we are to retain our independence and our freedom from government control and manipulation, we must, acting as responsibly and carefully as we [can], make the determination for ourselves. This is the way it has worked for 200 years, and I submit that though the press has not al-

ways been infallible, and has often been exasperating, this system has worked reasonably well and the nation still stands, and stands strong.

The ultimate question is where this power to determine what is or is not to be published should reside. I submit that the First Amendment resolves that issue—and the principles of democracy resolve that issue—by not giving the final power to the government.

But some of the reactions to my suspending Dan were so vehement that I felt that there was no use trying to explain. For example, in March 1976, a Louisville viewer wrote me a postcard stating: "I am certain that, like Eichmann, you are only doing your duty to your CBS bosses. . . . But what you are doing is despicable. . . . Schorr should be praised and celebrated by anyone who loves press freedom. . . . Please retract the vicious stand taken by CBS News and reinstate this man Schorr."

I felt it useless to try to explain: "'[L]ike Eichmann'? 'despicable'? 'vicious'? How can you expect a reply to an irrational postcard which deals with fundamental and perplexing issues? I for one can't give you a rational reply because you don't deserve one."

Another letter writer from Oakland, California, wrote me a letter beginning "Dear Quisling" and concluding, "You are a schmuck for not having the guts to rehire this great American."

I wrote back: "You make yourself perfectly clear. Yours sincerely, Schmuck Quisling."

• • •

On the usual questions of staffing—hiring and firing—I set general policies—relating to women and minorities, for example—and established a steadfast insistence that the first criterion was journalistic ability, experience, and professionalism. But in fact, while hiring, promotion, and firing were subject to my approval, I largely delegated those decisions, except for the key officers of CBS News.

I delegated in these areas mainly because those to whom I delegated—Gordon Manning, Bill Small, Bill Leonard, and others—were better equipped to judge than I. The head of a news division must try, as I tried, to make the organization a cohesive whole, and it is dangerous and destructive for it to split into separate fiefdoms. But the fact is that the various units—such as the *CBS Reports* unit or the *CBS Evening News* unit—must operate as a team with their own executive producer, drawing as much as they can on the resources of the entire organization. Recommendations from the executive producers, therefore, were given great weight, as were the recommendations of the bureau managers. And if Gordon Manning, Bill Small, or Bill Leonard approved in their respective areas, to the best of my recollection, I never turned down their recommendations.

My record in the few cases where I directly and actively intervened in hiring establishes that it was just as well that I delegated in this important area. While I do claim credit for hiring a few fine reporters—Michele Clarke and Susan Spencer are examples—I also must accept responsibility for one of the more conspicuous failures, when I hired Sally Quinn to coanchor the *CBS Morning News*. It was one notable black mark on my watch. Everybody has been blamed for that hire except the one guy who was responsible for it, which was me. It occurred when I was going through my period of discovery, finding out we weren't doing well by women at CBS News.

I had met Sally long before, when she had served on our staff during the 1968 political conventions. Later, she became a very successful reporter for the Style Section of the *Washington Post*. Her writing was first rate; her profiles witty, penetrating, and, where deserved, merciless.

While she was writing for the *Post*, she appeared for one week, along with a panel of other Washington women reporters, on Barbara Walters's syndicated daytime program called *Not for Women Only*. Sally was outstanding—quick, articulate, bright, perceptive. I persuaded Gordon Manning, then the hard news vice president, that she was just what we needed to coanchor the hour *Morning News*. We hired her.

It was disastrous. There had been great advance publicity, but on her first appearance on the *Morning News*, Sally had a high temperature and could hardly speak—and it was downhill after that. Although our staff worked with her, she just could not make the adjustment to television and we finally had to let her go.[8] Ultimately, Sally returned to the *Washington Post* and picked up where CBS had interrupted her, writing brilliant, sometimes wicked, profiles and accounts of the Washington scene.

Since it had been my general policy to leave the basic hiring decisions, even of anchors, to Manning, he got all the public blame for the gross mistake of thinking that Sally could become a television anchor. Gordon was innocent and blameless. I was guilty and blameworthy.

Diane Sawyer was a perfect example of the wisdom of my policy of delegating hiring to my betters. Diane had worked for a Louisville television station when she first came to Bill Small's attention. Later, she became an assistant in Ron Ziegler's press office during the Nixon administration, where Small again came to recognize her abilities—she was universally respected by the press corps.

---

[8]In the book she wrote afterwards, Quinn claimed that she never knew that the red light indicated which studio camera was operating.

When Nixon resigned, Diane went to San Clemente for a few years to work with Nixon on his papers and on his book. Bill Small came to me with a strong recommendation that we hire her as a correspondent. I balked. While I felt that nobody should be blacklisted for prior servitude—even for having worked in Nixon's White House—I felt that having continued to work for him was a bit too much.

I told Bill that even if she were as brilliant and literate as he said she was, there had to be some reasonable period of decompression. I did not want to hire her directly from working with Nixon. She should work somewhere else first to get back into journalism. Bill was persistent. He said that if we did not hire Diane, somebody else would, and we would lose her forever. With great reluctance, and against my judgment, I gave in. (We did take Diane—thank heavens—but in the late 1980s, she went to ABC News.)

Bill was right. Diane is probably one of the most thoughtful and well-read journalists I have ever met. She does her homework. She reads books—real books like Plato. She not only reads them, but she absorbs them and makes them part of her total experience. Soon, she became what I regarded as the best and most knowledgeable State Department correspondent any network ever had—and there have been some remarkably good ones.

After we hired Diane, six reporters in the news department of a New England television affiliate (whose manager, ironically, was a strong supporter of President Nixon and who had often criticized our coverage of Nixon and his policies) wrote me that "we are appalled." They wrote that Diane's "role in the worst press office in recent White House memory should, by itself, disqualify her from covering virtually any Washington assignment . . . We would also like to know why Ms. Sawyer's White House days didn't disqualify her for a Washington reporting job for CBS." With candor, they also wrote that "each of us is openly jealous of Ms. Sawyer," since she had not paid her dues as a local reporter as they had—and their goal was ultimately to be network reporters. I answered:

> Obviously, as you can infer from the fact that I approved her hiring, I cannot agree. It seems to me that you are suggesting that no matter what the merits of each individual, it is appropriate to disbar anybody because of prior employment.[9] Indeed, I received many dozens of letters advancing the same notion when we hired Bill Moyers. And I must reject the same

---

[9]I was less candid than the writers; I did not disclose that initially I had had some of the same doubts. Perhaps because, belatedly, I had seen the light, and possibly because I felt guilty about my earlier reservations, I did not come clean in my self-righteous reply.

kind of proposal which is a particularly virulent form of guilt by association and blacklisting.

The fact is, in our view, that Ms. Sawyer was fully qualified on the sole grounds which we ever consider—her abilities and experience as a journalist. Ms. Sawyer, a graduate of Wellesley, was a reporter for WLKY-TV in Louisville, Kentucky, for four years. Those of my colleagues in Washington who dealt with her when she was in the press secretary's office of the White House found her to be honest, talented, intelligent, and highly qualified. In the circumstances, it seems to me to be unethical and entirely lacking in compassion to conclude that because of her work in and with the Nixon administration, she should be barred, without any indictment or conviction, from following her chosen profession. Indeed, it is our view on the basis of the reports that Ms. Sawyer has done for us that she is entirely qualified.

I note that you do not claim that Ms. Sawyer is not impartial but only "that the appearance of a conflict of interest will be seen by many of your viewers. Even the appearance of impropriety should be avoided." I must wonder why you did not raise the same question concerning Mr. Moyers. And I am sure, had I been able to persuade Ed Murrow to come back to CBS News after his service with the USIA for President Kennedy and before he died, you would not have invoked any such rule of avoiding any appearance of impropriety.

After I left CBS News and after Don Hewitt had resisted hiring a woman as coanchor for many years (except for his agreement to include Michele Clark), he added Diane to *60 Minutes*. Don has said that he added Diane not because she was a woman and not because she was a beautiful blond, but because she was a great reporter. Don has said he would have hired her even if her name was Tom Sawyer. Don had the wisdom to choose Mike Wallace, Harry Reasoner, Morley Safer, and Ed Bradley. While Don is occasionally given to colorful overstatement, he knows great talent when he sees it.

If I had had my way and had not deferred to Bill Small, CBS News would have lost a superb reporter, who, had she stayed at CBS News, in my view, would someday have been the first *CBS Evening News* woman anchor—after Dan Rather retired.

Part Five
Editorial Philosophy

In his lead-in to his interview with Reagan last night, Cronkite said, "Where does Reagan stand on the issues? In a nutshell, on the far right."

This bothers me a great deal—on two grounds.

First, since we are about to hear Reagan's positions on the major issues, Cronkite's characterization is both superfluous and presumptuous. Why not let the viewer make up his own mind after listening to Reagan?

Second, the "far right" reference is debatable indeed—at least on the basis of the Reagan statements which we included in the broadcast. When we say "far left," there is an implication of something pretty close to communism, the SDS [Students for a Democratic Society], the Weathermen. The term "far right" similarly has the implication of great extremism—the KKK [Ku Klux Klan], the Billy Hargis type, the Falangists, the American Nazi Party, and military right-wing juntas.

To me, Reagan is no more "far right" than McGovern is "far left." Cronkite's sentence which followed that "Reagan preaches the gospel of fundamental conservatism" is more accurate. I do not think that "fundamental conservatism" can be equated with "far right."

24

Letters from the Editor

The press must examine its own performance, to separate out the foolish and destructive criticism from the genuine and constructive . . . the press must be concerned with public opinion. For with its guaranteed press freedom, the American people have a right to expect responsibility. . . . Not government-enforced responsibility, because the First Amendment says that the press is not responsible or accountable to government. What it does not say is that the press be accountable to no one. It is accountable to everyone but the government.

—*University of California Commencement, Berkeley, May 5, 1984*

I SPENT WHAT MY COLLEAGUES at CBS News, and especially my secretaries, undoubtedly believed to have been an inordinate amount of my time reading and answering mail from viewers. It is dangerous to count letters and regard them as representative of all the people out there. They are not, because most viewers, listeners, and readers do not ordinarily write. Normally, only the most vocal and angry critics write. Letter writers are not a scientific sample of public opinion. Even if they were, news cannot and should not be edited to suit the popular fancy.

Nevertheless, I believed that attention should be paid to viewer reaction and that to the greatest extent possible, I ought to reply to mail addressed to me. It was important, at the very least, to keep aware of the main strains of criticism. Accordingly, the Audience Services Department of the Broadcast Group analyzed all the mail concerning the CBS News Division, provided me with weekly counts of the issues dealt with and the pro and con numbers. They also replied to the more routine mail not addressed specifically to me—or, when the mail involved an issue to which I had addressed myself in personal replies, answered it along the lines of my reply.

But often, those who wrote were not satisfied with Audience Services' replies. They would write again—to me—insisting that they were entitled to more. They wanted to be assured that their views were brought home to me. Because broadcasting is such an extraordinarily one-way street with not even a regular letters-to-the-editor opportunity,[1] it was important, as a safety valve at least, to try to respond to mail.

I have heard some stiff-necked and misguided editors and publishers insist that nobody has a right to look over their shoulders. I disagree: I believe that blessed as we are with the constitutional free press guarantee, we should voluntarily and conscientiously accept the principle that because the government is thus barred from looking over our shoulders, everybody else has the right to do so. News organizations are frequently accused of being arrogant. I believe this is due to the frustration the public feels when its complaints and criticism are met only with silence. (Although I concede that in many cases, letter writers would be satisfied only with an abject confession of error.)

But aside from the aspect of public relations, I felt that reading and answering viewer and listener mail was good discipline for me, and perhaps, educational for the letter writer. It was good discipline for me because, in responding, I had to reexamine what we were doing and why we were doing it. And in replying, I was optimistic enough to believe that at least in a few cases, I could throw some light for the viewer or listener on what the news process was all about. It was an effort on my part—probably quixotic—to show that I could shorten the great distance between news organization and news consumer, to persuade the consumer that we were not some huge remote and mysterious bureaucracy which acted whimsically, indifferent to and contemptuous of those who viewed or listened to us.

And so, early on, it became my practice to answer as many letters addressed to me as I could. But in addition to all these philosophical

---

[1]Over the years, I struggled with (1) a letters to CBS News broadcast series—the broadcast equivalent of print's letters to the editor, and (2) *Inside CBS News*. For this series, senior news management and correspondents made appearances around the country to answer questions put to us by members of the public. These sessions were taped and edited and then broadcast on the network. Both were important and useful series. I regret that they have been abandoned, although there is still a letters-to-the-editor segment on *60 Minutes*.

reasons, I devoted so much time to answering letters because I had fun doing it.

In May 1975, a viewer from Fairfax, Virginia, wrote a strong letter to Eric Sevareid, condemning him for having stated that "Europe ignored Israel's plight during the oil crisis." The writer had written, "Well, Eric you blew it!!!! What plight? Who created the situation that brought on the crisis?"[2] After receiving a boilerplate reply from Audience Services, the writer then turned to me, writing that

> the establishment of a[n Audience Services] department . . . has not enhanced the audience-medium interaction but only increased your bureaucracy and removed the audience at least one step. . . . [W]e should get more than the catch phrases and buzz words which are the trade mark of groups like Audience Services. Cummon, Mr. Salant. A man of your many talents can be more imaginative and influential in directing policies of CBS. Please! if your answer is to be handled by [Audience Services], Forget it!

My reply:

> I am afraid that you are wrong when you state "a man of your many talents can be more imaginative." I've struggled with the problem of how to deal with audience mail for over twenty years and I have not found a wholly satisfactory solution.[3]
>
> I can well understand why you should feel disappointed and disenchanted when you write a letter and get a more or less general reply from Audience Services. . . . But have a look at how complex the problem is: On an annual basis, audience mail to CBS News comes at about the rate of 150,000. Letters to Sevareid total somewhere in the neighborhood of 5,000 to 10,000 a year. Now I ask you—how am I, or Sevareid, or Cronkite, or anybody else with operating functions within the News Division, to answer all of these in a way that will satisfy people who write?
>
> The compromise we have developed in recent years is the Audience Services unit. I believe that it is a good deal better than nothing, but not quite perfect. . . .
>
> If you have any better ideas, don't hesitate to share them with me.

---

[2]The writer had sent a copy of his letter to the National Association of Arab Americans. His letter complaining that Eric was pro-Israeli and anti-Arab was in sharp contrast to other letters which I received charging Eric with being anti-Semitic and anti-Israeli. As we will see, contrasting letters about the same broadcasts attest to the accuracy of the cliché that often, bias lies in the eyes of the beholder.

[3]I became concerned with the problem of how best to answer audience mail when I was a corporate vice president, before I went to CBS News. As a result, the Audience Services Department had been established.

The writer was as adamant about his right to receive personal replies from those to whom he had addressed his complaints as he was unpersuaded by my letter. He accepted my invitation to share his "better ideas" with me. He wrote that while he appreciated "the dilemma," he would "expect that your network receive[s] voluminous mail. If not, you would be ABC."

He concluded, "I appreciate your taking the time to answer my letter. I, in your position, would make the Cronkites, Sevareids et al. earn their buck. . . . Let [Audience Services] handle the routine: make the stars answer the thorny."

We were at an impasse. I had already explained that the volume of mail received by the "stars" precluded their taking the time from their journalistic duties to answer most of their mail. While the "Sevareids, Cronkites et al." were entirely capable of walking and chewing gum at the same time, no human being could perform their functions as journalists and answer even the nonroutine mail simultaneously. I invoked my general one-bite-at-the-cherry policy in replying to letters and did not answer further.

In August 1975, a viewer from Bridgeport, Connecticut, wrote me a letter criticizing a *CBS Morning News* interview. He wrote in the course of his letter that he was

> a realist and I also realize the futility of a letter to you which does not say "mea culpa." . . . I realize that my letter is placed in a stack with others and the replies I get from CBS are probably from an "automatic" letter writer. Nevertheless, the fact that I communicated my concerns to you, and hopefully many others will also, so that collectively, we will strike a responsive cord [sic] which will result in an unbiased, honest and fair presentation.

While I replied to the writer at some length on the substance of his complaint about the interview, I also wrote:

> Perish the thought—I will never insist that anybody who writes me must say "mea culpa"—I wouldn't even suggest it. [After a discussion of the writer's charges] Just in case you persist in your unwarranted suspicions, this letter is being dictated by me and typed by my secretary. Both of us are flesh and blood indeed and neither of us is an "automatic" letter writer. I may be a compulsive letter writer and my secretary may be an overburdened and reluctant typist, but we are anything but "automatic."
>
> P.S. What is a "responsive cord"? I never had a piece of string or a load of wood that answered me back. Perhaps yours was not a lost chord—only a lost "h." Unimportant—except that this may give you some sympathy for human fallibility, to which all of us are subject—both you and I.

In some cases, I refused to answer on the merits of a letter writer's charges. In January 1973, a viewer from Memphis wrote, objecting to a story we had done about a military officer who had been the victim of stress. The viewer concluded his letter, "Why don't you show the men who are faithful and dedicated—fighting to save even traitors like yourself?" I wrote back:

"Normally, I, or one of my associates at CBS News, try to answer all letters from viewers that we receive. I am making an exception in your case. I will not answer your letter on the merits. If you want to know why, have a look at your last sentence."

•   •   •

Some viewers and listeners wrote me such unpleasant letters that I should have ignored them. But it was too tempting, and so I replied in kind. It was enjoyable therapy for me.

In response to a 1972 letter from a Torrance, California, viewer—who, in reply to my earlier response to him, wrote that "it was a pleasure to read your letter . . . its total lack of content discloses your true thinking: A total vacuum"—My answer (in its entirety): "Yup."

In September 1968, after the FCC had announced that it was inquiring into our coverage of the 1968 Democratic Convention[4] and I had issued a statement expressing my concern about the serious First Amendment implications of the FCC action, a St. Petersburg viewer wrote me that he hoped that the FCC would "make you straighten up or drop out" and that "my heart bleeds for you! Hurray for the FCC!" I replied:

"I suggest that someday you take a little time out to study what the First Amendment of the Constitution, which I know I support, and which I assume you support, is all about.

"Your heart can stop bleeding for me. I don't think I want your blood."

In November 1972, during the Watergate period, a viewer from Torrance, California, addressing me as "Dear Creep," wrote that he was convinced that "a plot cooked up by the *New York Times*, CBS, and the *Washington Post* really did exist." He called us a "bunch of left-wing bastards" and said that we were "using old freak Cronkite to get

---

[4]The FCC proceeding was ultimately dropped with no action against CBS.

your propaganda across as a true news story not just something dreamed up in the sewer by Salant, Stanton and Company."

We were, the writer said, a "bunch of over educated bastards" and that he would write the FCC to urge that "they revoke CBS licenses. . . . Luckily the people saw thru your crap and voted the right way [for Nixon and Agnew]."

I answered: "Well—so somebody finally found out the truth."

With disturbing frequency, I received virulently anti-Semitic letters. For example, in 1971, after the broadcast of "The Selling of the Pentagon," a Cincinnati viewer wrote me:

> To put a liver-lipped misfit like you before a mike to lisp out arrogant defiance against the only agency left in this World powerful enough to oppose the bestiality of Communism, puts CBS right in character; just an insidious agency dedicated to superimposing Jewish domination upon our government. . . . If the U.S. were fighting in Israel, the networks would be cheering Pentagon policies; getting a lot of Gentiles killed fighting a war for the Jews. Just the same machinations used in WWII to get them off the hook in Germany.

There was lots more in the letter about the perfidy of Jews throughout the world. For this letter, and letters like it, I borrowed from the late Senator Steven Young of Ohio:

> I am attaching herewith a letter which I have received [the letter the viewer had written me]. I call it to your attention because I am sure that you will want to know that some obscenely anti-Semitic racist is writing letters of this sort and demeaning your good name by signing it to his letter.

Or in response to similar anti-Semitic letters, I used a variation of that response: "I am sure that you want to know that somebody is writing anti-Semitic letters and signing your name. I am sure that you would not countenance this and that your signature was forged. You may want to refer the matter to your local postal authorities and local police."[5]

A Petersburg, Virginia, viewer wrote me in December 1971, attacking CBS News for its alleged lack of objectivity. He wrote that he did not think that we "could do a straight reporting job on a rainstorm. . . .

---

[5] I used the same kind of reply to those who wrote obscene letters—in the rare instances when they signed their name and provided an address.

At his retirement party in April 1979, Salant and Bill Leonard, his deputy and his successor as president of CBS News, exchange gag gifts. Leonard signed a retirement photograph: "Two guys looking back over the years—and happy about them." Leonard said, "The happiest days of my working life were the years that I spent hand in hand with Gordon Manning trying to help Dick Salant run CBS News."

After Salant retired from CBS in April 1979, he was given the Gold Medal Award by the International Radio and Television Society (IRTS) at a black-tie dinner in New York City.

Salant shakes hands with 60 Minutes correspondent Ed Bradley at the IRTS awards dinner following his retirement from CBS. It was Salant's policy to try to recruit and hire more women and minorities at CBS News than the network had in the past.

Charles Kuralt, the anchor of CBS Sunday Morning, *speaks with Salant at the IRTS awards dinner in New York.* Sunday Morning *was one of many programs conceptualized during Salant's tenure. The most successful of all of Salant's launches was 60 Minutes. Other programs he started included:* CBS Morning News, In the News, Inside CBS News, 30 Minutes, *and* Your Turn: Letters to CBS News.

Salant, right, with Harry Reasoner and Mike Wallace after a tennis match.

Salant in his office at NBC in Rockefeller Center in New York City. After he retired from CBS, Salant spent the next four years at NBC as vice chairman.

After Salant moved from CBS to rival NBC in May 1979, he received this photograph with a note from James Rosenfield, a former colleague still at CBS: "Dick, can you find the mistake in this picture?"

In a typical lecturing pose, Salant, fully retired and shown here on vacation at Martha's Vineyard about 1988, has a discussion with grandson Ben Carpenter.

I have very little faith, and very little respect for the network and its principles."

I answered: "I have your December 21 letter and have read it. Yours sincerely."

In the summer of 1974, President Nixon went to a summit meeting in Moscow. Reporters accompanying the president, including the reporters for the three commercial networks, used the occasion to interview Russian dissidents. To get our stories back to the United States, we were obliged to use Russian studios to send out our film stories to the satellite. As each of the networks was transmitting material for the satellite, the screen suddenly went black. The Russians blamed it on technical difficulties.

In fact, the Russians at the studio from which we were transmitting pulled the plug the moment our stories about the dissidents began. Each of the networks, on the evening news broadcasts, showed exactly what happened at the receiving end in the United States—the film and voice immediately being cut off, to resume when that part of the coverage was finished and our coverage went on to another subject. We all believed it was a vivid and dramatic way to demonstrate how censorship worked and the contrast between the Soviet-controlled press and our free press.

But in July 1974, immediately after this episode, a San Francisco viewer wrote me that "news media people from the United States are over there trying to stir up trouble. I'm glad the Soviets 'pulled the plug' on news media shit-stirrers. If authorities would do the same in this country, we would all be better off. . . . You stink! . . . P.S. You're welcome to pass this one on to your arrogant, know it all, media fuckhead cronies!"

I applied the Senator Young tactic: "I owe it to you to inform you that someone is writing obscene letters in your name. A copy is attached. Yours sincerely."

Unabashed, the writer replied, again supporting the Russian action and stating,

> Your dirty cloak of prissiness doesn't do much to shield you from the shame you must feel in your profession now it has been brought so low by the kind of people who infest it. I don't know why Bill Paley doesn't terminate the whole worn out, lock step, dull pack of you and hire a completely new cast more in tune with the people. There. I didn't use any dirty words. Is that better?

My reply must have at least tied my record for brevity. I answered, "No."

Two and a half times longer was my answer to an August 1974 letter from an Evanston, Illinois, viewer who objected to my having reassigned Dan Rather from the White House (shortly after Nixon's resignation) to anchoring *CBS Reports*. The viewer asked me, "Are you nuts?"

I answered, "Maybe."

A viewer from Dunn, North Carolina, wrote in March 1976, sharply critical of our political coverage. He referred to us as "you bastards," demanded that I tell "old Walter [Cronkite] to keep his half-assed opinions to himself," and cited Jerry Rubin as his authority for the allegation that CBS News had "finance[ed] . . . his escapades at the 1968 Democratic convention."

I answered: "Sorry—but people who call me a 'bastard,' characterize Walter Cronkite as 'half-assed,' and take Jerry Rubin's word for anything are not worthy of response. Your letter tells me more about your biases than I care to know."

The letter writer resented my having replied to him. He returned my letter and appended a note, "I was not soliciting a response in my letter to you. I was merely expressing a well-founded opinion."

I could not win: People were angry if I did not answer; others were angry if I did. (Although, as evidenced by my responses reproduced in this section, my answers were not always well calculated either to make friends or influence people.) But whether it is broadcasting the news or writing letters about it, some people are bound to get angry all of the time.

In August 1973, a viewer from Great Neck, New York, wrote a bitter letter complaining that we had neglected to report on the plight of returning Vietnam veterans and advising me that I was an ass, a eunuch, and that CBS News needed someone with balls. I was provoked:

> You may think we need someone with balls. I think we need someone who has the common sense, if not the decency, to look and listen before he shouts. The fact is that on April 4, 5, 6, 9, and 10, 1973, on the *CBS Evening News with Walter Cronkite*, we did a special five-part series on the plight of the Vietnam veterans—covering the points you make in your August 13 letter.
>
> Why do people like you weaken your very excellent cases by assuming that you have a total monopoly on wisdom, good sense, and compassion—and that everybody else is an ass or a eunuch?

In April 1974, a New York City viewer who was a magazine editor wrote a very amusing letter, identifying himself as a "civilized man who reads books, sometimes dipping into Yeats and Plato," and who, he wrote, "hold[s] my farts until I reach privacy."

He objected to our coverage of President Nixon's visit to an Ohio town devastated by a tornado; Nixon's remarks at the scene, the writer insisted, were empty and meaningless and so the president's visit was not newsworthy. The writer also objected to the fact that we reported Hank Aaron's hitting his 715th home run, breaking Babe Ruth's record. These reports were, he wrote, "C-R-A-P." The letter was too delicious to ignore, and so I wrote,

> You are indeed good at dyspeptic letters—and besides I am not at all sure that you aren't right. But to an awful (and I do mean awful) lot of people, Hank Aaron's 715th was a piece of history. And the typical performance of the president—yours as well as mine—in Xenia was certainly newsworthy and revealing, as your own reactions seem to indicate.
>
> Just remember that one man's C-R-A-P is another man's F-E-R-T-I-L-I-Z-E-R. As we used to say when we got finished freely translating it from French—each to his own crap.

In August 1976, as the presidential campaign was getting under way, a viewer from Wadsworth, Ohio, addressing me as "Dear Richard," made a number of points: (1) he did not like the "constipation commercials" on the *CBS Evening News*; (2) he offered to use the constipation remedies advertised on the broadcasts only if we stop "using three-fourths of your time quoting Senator Dole, or discussing the count in the Mississippi delegation" (he was also "sick of seeing Gerry [President Ford] . . . say some bland nothing"); (3) our news broadcasts "are geared to . . . sickly, retired nobodys" instead of trying to attract "the eighteen to thirty-year-olds." He had stopped watching CBS and now watched PBS only. He urged me to read his letter because "your public relations aide is too constipated to read this." My reply:

> Well, one thing—you do make yourself perfectly clear. You give me a lot to chew on—and a lot to throw up on. How do I answer without any hopes of persuading a mind shut like a steel trap?
>
> You're busy (I hope); I'm busy (I know)—so I'll make these points very briefly:
>
> 1. I did read your letter, and I have no public relations aide—constipated or otherwise.
> 2. I am responsible for the news content of our news broadcasts and have nothing whatever to do with commercials. That's the way it should

be—a church-and-state relationship. In return for the salespeople never touching what CBS News does, CBS News leaves the commercials alone. It's a fair deal, and better all around.

3. Senator Dole, the count of the Mississippi delegation, and what President Ford says are all news. We don't include or exclude depending on what we like to hear. Our judgments are based solely on newsworthiness.

4. We don't "target" our audiences to any segment of the adult population. We just assume we have an intelligent audience—of whatever age. Including you—but I guess we missed on the latter—which I regret.

5. I like PBS, too.

On Thanksgiving 1975, we broadcast a piece—in doggerel—on turkeys—not favorable to them and their intelligence. Months later in 1976, the executive vice president of the National Wild Turkey Federation (whose address was Wild Turkey Building, Edgefield, South Carolina), wrote me an angry letter charging that we had maligned "this magnificent bird," demanding that we apologize to the wild turkey and its supporters, and requesting that as a public service we broadcast a sixty-second "commercial" telling the truth about wild turkeys. I could not resist taking that one on:

If the wild turkeys ask for time to reply under the personal attack doctrine, I will consider the matter. But certainly if they do, we will have established they are hardly stupid. In fact, if any bird can read that government regulation and then communicate the demand to me, they may be irritating but they are indeed extraordinarily intelligent—or at least literate.

Meanwhile, I would note that it seems fairly clear to me that our piece was dealing not with wild turkeys, but domestic ones—which you concede are stupid. I thought that the whole thing was pretty funny, and I am distressed that the wild turkeys prevailed on you to be their spokesman. And in any case, it seems to me that wild turkeys may be very bright, as you say, but they sure ain't got a sense of humor. They also seem to take a while to react: After all, your letter is dated April 23—five months and one day after the story was broadcast. Wild turkeys may be intelligent, but they sure are lethargic.

Wild turkeys, domestic turkeys and doggerel writers unite—you have nothing to lose but your sense of humor.

25

What Is News?

Our pursuit must be of the truth—and I passionately believe that if we superimpose on that objective a further criterion of judging what is "good" or "bad" for our audience, we stop being journalists and start being deities or tyrants or propagandists. So especially in news, we must make our judgments in an atmosphere of what one of my colleagues at NBC called "enforced innocence."

—Salant Papers

LETTER WRITERS OFTEN ASKED about the definition of news and the criteria for news judgments—matters which in the earlier years of my tenure puzzled me as well. In response, I tried to provide some outline of what is and what is not news, and what the criteria are.

In May 1969, a troubled viewer wrote me a letter which raised many of the basic issues of the definition of news. She wrote:

Would you be kind enough to tell me what constitutes news? Is it the spectacular? Is it the disobedience in all phases of life? Is it a detailed report of life out of focus? Of people who have lost their perspective? Is it the ugly and seamy side of life? Is there no place in the news for the positive and the good? No place for acts of courage and unselfishness?

Many years ago, a young reporter for the local newspaper visited a group of Junior High School students who were interested in finding out why the things they did to help humanity, their standards, their achievements, were never published. I served as adviser to this group. The reporter answered, "These things are not news. No one wants to read them!" If this is true, as is indicated by every newspaper and TV News Program, then surely the incentive to be all that is good is removed. One sees cameras exploiting misbehavior and law-breaking, but sadly lacking when young people achieve goals. What does constitute news, Mr. Salant? I am not trying to be facetious—merely inquisitive.

It was a sincere letter with good questions. I had no definitive answers, but I replied:

Long ago, when I first entered this mysterious field of journalism, I asked the same question of one of the great editors. He pierced me with a withering gaze and said, "If you have to ask, you don't belong in the business." Nevertheless, I think now, as I thought then, that the question is a legitimate one which defies explicit definition.

Let me turn to some of your specific questions. News may or may not be "the spectacular." If it is three astronauts coming within ten miles of the surface of the moon and transmitting color television pictures back, news certainly is "the spectacular." If it is a very expensive Fourth of July fireworks display, news is not "the spectacular." In other words, the mere fact that it is spectacular does not necessarily make it news.

"Is it the disobedience in all phases of life?" Again, it may or may not be. If it is civil disobedience which may change the fabric of a nation's society, as was Gandhi's or even Martin Luther King's, it certainly is news. But if my ten-year-old daughter declines to turn the television set off and go to bed, that is civil disobedience but it is hardly news. On the contrary, if she did turn off the television set and go straight to bed, that would be news!

Next, "Is it a detailed report of life out of focus?" It depends on whose life, and how many lives, and whose focus. If it is the life "out of focus" of millions of poor and hungry and alienated in the ghettos, it may well be news. If it is my feelings of weariness and frustration at the end of each day, it is not news.

Is it a report of "people who have lost their perspective?" It depends on how many people, and whose perspective, and what the impact is on the structure of our society.

Next, "Is it the ugly and seamy side of life?" It may very well be—if it involves hunger on the part of millions of people, or living among rats, or the stories of man's inhumanity to man if enough men are involved.

You ask whether there is a place in the news for the positive and the good and for acts of courage, integrity, and unselfishness. Of course there is nothing that gives us greater pleasure than to report on the positive, the good, the courageous, and the unselfish. We seek those stories, and we like to tell them. But they cannot be isolated items[1] because isolated

---

[1]The luxury to have second thoughts leads me to the conclusion that I was wrong in writing that such stories cannot be "isolated items." Of course, "isolated" individual acts of courage, integrity, and unselfishness may be news—and do find their way even into the twenty-two minutes of national and international news on the networks' evening news.

acts may not be news. I am afraid that too many people regard news as mirroring life itself. But it does not. By and large, life goes on with most people behaving the way they should, doing their duty, not hurting anybody else. But as another editor has wisely observed, the fact that it is not news that most people do go about their business quietly and do perform their duty as they should, should be a comfort to all of us. Wouldn't this world be in an awful fix if so few people went about their business and their duties in a quiet, orderly way that that would be news?

I am reminded of the way a print editor addressed himself to this problem: He wrote a fictitious article which would satisfy those who want the normal and the good to be emphasized and the bad to be buried. The article, roughly, was this: "Today at the ABC High School, 2,322 students were in their classrooms studying and learning." He went on and on about the studying students. At the end of the article came this one sentence: "Meanwhile, one student, John Smith, walked into the office of the principal and stabbed him to death."

The fact is that news is the unusual, the aberrant, the out of the ordinary.

Perhaps the whole definition of news should be reexamined, but the definition is not ours and it doesn't belong to 1969. It goes all the way back to the beginning of news. Even history itself treats the violent and aberrant . . . as the key points in man's progress: Note the behavior of that wild little handful of young people who painted their faces, and put feathers in their hair, and went out into the Boston harbor, and without regard to private property, dumped all that tea.

• • •

A persistent notion, reflected in letters I received, was that whatever the writer found distasteful or unpleasant would go away if news only ignored it—a notion which carried the "out of sight, out of mind" concept to its final step—out of existence. And so we were urged to delete unpalatable events or people from the face of the earth by not covering them in the news.

In February 1968, a Salt Lake City viewer wrote that "the realistic coverage of the Vietnamese War on TV in picture and sound is not only in bad taste, but a strong and determining factor in molding the hearts and minds of people in this country and abroad in a negative way." He wrote that it was our responsibility "to change this negative and demoralizing presentation of human beings killing each other."

Accordingly, he proposed "the recall of all CBS news cameramen and their crews from Vietnam and a policy announcement by the president of CBS that in the interest of peace in the world, the showing of war films will be discontinued. . . . Here is your chance to be a pioneer in shaping the course of human events—take it!"

I answered:

I can only say that your suggestion is most provocative and interesting. But we are a news organization and our profession is news. I suspect that it can be argued that a great many unpleasant and unpalatable things and people would disappear, or at least the American public wouldn't have to worry about them so much, if only newspapers and broadcast news organizations boycotted them.

But a responsible news organization cannot play that game: We cannot try to eliminate events and people by pretending that they don't exist. I assure you that we do not enjoy reporting about the war. But there is a war on and the people have a right to know as much as possible about it. And hence, we owe the American public the obligation to report as responsibly as we can.

Actually, I do not believe that the Vietnam War would come to an end if we pulled back all our reporters and cameramen from there. Perhaps if some higher power could guarantee that all wars, including the Vietnam War, would end by so simple and money-saving an expedient, I might be sorely tempted.

That viewer was not alone in wanting us to stop reporting on the Vietnam War. His desire was to end war. But in April 1975, the president of a radio broadcasting company in Delaware went on his station's air to call for an end of reporting the still-continuing events in Indochina, because, he said, he and many others were sick and tired of hearing about the happenings in Southeast Asia. He sent me a copy of his station editorial. I commented:

My first reaction was that you couldn't be serious—but I guess you are because you expressed your views over your own air. You obviously bring to bear viewpoints other than journalistic viewpoints, on the issue of whether or not the events in Indochina are newsworthy. Our only criteria must be journalistic ones.

I, too, am sick and tired of the Indochina story, although I confess more sick than tired. But I do not think that there is a responsible professional journalist who would agree with you and who would think that it would go away if we in the news only ignored it. The fact is that by any standards, journalistic or historical, the Indochina story is one of the major stories of the current decade. It is a tragedy of surpassing importance. Its lessons will be examined and debated for years. The United States has invested billions of dollars in the war in Indochina, and more important, 50,000 American lives. The story appears now to be reaching its climax and its shattering end. It is, and should be, a matter of immense national interest and national debate. We would be abdicating our journalistic responsibility and our basic mission to inform our viewers and listeners if we followed your advice and pretended it wasn't there just because "we want out." "Forget Southeast Asia" may be sensible political advice, but it is intolerable journalistic advice.

• • •

Intertwined with the notion that unpleasant news should not be covered was the proposal, expressed frequently in my mail, that news ought to be avoided if it might give viewers or listeners "bad"—antisocial—ideas. These letter writers, in effect, urged that we superimpose on normal news judgments additional societal judgments concerning the consequences of our reporting. Either we should make our news judgments to teach moral lessons or avoid reporting news if the consequences might be undesirable—by the writer's standards. These notions took a variety of forms and covered a wide range of subjects which the writers thought ought to be emphasized in our news judgments or ought not to be reported because of the harmful effects.

For example, in 1977, *60 Minutes* broadcast an exposé showing how easy it was to get a false passport. Through hidden cameras, the piece showed how *60 Minutes* personnel easily obtained false birth certificates, drivers' licenses, and credit cards—and then used them to obtain false passports. Many letters criticized us for showing the public how they could commit these crimes (similar complaints were invariably received whenever CBS News did a story on the ease with which laws could be broken or security breached).

The president of a San Diego bank wrote me, criticizing our *60 Minutes* piece, calling to my attention the negative side effects of the story. He stated that as a result of the story, "two women prepared a complex fraud scheme and proceeded to implement the plan here. . . . [M]any times you are actually planting ideas in the minds of potential criminals, or worse—showing them how to accomplish such a scheme." The issue the banker raised is not always an easy or foolish one. I replied:

> I cannot agree with you that serious problems in our society today, when they have become of sufficient magnitude and frequency that the public ought to know about them, should not be exposed by journalists because of the danger that they might give the people ideas to imitate the behavior which we are exposing. I recognize that this is an issue which is often raised and discussed. The assumption is that if we as journalists never mention these things, they would go away. The contention arises time and time again over countless issues. Many of my Southern friends used

to contend that we should not cover sit-ins in public restaurants since seeing people do this was "contagious." Others have contended that we should not report on actions by hijackers or terrorists,[2] etc.

But in general, as journalists, it is our job to report on what is important so the public through their legislators or others can see that remedies are found.

In the particular case, we had determined through our research and through talking to many people that the dangers of obtaining by fraud complete sets of IDs by false names were real and widespread. Indeed, we were encouraged to engage in our investigation by the head of the Passport Division of the State Department. And, as a result, at least in part because of our report, remedial action has been taken. That, I submit, is one of the things that investigative journalism is all about. If the public is never told about the danger, and its frequency, nothing will ever be done about it. And so it is my own thought that it is our responsibility not to put our heads in the sand but to report such matters.

In April 1968, the *CBS Evening News* included film of the public execution by the South Vietnamese government of a South Vietnamese soldier accused of corruption. The dean of a Michigan university criticized the broadcast, writing that

particularly in these troubled times, it appears not in the public interest to show to millions of people the death of a man before a firing squad. . . . I do not believe it either good taste or good public policy to offer the sight of a man slumping down in death in an execution. Could you not edit such film more carefully?

I answered:

I concede that the question is not free from doubt, and the very fact that you take issue with our inclusion of the film segment establishes that thoughtful and responsible people can disagree with our judgment. Perhaps it would be helpful if I described briefly our rationale (and I assure you we thought carefully before we included the segment). The nature of the South Vietnamese, their development, their mode of living and governing, and their attitudes are of great importance to people in the United

---

[2] I had specifically addressed myself to the issue relating to terrorists in an April 4, 1977, addition to the "CBS News Standards": "CBS News will continue to apply the normal tests of news judgment, and if, as so often they are, these stories are newsworthy, we must continue to give them coverage despite the dangers of 'contagion.' The disadvantages of suppression are, among other things, (1) adversely affecting our credibility ('What else are the news people keeping from us?'); (2) giving free rein to sensationalized and erroneous word of mouth rumors; and (3) distorting our news judgments for some extraneous judgmental purpose. These disadvantages compel us to continue to provide coverage."

States. They are not only our allies; more than that, we have committed over one-half million men and $30 billion a year toward helping them win the war in order to permit them to determine their own future.

In these circumstances, we felt it was relevant and newsworthy that the South Vietnamese government chose to make a public spectacle of a public execution, to which the victim's family, as well as members of the public were invited. This, it seems to us, throws a good deal of light on what our problems are in South Vietnam and why it is so difficult for us to try to impose our standards on a nation whose standards are rather different from ours.

You suggest that you would have no objection to our reporting the news of the execution and that the thrust of your objection is that we included the sight—that is, the film—of the execution. But we are in the television news business. You are asking us to abandon our primary tools and to limit ourselves to reporting what happened secondhand, thus depriving the viewers of what television has to offer first of all—the ability of the American viewer to see for himself with his own eyes.

I concede, there are times when a picture is so vivid and so sensational that we limit ourselves to the word rather than the sight. But these circumstances must be extraordinary. What we did here, instead, was to use only what we call a long shot and to avoid a close-up; further, we cut a lot out of the sight of the man slumping down in death so it [the film] was only a second or two. In other words, we felt it important to make the point visually, but not to dwell on it.

Your thoughtful letter, however, makes me wonder whether our decision was right.[3]

• • •

The day after Election Day in November 1972, when Richard Nixon won by a large margin, the general manager of a Tennessee CBS television affiliate wired me: "It is hoped that the mandate to Nixon by the American people will possibly convince most at CBS News that their liberal leanings and reporting do not coincide with those of their viewers. Wipe Eric's tears and shift him to analyzing the situation in Outer Mongolia from the scene."

---

[3]The question of broadcasting pictures of violence (or other kinds of scenes, such as those showing emotions of families struck by tragedy) is a difficult one, as I stated in this letter. Sensational pictures for their own sake—such as bloody close-up pictures, adding nothing to important information—ought to be avoided or edited. When a group of nurses in Chicago were murdered in their beds and the police allowed us in to film the scene of the crime, the color pictures of the bloody sheets and shoes of the nurses were so vivid that we broadcast the pictures in black and white, instead of color. On the other hand, a documentary on safe driving or drunken driving may justifiably include gory scenes—the consequences of such driving are an important part of an important social phenomenon and should not be sanitized.

With the restraint which dealing with affiliates compelled and ignoring the slap at Eric Sevareid, I wrote the affiliate about the nature of news and its relationship to "popularity":

[T]he wire may be interpreted to raise a fundamental issue to which I owe it to both of us to address myself in order to avoid any misunderstanding about where I stand.

The question is whether the mandate that any politician or news event represents permits or requires news reporting to "coincide with [the views or wishes] of [their] viewers" or readers or listeners. I strongly believe the answer is negative.

As I have stated publicly a number of times, sound journalism cannot be conducted by the numbers or by holding a finger to the wind to see which way the popular winds blow. And that is true no matter who or what gets a popular mandate—whether it is something or somebody you are for or against. No great editor who has ever gone down in journalistic history and no professional journalist or observer has ever suggested that one's reporting ought to take into account whether that reporter pleases or displeases the majority or accords or doesn't accord with what the majority would like to hear. I am sure you are not suggesting to the contrary, for any other principle would be antithetical to everything that professional journalism, and hence CBS News, stands for. We must call them as we see them—as accurately and objectively as human fallibility permits. Umpires cannot call them by measuring the decibels of the shouts of the crowd—calling them one way for a ball team when it's playing at home and another way when it's playing away. Nor can journalists.

Of course, there can be reasonable disagreement on whether we have achieved our basic goal of fairness, balance and objectivity. I believe that on the whole we have; you, I suspect, believe that we have not. But I hope that there is no disagreement between us on whether our news judgments, fairly arrived at, should be shaped or judged by whether such judgments coincide with those of [our] viewers. Surely, if we believe in independent, professional, sound journalism, we must agree that the answer is that it should not, and cannot.

• • •

The issue whether a news organization's judgments should give priority to information which the people of a democracy need to know, on one hand, or to what will interest and titillate them, on the other, is a fundamental and underlying one—both for print and for broadcast. Increasingly, in recent years, the greater weight—while not publicly articulated—seems to have been given to what interests people rather than what informs them. News proprietors and many editors seem to believe that higher circulation and ratings depend on giving the readers, viewers, and listeners what they want. My strong views in favor of need rather than want as the basic criterion were set out in public speeches, interviews, and in a typical exchange of letters in June 1977.

A Denver viewer wrote me, noting that in a newspaper interview I had said, "Journalists ought to tell people what they ought to know." She wrote:

> Your arrogance is exceeded only by your effrontery. Who gave you the knowledge, know-how, brains, perception, imagination, authority to know what I, or anyone else, "ought to know." This is the most danger- ous statement I have read, or heard, in a very long time, at a period in our history when opinions and statements are flung about like confetti. Get with it—get off it—and *never, never* forget that, only by the grace of your license, are you allowed to make millions, by using the airwaves owned by *all* of us. One's only hope for sanity in this world is that persons of your stripe will dig your own grave in the media.

I answered:

> I am sorry that I have "disgusted" you and led you to conclude that my "arrogance is exceeded only by [my] effrontery." With that kind of lan- guage so strongly stated, I am hardly optimistic about persuading you. You obviously have made up your own mind.
>
> Nevertheless, I do not take a word of it back—I feel strongly that it is a journalist's function to tell people what they ought to know, and not take public opinion surveys to find out what is most interesting, titillating, and amusing, in the way of news. It has always been the function of editors and other journalists to choose those news stories which are most important, and the fact that many people may not initially be interested in them can- not deter us. I am afraid that that is elitist, but it is the true profession of journalism, and, indeed, the important function of telling people what they need to know is why our Founding Fathers included the First Amendment protection of the freedom of the press in the Constitution. . . .
>
> I regret that I have displeased you so.

The same issue arose in the context of a specific case—the treat- ment of two concurrent and disparate stories involving the Panama Canal and the death of Elvis Presley. On August 16, 1977, when the question of the Panama Canal Treaty was being debated in the United States, President Ford announced his support of the treaty. On the same day, Elvis Presley died. On the *CBS Evening News* that day, our lead story was the treaty and Ford's statement; Presley's death came lower in the broadcast—and was shorter. ABC News led, at consider- able length, with Presley. I was so pleased with our treatment of the two stories that I sent a note congratulating the *Evening News*.

But much of the mail I received was critical of our judgment. Viewers wrote to say that we had shortchanged the Presley story. A viewer from Falmouth Fortside, Maine, wrote me, saying:

> Having been an avid viewer of CBS News for many years, it was with a great deal of surprise that I tuned in last night to find the Panama Canal beat out the death of Elvis Presley. I don't know who is responsible for making this type of decision but whomever made that one obviously did not have his finger on the pulse of the American people. . . . I believe this to be the biggest oversight and the worst judgment that CBS news has ever shown in all the years I've been watching.

I replied:

> We here at CBS News believe strongly that the primary function of American journalism is to provide facts and viewpoints concerning the major issues and happenings of the day so that the American public can make up its own mind in guiding the future of this nation. Hence, we believe that it is our primary responsibility—and indeed the responsibility which underlies the First Amendment—to deal with what the American people ought to know.
>
> There is no question that one of the major issues of the day—the resolution of which will have important long-term consequences to this nation and indeed to South America—is the Panama Canal and the agreements which have recently been reached. It is an issue which came very close to determining who the Republican nominee for the presidency was in 1976.[4] It is an issue on which the people of this nation have strong feelings and are seriously divided. In these circumstances, I believe that our judgment in giving the Panama Canal story priority over the death of Elvis Presley was not only correct, but in the fulfillment of our duties and responsibilities.

•   •   •

A persistent demand which appeared in our mail was that our news broadcasts ought to raise the level of American taste or serve as an educational tool. My view was that this would require us to depart from professional news judgments.

An example was the exchange in January 1972 between me and the publicity director of a college of the arts at a Midwestern university. The official had written that:

---

[4]Ronald Reagan, Ford's major rival for the 1976 nomination, had opposed the Panama Canal Treaty.

at a time when the predominant cry is for peace and beauty and a lessening of violence and injustice, it seems strange that artistic ventures such as concerts, plays, dance programs, and art exhibits are all but ignored by the media. . . . the broadcast media choose to concentrate on other matters. . . . Could not a peaceful and beautiful revolution be staged if the media chose to devote a segment of each "news" broadcast to activities in the various arts areas. . . . We truly think that a change in the entire complexion of today's life styles could be affected by such attention. . . . You could change the world!

It was a cri de coeur, but I turned a deaf ear:

We have, over the years, considered expanding our news coverage of the arts on our television news. But each time we have found that at least so far as reasonably regularized news coverage is concerned, there is an insuperable obstacle—and that is that concerts, operas, plays, and art exhibits are essentially localized and hence are ordinarily not national news stories. Unless there is some extraordinary news impact to a play or art exhibit, for example, it is futile and frustrating to tell people in Los Angeles or Des Moines about something they can attend only in New York. Hence, the kind of continuous news coverage of the arts which I think you are calling for has to be provided by local stations on a local basis, rather than by a network.

I would further point out that at least as far as the Evening News is concerned, we only have a half an hour to cover the major national and international events, and it would scarcely do to sacrifice our reportage in those areas in our network news broadcasts.[5] . . .

I ought to emphasize that I believe you mistake the function of news and news judgments. You seem to believe that we ought to devote time to the arts because if we did so we would bring about "a change in the entire complexion of today's lifestyles." In this way, you conclude, "You could change the world!"

I can think of few things more dangerous than for a news reporter or editor, as distinguished from an editorialist (and CBS News does not editorialize), to abandon objective news judgments and seek instead to select—and exclude—news stories in order to "change lifestyles" or "change the world." That is a power too great for us to seek to exercise; I for one am not qualified. We are journalists, seeking to reflect that which is truly newsworthy. We are not deities who have any right or qualification to shape our news judgments by some beneficent motive to improve the breed. That is a task that belongs to preachers, teachers, parents, statesmen—and not to fallible and mortal journalists.

---

[5]The ninety-minute *CBS Sunday Morning* program with Charles Kuralt began broadcasts in early 1979. It has consistently covered, at considerable length and with great skill, newsworthy stories about the arts.

26

What Is Bias?

*Roger Mudd once said that I had "fairness and balance" writ-
ten on my forehead.*

—Salant Papers

MOST OF MY ANSWERS TO MY MAIL were not curt, or nasty, or
intended to be funny. I used my responses in the hopes that I could explain what our standards and objectives were and why we had done
what we had done.

In October 1973, after President Nixon had attacked the networks
for biased coverage of his presidency and the Watergate story and I had
issued a public response, a Minnesota affiliate—a good friend of
mine—wrote me that while I "may be absolutely correct in [my] response, the public is not with us. . . . [T]here is very little feeling in
the minds of most of the people that the networks have been fair."

He wrote that the head of the largest bank in his city as well as the
former president of the local Chamber of Commerce and one of the
city's largest contractors all "castigate[d] the manner in which our reporters deliver the news. . . . [T]hey feel[1] the attitude of our reporters
is absolutely unreasonable, unfair, and that television must be punished. . . . I think the industry is going to have to pay dearly for the
bias the public feels exists."

Since he reflected a viewpoint shared by many other affiliates, I
replied at some length:

---

[1]In citing as his proof of bias and disapproval the fact that the bank president, the
Chamber of Commerce officials, and the contractor found bias and disapproval, the affiliate also reflected a theme often appearing in critical letters, i.e., "all my friends," or
"everybody I know" agrees with the letter writer's views. Even if true, that hardly represents a good sample—like-minded people tended to circle the wagons together.

Too often, human nature causes some of us—certainly including my-self—to reject as biased or inaccurate facts which we do not want to accept and which we find disagreeable. Bias too often acts as an uncontrollable filter which rejects for us those alien facts and views which are contrary to our own deeply held predispositions and convictions. . . .

I do not say that we are infallible—because we are not.

I do not say that we have made no mistakes—for we have.

I do not say that we have always achieved objectivity, that we have always been fair, that we have always been balanced—because we have not.

But I am convinced, on the basis of knowing our people and what motivates me and them, that our failures are not for lack of the recognition of the desirability of objectivity or for lack of trying to achieve it. As Mr. Paley said a long time ago, it is humanly impossible to achieve objectivity 100 percent of the time, but if one tries all the time, one can achieve it more often than if one does not try. And I assure you, and your friends, that we do try. . . .

But I should say in any event, and with great sadness, that given the turmoil in our society today, the loss of civility in citizens and political dialogue, of intolerance for points of view other than our own, I simply do not believe that it is possible to do a proper, independent, and worthy journalistic job and at the same time be loved by everybody, or even sometimes, by most of my friends. There are those—many of them, including me—who believe that honest journalism and a desire to please all of the people all of the time or even most of the people most of the time may sometimes be, and are, incompatible.

Honest journalism, necessary for a meaningful democracy since it is the foundation of informed citizen judgments, cannot be conducted by holding a wet finger to the wind and letting the wind blow the facts in whatever quarter the wind directs. It is not honest journalism—it is not journalism at all, but professional prostitution—to provide the people only with those facts that they want to hear in their version. If history, from the Old Testament on, tells us anything, it is often that the truth teller is not, and cannot be, the most popular man in town. It is the fate of the honest messenger to be killed—or, worse than death, to be scorned and spat upon.

I hope and pray that these passions someday soon will die down and you and your friends and other good men and good historians will look at what we have done and conclude that we have served democracy and the truth better than you currently think. For if I am doing as badly as you and your friends think, I am committing an intolerable disservice to what I always thought this country and I stood for, and I don't belong in this job.

In December 1971, a professor in a Department of Communications at a border state university wrote me with what he called "a plea for help." He wrote:

My students ask me to define bias as it applies to television news.
... What they are asking is, must they take what they see on television
news as being completely objective, without bias, unslanted and as the
unalterable truth? ... Would you be kind enough to define bias so that
we, as laymen, may apply it to what we view on the networks and be able
to decide for ourselves if there is bias.

I answered:

"Bias" is defined precisely the same "as it applies to television news" as
it is defined when applied to all other news—print or radio. It is, as surely
you must know, personal, political, or social prejudice—a refusal to accept or report facts which do not fit in with personal preconceptions. Any
editor whose personal views color his professional judgments of what is
newsworthy and whose social or political views govern selection or exclusion of news stories is biased and unprofessional. So too, a reporter
who reports only those facts which please him or suit his personal fancy
is biased and unprofessional.

I would most emphatically urge that nobody—your students or anyone
else—ever accept any report, whether on television, on radio, or in print
(with the probable exception of from the pulpit) as "the unalterable
truth." All of us truly dedicated to the profession of journalism try to
come to "the unalterable truth" as nearly as we can, but we are all human, and hence we are fallible. I would advise anybody to read as many
diverse newspapers, newsmagazines, and journals of opinion[2] and to
watch as many diverse television broadcasts and listen to as many diverse radio broadcasts as he possibly can so that he can choose among a
multiplicity from which the truth will emerge.

And I would urge everybody to keep in mind that bias, like beauty, often lies in the eye of the beholder, the reader, the listener, the viewer.
And so the reader, listener, or viewer should try to take his own biases
into account in trying to determine whether a news report is biased or
whether the individual is.

• • •

A recurrent theme, which still persists in the current conservative
literature, was that all reporters are "liberals" with "conservatives"
excluded. In May 1975, a viewer from Burlington, Indiana, wrote me,
asking if a Dan Rather *CBS Reports* which examined whether IQ tests

---

[2]Because I so strongly and genuinely believed in the value of diversity of opinion,
when I learned that *National Review*, Bill Buckley's journal of opinion, which was often
critical of CBS News, was in financial trouble which might threaten its existence, I sent
a contribution to Buckley. Some time later, at a banquet which I attended, Buckley sent
a note to my table: "I know Salant is not a Communist."

were fair and accurate measures of intelligence was an example of our "liberalism." He wrote that

> I can probably assume that you will arrogantly ignore this letter. . . . The overwhelming point, to which I have never heard or read any network spokesman addressing himself to, is simply this: Name one conservative newsman . . . on your network or either of the other networks. It can't be done. You do not hire newsmen unless they are liberals. . . . I will be anxiously awaiting your list of conservatives who work for the networks. Ha, ha.

I found it ironic that conservatives, including some in the Reagan administration, who called for our applying a political test with a view toward balancing "liberals" with "conservatives" by seeking out and hiring "conservatives" are the very ones who oppose affirmative action and demand that hiring in other fields be "color-blind." Affirmative action on behalf of conservative newspeople is apparently desirable. In any event, I replied:

> I have the feeling that neither of us will get very far in persuading the other.
> I simply cannot answer your demand that I should "name one conservative newsman" who is a staff member of CBS News. Nor can I name any "liberal" newsman. I do not inquire into the politics of our reporters, since I do not believe it is any of my business. Nor do I believe it is relevant. A professional journalist is a professional journalist because he puts aside his personal views and reports the truth as nearly as is humanly possible. Among those of us who still believe in objective journalism, that is what a reporter is paid for.
> You cite our recent *CBS Reports* on the IQ tests, but I am blessed if I know why the issue related to the efficiency and meaning of these tests is, or should be, a "liberal-conservative" issue. What is "liberal" about believing that IQ tests have been misused and misinterpreted? What is "conservative" about believing that IQ tests are successful in identifying who is or should be at the top of heap?
> Finally, you are absolutely 100 percent wrong in stating: "Of course, you probably think it is impossible to disagree with the CBS point of view!" We are human, hence we are fallible and we err. Do you?

On an earlier occasion, I had dealt with the issue of inquiry into a newsperson's personal politics more fully in a different context. In July 1971, a graduate student at a major Midwestern university wrote me that "lost in the claims and counterclaims about alleged television news bias is this simple question: 'What are newsmen's political opinions to begin with?' . . . Broad generalizations about bias can not be made without knowing newsmen's beliefs."

Accordingly, the student wrote that for his master's thesis, he conducted a survey of television newsmen's political beliefs. He sent me a summary of the responses which, he said, "refuted much of the recent criticism aimed at TV news. Newsmen were not locked into one set of political beliefs. Instead, they had about as many opinions as there were newsmen. It is a healthy sign that news is being handled by men with varying political opinions."

He asked for my comments and also attached his résumé and applied for a job with CBS News. I replied:

> Since you ask for my comments, I will tell you candidly that I am deeply disturbed about some of the implications of your study. I find it, for example, appalling that some of the respondents [to the student's questionnaire] who purport to be journalists nevertheless admit to having contributed to political campaigns, helped campaign for a candidate, and indeed held positions in a political party or ran for political office. If they did any of these things while they were journalists, I am shocked. I am old-fashioned enough to believe in the importance of objectivity and to reject the notion of subjective journalism. I can only tell you that activities of this nature are totally contrary to the policies of CBS News.[3] . . .
>
> Most important of all, I am deeply disturbed by what seems to me to be your basic premise that bias in reporting can be determined by ascertaining "What are newsmen's political opinions to begin with?" This is a notion which I reject and it is precisely why I refuse to inquire into the "political opinions" of any applicant for a job with CBS News. The test must not be the test of a political litmus paper; it must be a journalist's work output. I don't care how a newsman votes just so long as how he votes is not ascertainable by an examination of his reporting.
>
> This is a subject to which I have addressed myself a number of times, and perhaps I can best summarize it by quoting from one of my speeches:
>
> "It is not easy to be objective. Every man worth his salt feels strongly about the great issues of the day. But I submit that the true journalist—the only journalist who does real honor to this honorable profession—is the one who applies the same skepticism or the same credulity to those whom he likes as to those whom he dislikes, to those viewpoints he detests as to those with which he sympathizes. He must be just as ready to report a fact that runs counter to his personal predilections as he is to report a fact that advances those predilections."

•   •   •

---

[3]The policy was embodied in the "CBS News Standards," which provided: "Employees who, in their private capacity, take a public position on a controversial issue, including participation in a partisan political campaign, will either be removed from handling the news involving that issue or, if such reassignment is not practical, be required to take a leave of absence. The rationale behind this policy is that an employee who takes such a public position loses, at the minimum, the appearance of objectivity."

Too often, charges of bias were based on seeing or hearing what was not in fact said on a broadcast, or, conversely, on not seeing or hearing what indeed had been broadcast. For example, amid the hundreds of letters we received accusing us of bias against the American role in Vietnam, I received a letter in February 1968 from a San Francisco viewer, reacting to a documentary we had broadcast on the Vietcong, and showing some of the cruelties and atrocities perpetrated by the VC.

The viewer objected and asked, "Don't you think that you should give equal time to the other side. I'm sure it wouldn't be too difficult to find an hour's worth of film depicting American atrocities and destruction in South Vietnam." She wrote that our broadcast was "irresponsible" and was "propaganda." It was a good example of a letter which demonstrated the writer's own biases.

I replied:

Well, at least your letter is refreshing because it is different.

Almost invariably for the past year the letters I have had from viewers complaining about our Vietnam coverage have been precisely opposite from yours. They have bitterly complained about our reporting on the cruelty and brutality on the American and South Vietnamese side of the war. You may recall our news report of the U.S. Marines burning down villages with Zippo lighters; of our GIs cutting off the ears of the Vietcong; of the disposition of Vietcong corpses by collecting them in a net and then attaching the net to a helicopter and flying the bodies off. So too, we have reported many times on the tragedy of the war involving the injuries and deaths of civilians caused by our side as well as their side.

Invariably, these reports have elicited angry mail asking why we never show "the other side"—the atrocities and brutality of the North Vietnamese and the Vietcong.

It seems to me quite clear that we have reported factually—that war is brutal on both sides. This, we believe, we must do because as you state, it is indeed our "responsibility to show Americans what is really going on." And what is really going on is that war is a brutal thing—and brutalizes both sides. I do not think it would be responsible for us to ignore the brutalities on the Vietcong side.

———————

Many letter writers exemplified my eggplant–chocolate sundae analogy:[4] There were writers who ignored (or missed) the viewpoints

———

[4]When I like something, like chocolate sundaes, then I can't get enough of them; but when I hate something, like eggplant, then even a tiny bit is too much. The same preferences apply to reactions to the news: If people like it, there's not enough, and if they hate it, any amount is too much.

with which they agreed but selectively retained, and were angry about, the coverage of viewpoints with which they disagreed. In other cases, often one set of viewers attacked us for not broadcasting what in fact we had broadcast, while another set of viewers, with different mind-sets, attacked us for having aired the same broadcast. These were examples of the you-can't-win phenomenon—one person's meat is another's poison.

In July 1974, as Watergate was nearing its climax, James St. Clair, Nixon's legal counsel, held a press conference to answer the charges against the president. CBS News broadcast the press conference in full on the television network. The vice president of an organization named Women Speak Out for Peace and Justice sent me a telegram from Cleveland, Ohio, stating, "1,600 Greater Cleveland Women are appalled at CBS's kowtowing to Nixon, giving free time to one of his agents to sway the public at a time when impartiality should be maintained."

Concurrently, a Halotes, Texas, viewer wrote me, "You have succeeded in your plan to destroy our president. We believe you have destroyed our country in doing this. Why didn't you show Mr. St. Clair's press conference?"

To the Nixon supporter who complained about our not carrying the St. Clair conference, I wrote:

> Your . . . note baffles me and gets me a little bit mad. Do you have any idea how grave a charge you make, and what it means to me personally, when you refer to "my plan to destroy our president" and state that I "have destroyed our wonderful country"? Cannot reasonable people disagree without such extreme and baseless charges?
>
> I must tell you in all candor that I cannot take your criticism seriously when you impugn my motives and my patriotism.
>
> Nor can I take them seriously when you are so wrong on the only fact that you try to state. You write, "Why didn't you show Mr. St. Clair's press conference?" Well, you are wrong about that, too, because we did— we were one of the two television networks that carried it full, live, as it happened.

Since affiliates are free to carry or reject any network programs, in all fairness to that critic, it is possible the local station serving the area in which she lived chose not to carry the broadcast. But that was a matter which, under FCC regulations, was not, and could not be, under network control.

To the anti-Nixon complainant, I replied, with excessive testiness:

> Oh, come on now. Telegrams like the one you sent me don't move me a bit because I am in the news business and my job is to exercise news

judgments objectively and not just cover the people with whom I agree and events that further my causes. I may make mistakes, but they are errors of judgment, and so I very much resent your accusing me and my organization, in deciding to carry St. Clair's press conference last night live, as constituting "kowtowing" to the president. That is one of the dirtiest words you can think of when you apply it to a newsman.

We don't kowtow to anyone—not to the president and not to you. We won't be bullied—by anybody—into not carrying what we think is newsworthy or carrying what we think isn't newsworthy. I agree fully that "impartiality should be maintained," but it is apparent that your idea of "impartiality" is permitting the public to hear only what suits your predilections. That's not journalism. In fact, it isn't justice.

Usually my passionate lecture on bias, objectivity, and the functions of honest journalism went for naught. Many if not most of those who have concluded that there is bias cannot be persuaded that there is none. But in my letters to viewers and listeners, in one way or another, I kept on trying.

27

Defending the Anchors

On its best days, the evening news is brilliant; on its good days, which are more common than its bad days, it is surprisingly informative. Over the years, it has evolved into a unique art form of journalism. . . . Only network news provides to everybody the common data base needed by a democracy and its citizens.

—Benton Lecture, University of Chicago, March 3, 1988

CBS ANCHORS, BECAUSE OF THEIR VISIBILITY, generated many letters from viewers. Perhaps no broadcast by Walter Cronkite created quite so much of a stir as Walter's special half-hour "Report from Vietnam" on February 27, 1968, at the conclusion of the Tet offensive. In that broadcast, Walter summarized his observations after having covered the offensive. He concluded with these words:

[I]t seems now more certain than ever that the bloody experience of Vietnam is to end in a stalemate. . . . It is increasingly clear to this reporter that the only rational way out will be to negotiate, not as victors but as an honorable people who lived up to their pledge to defend democracy and did the best they could.

Recognizing the confidence the public had in Walter Cronkite, President Lyndon Johnson supposedly said when he heard this broadcast that if the Vietnam War had lost Cronkite, then the war, without public support, could no longer be won.

The Cronkite report stimulated a lot of mail. An unusual letter came from a Cambridge, Massachusetts, viewer who wrote that he agreed with Cronkite's conclusions but he was troubled by the "implications" of the policy that permitted him to say it. I wrote back to him: "You are one of the very few people who have ever written in to suggest that 'perhaps I agree with everything you say, but I am not sure about your right to say it.' It takes a special and very valuable kind of objectivity to raise that question."

And I explained to him the difficulty of rulebooking a reporter like Cronkite, who, based on his firsthand observations, may have crossed the line, in a few sentences, from analysis and interpretation into personal editorializing.

A different kind of letter, but one making the same point about editorialization, came to me from the executive vice president of a broadcast group which owned television stations affiliated with the CBS Television Network. Unlike my Cambridge correspondent, the broadcaster was in sympathy with the Johnson administration's policies in respect of Vietnam. He wrote:

> I must admit I was somewhat dismayed when he summed up the situation by delineating a position of surrender on the part of the United States to solve the problem in Viet Nam. . . . What bothers me is the fact that this tail end appraisal by Cronkite was . . . what we would consider an out-and-out editorial position, without labeling it as such.

I did not find it easy to give him a wholly convincing reply:

> I genuinely appreciate your taking the time to write me about the Cronkite Vietnam broadcast; even more do I appreciate the fact that you raise the issue head-on and with full candor. I think this kind of dialogue can be helpful to all of us at CBS News.
>
> In all good conscience, I cannot say that the point you raise about Walter's conclusion on his February 27 special (transcript of which I am attaching) is not a real one. This whole difficult and delicate business of the precisely right line to draw between permissible factual conclusions, on the one hand, and impermissible editorial judgments and exhortation, on the other hand, is a perplexing and troublesome one which has plagued broadcasters for many years and, judging from the literature on the subject, has plagued almost every newspaper editor.
>
> Actually, I think that the issue is raised not by the bulk of Walter's conclusions. . . . Only . . . five or six lines . . . present problems. All the rest of the conclusions, it seems to me, are really no more than factual conclusions, based on firsthand observations and hundreds of interviews in Vietnam, rather than editorialization. And, as you will see from the transcript, Walter specifically introduces the conclusion as "specula-

tive," "personal" and "subjective." And he also made clear that even as to the most doubtful sentence . . . that is the way it seemed to "this reporter." Therefore, I do believe that this was labeled as personal opinion rather than as straight news.

I let the conclusion go as Walter had written it (with a few minor changes which I had suggested) because I felt there are some extraordinary occasions when our senior correspondents should, on the basis of personal survey and observations, be given permission to state conclusions. We do that on our annual "Correspondents' Report" and we have done it on rare occasions on other kinds of personal reports.[1] And we try to label them as departing from the usual broadcast and as constituting personal opinions and conclusions.

• • •

We assigned Dan Rather to the White House when Lyndon Johnson became president. He continued there throughout the Nixon administration. A tough and courageous reporter, Dan carried out the principle which he had so often expressed—that a reporter should be neither a lapdog nor an attack dog, but a watchdog. His reporting at the White House during the Nixon years drew much criticism—and praise— from many quarters—before, during, and after Watergate. Even his reassignment after Nixon's resignation gave rise to much mail.

I received many letters about Dan after an incident which occurred at the annual convention of the National Association of Broadcasters [NAB] in March 1974. At the convention, President Nixon held what he called a "press conference," attended by members of the broadcasting industry and by the press, including those from Washington who regularly covered the White House. Members of the NAB board sat on the stage behind the president. Questions were asked both by local reporters and by members of the regular White House press corps.

Afterward, the event was described in an editorial published by the *Watertown* (New York) *Daily Times* (which owned the Watertown CBS Television Network affiliate). The editorial was entitled, "Radio-TV Claque."

President Nixon appeared before the National Association of Broadcast- ers Convention in Houston. The result was a mild success for the President and an embarrassment for radio and TV.

Using the format which permits others than members of the White House press corps to quiz him, the President submitted to questions . . .

---

[1]The most notable occasion on which CBS management delegated to a senior correspondent the right to state editorial conclusions was Ed Murrow's famous McCarthy broadcast. This policy of exception for senior correspondents was in fact decided after the McCarthy broadcast and applied retroactively to it.

The audience was composed of owners and managers of radio and TV stations. Incredibly, they gave hearty applause to every answer by the President, not mattering if the answer was a banality or an evasion of the question. It was as if the President had brought his own claque.

Most disturbingly, strong applause greeted a reporter's question of whether the country might not be better off if the Watergate story had never been revealed at all.

The broadcasters who attended the President's appearance might be well advised to now employ "instant replay" and appraise their own performance in Houston.

It was in this atmosphere that President Nixon recognized Dan Rather. When Dan stood up, there were boos and applause. Before Dan could ask his question, President Nixon asked him, "Are you running for something, Mr. Rather?" Dan replied, "No sir, Mr. President, are you?" Dan then asked his question—a tough one about Watergate.

Affiliates, other broadcasters, and the public all wrote me reacting to the extraordinary episode. As an NAB official wrote, "The criticism is really an accumulation of feeling about Rather, which his relatively innocent remark triggered." Some of the letters I received from CBS affiliates demanded Dan's reassignment. To such a demand from the president of a Southeastern affiliate, I replied:

You characterize Dan's "performance" at the NAB conference as "unprofessional"; you state that "Dan's personal feelings show through"; and you urge that "this sharp young man be reassigned somewhere else—at least until Richard Nixon leaves the White House." . . .

[T]o comply with such a suggestion would not be the right thing to do.

I wish, and I suspect that Dan wishes, that what happened at Houston hadn't happened. But just have a look at the circumstances that occurred there and tell me whether you can be certain that you might not have made some inadvertent remark. I know that I am not certain that I wouldn't have. There was plenty of "unprofessional conduct"—all around. I believe that the major stimulating unprofessional conduct was that of those who were attending the NAB meeting, who, forgetting their own professional obligations to their colleagues in the news departments [the members of the Radio and Television News Directors Association, who participated in the questioning of the president] and to the president of the United States, turned themselves into a cheering and booing audience, which was entirely inappropriate for a press conference held by the president with serious journalists. Greeting Dan Rather, when he stood up, with boos and cheers upset the president; I strongly suspect that that unseemly performance led the president to ask a question ["Running for something, Mr. Rather?"] which shouldn't have been asked. Dan, in turn, thrown for a loop, asked a question ["No sir, Mr. President, are you?"] which would better have been unasked. But given the inappropriate behavior of the audience, I blame neither the president nor Dan.

I continue to believe that Dan is one of the best reporters in the business. He does not dislike the president. He knows full well that the cornerstone of our policy is objectivity and that whatever his personal feelings in any event, he must be objective—he must ask the same tough questions of those he likes . . . as of those he dislikes, of those with whom he agrees as of those with whom he disagrees. All of us slip sometime, but I think that Dan overall has done a superb job.

I have full confidence in Dan. I believe at least as many people—public and professional—share my views as share your view about Dan. But it would be wrong in any event to make this a popularity contest. Dan is doing his job, and that's enough for me. And so I must decline your invitation [to reassign him].

Along with the affiliates, viewers also wrote letters criticizing Rather and demanding that he be fired. A typical viewer's letter came from Hawthorne, New Jersey. The viewer wrote that the "so-called news correspondent" Dan Rather was "crude and disrespectful to the office of the Presidency. . . . I suggest that the CBS News department either curtail Mr. Rather's operation or demand a public apology. . . . I would appreciate an answer to my letter with your comments."

Two weeks later, the same viewer sent me a registered letter, noting that I had not yet answered him and stating, "You can be assured that unless I have an answer . . . [by the end of two weeks] I will issue a letter to the editor of the *New York Times, New York Daily News* and the local North Jersey papers."

His impatience tried my patience; I huffed back (by ordinary mail):

We have received well over 3,000 letters relating to Mr. Rather and his response to a comment by the president in Houston. If you insist on getting all the way in front of all the other people—OK, but you're going to get a much shorter and ruder response than you would have gotten otherwise. And that is particularly so because I don't scare easily and I resent ultimata from anyone, including you. Your threat to "issue a letter to the editor of the *New York Times, New York Daily News*, and the local northern New Jersey papers" doesn't scare me a bit.

Mr. Dan Rather was not "disrespectful to the highest office in our country." It wasn't the office, it was the incumbent who made the provocative remark to Dan Rather and to whom Dan Rather replied. If you can't distinguish between the office of the president and the officeholder, just say "the office of the presidency of the United States" and "Warren G. Harding" all in one sentence. Now do you see the difference?

I have no intention whatever of acceding to your demand that I "either curtail Mr. Rather's operation or demand a public apology." I do not believe that either action is warranted.

I also received letters supporting Rather. There was one letter from a woman in Charlotte, North Carolina, who says she admired Dan Rather from the time she had seen his coverage of Hurricane Carla for the Houston station before he came to CBS News (coverage which first attracted our interest in Dan). She wrote that if I fired or reassigned Dan, she would streak naked though my office. It was a dilemma, but I resolved it:

> Some letters turn my stomach; some I appreciate; some I am grateful for; but mighty few do I enjoy. Yours is one such letter, and I am grateful indeed.
>
> Yes, I saw Dan's coverage of Hurricane Carla, and that's why he is working for us now. [As to the demands of affiliate station managers] that I fire Dan Rather: No chance.
>
> But, for the first time, I am tempted—and by you—to take Rather off the air. Up to now, I have been adamant, but that is because nobody has offered to streak through my office if I do so. Oh well—I will have to get Satan behind me. Not even the tempting prospect of my own personal streaker will cause me to abandon Dan.

In the summer of 1974, after Gerald Ford had succeeded Richard Nixon, I asked Dan Rather to leave his assignment at the White House to anchor our *CBS Reports*. Since Ed Murrow, we had not had a documentary series anchored by a single correspondent. It was an important role; I was eager to reemphasize that documentaries were a vital part of CBS News broadcasts, but Dan hesitated.

After Bill Small and I went to visit with Dan and his wife at their home in Washington, and after I had made it clear to them that the reassignment was not a forced one but that the choice was being left to Dan whether he would remain at the White House or would come to New York for documentaries—with the same substantially increased salary in either case—Dan agreed to accept the New York role.

But rumors, fueled by a column by the *Chicago Tribune*'s broadcast critic, were widespread that the change was a demotion for Dan and punishment for his Nixon coverage. The result was mail from a wide range of viewers decrying our treatment of him.

A priest who was the director of a school for boys in Terre Haute, Indiana, wrote me that he had read the *Chicago Tribune*'s "disturbing" article concerning Dan Rather and that the article

> indicates that CBS News is bending to outside pressures . . . If a further explanation would not be forthcoming, I would have to accept as true the statements made in the *Chicago Tribune*. That would cause me to question the integrity of the CBS News Department, and I can assure you that I would no longer remain a viewer.

In my reply, I wrote:

I appreciate your courtesy in giving me the opportunity to comment.

It deeply saddens me to have to say about a fellow journalist that the pieces in the *Chicago Tribune* concerning our White House assignments were shocking examples of journalistic irresponsibility. To put it bluntly, the articles were false and were written in violation of the elementary rule that a good journalist make an affirmative effort to determine the facts on both sides before he rushes to judgment. And we know for a fact that the author of the *Chicago Tribune*, in this matter, did not bother to check with any of us here on any of the basic facts.

The salient facts are these: . . . Dan Rather will leave his White House assignment but not—and I cannot emphasize this too strongly—as a result of any pressures from any sources on me or on any pressures by me on Dan. After all, if I were to succumb to such pressures I would have done so a long time ago: For five years those pressures from the White House[2] . . . and from some, but by no means all, of our affiliated stations were strong and I consistently rejected them. Why in the world, when those pressures no longer exist, would I now succumb?

In any event, as is customary when there is a change in administration, we review our White House assignments. Two weeks ago, I had lunch with Dan Rather and told him that the job he had done was superb and that he could either stay at the White House in his current assignment—at a substantial increase in salary—or he could take on a new assignment [as] anchorman of our *CBS Reports* . . . plus anchorman on our Saturday and Sunday news, at the same substantial increase in salary. (I didn't want to make him an offer he couldn't refuse.) Dan decided he would try the new assignment because he regarded it as something new and important, and as an advancement.[3] I do hope that my record here as president of CBS News over twelve years will lead you to give me some benefit of the doubt in this matter: I have not, and I never will, make assignments as a result of pressures of any kind—or even public opinion polls.

The kind Father wrote back thanking me "for your time in responding to my questions. I do find your response most satisfactory. It is most heartening to me to be able not only to keep but to reaffirm my belief in the integrity of your news operations." Demonstrating once

---

[2]The reference to White House pressures concerned the conversation I had with John Ehrlichman. At the time I wrote this letter, I still believed that Ehrlichman's suggestion about assigning Rather back to Texas was seriously intended. As I have described in an earlier chapter, I have since become persuaded that Ehrlichman did not so intend it, and I had foolishly precipitated the conversation about Rather.

[3]The assignment to New York, of course, led to his reassignment a year later to *60 Minutes*—from where, when Cronkite retired, Rather moved to anchor the weekday *CBS Evening News*.

again that, occasionally, it is worth the time and energy to reply to viewer mail by more than form acknowledgments.

But some skeptics preferred to believe the worst about Dan's reassignment. A Glens Falls, New York, viewer wrote that Dan's

> Saturday broadcast[4] is all he got for doing such a superb job all during Watergate. . . . We got to trust him. His apparent reward from C.B.S. was to send him into oblivion. You have made him another Watergate casualty. . . .
>
> None that we know believe that the assignments offered to him after Watergate were meant to be promotions. There was no need of replacing him at the White House for he was the one person covering C.B.S. news who should be rewarded.

My reply:

> Sorry that all your friends agree with you in refusing to believe that Dan's new assignments were meant to be promotions. I know they were. He knows they were. Jean, Dan's wife, knows they were. Dan's bank knows they were.
>
> We also told Dan that any time he wants to go back to the White House, he can do so. As a matter of fact, as far as I am concerned, I would be delighted if he went back as president of the United States.

In 1973, at a CBS management meeting which officers of the company and all division officers attended, an officer of another division asked me who would replace Walter Cronkite as *Evening News* anchor. I was reluctant to answer; I tried to pass the question off. First, I replied that one of the few happy consequences of my mandatory retirement scheduled for 1979 was that Cronkite, younger than I, would still be anchoring the *Evening News,* so I would not have to make that excruciatingly difficult decision—my successor would have to make it.

The questioner was persistent: What if Cronkite were hit by a truck today? My answer: I would sue the truck company. Questioner: Yes, but who would take Cronkite's place? I still bobbed and weaved: I answered "Ed Asner"—the actor—because I knew it might get out if I said anything. But that did not do it. I was told by a senior officer that this meeting was all in the family; and I was supposed to answer these questions seriously—"Dick, you just can't treat people this way . . . be honest." I feared it was a leaky family, but finally I did answer the

---

[4]Either the letter writer had neglected to watch the *CBS Evening News* on Sunday, which Dan also anchored, or the local affiliate did not clear for it.

question—I said "Roger Mudd," and sure enough it was in *Variety* the next Wednesday. I don't think Dan has ever forgiven me for that.

Some time later, a University of Minnesota professor wrote that it would be "a serious mistake to appoint Roger Mudd as Cronkite's successor. . . . Clearly no one could ever replace Walter Cronkite—but if anyone does it should be Dan Rather."

My squirming answer:

> I have only said—about a year ago—that if on that particular day, Cronkite were hit by a truck, Mudd would be his replacement; I also said that I could not speculate who the replacement would be a year from then or two years from then.
>   That still stands. So don't give up.

It has seemed to me to be a major irony that when the Nixon White House was Dan's beat, he was the particular target of many of our affiliates who wrote furious letters demanding that he be fired. But after his great success when he was later assigned to *60 Minutes*, and even more, after he succeeded Cronkite as anchor of the *CBS Evening News*, for many years maintaining its ratings lead over the competition, he became the affiliates' hero, and they discovered that he was just fine after all.

Nothing succeeds like ratings success. The critical affiliates were wrong about Dan the first time around, right thereafter—evidence once again that a good, probing, thorough messenger gets blamed for the message.

•   •   •

I first ran across Mike Wallace when he was doing *Nightbeat*, a television program on the old New York Dumont station. Mike interviewed his guests, one-on-one.[5] One night, I was the guest. Like so many idiots before and after me, I just knew that I was smarter than Mike and that he couldn't lay a glove on me. Sure enough, he lacerated me. But he did it fair and square. It was the essence of Mike: He didn't bully; he just cut through my obfuscations, exposed my fallacies, and got to the heart of the issues. He didn't win; the cause of an informed public did.

So when Mike came to see me in 1962 to tell me he would like to get back into journalism, I remembered that interview and I was impressed by how serious he was about journalism. When he was willing

---

[5]*Editors' note:* These comments by Salant on Mike Wallace are taken from a speech Salant gave before the Museum of Broadcast Communications on September 23, 1989, in Chicago.

to work for a serf's wages—he remembers it as $40,000 a year, but I prefer to misremember it as $50 a week—we took him onboard.

Some of my news colleagues had doubts about the nonjournalistic portions of Mike's résumé. They believed he had forfeited the right to reenter journalism because he had acted in a play, he had done some entertainment shows on television, and he had made television commercials for Parliament cigarettes. Whatever Mike had done, I knew that my journalistic résumé was much skimpier than his.

Mike promptly established himself as belonging in the great tradition of CBS News. He anchored the early *CBS Morning News*, when it was the first half-hour news broadcast on television. Another great Wallace landmark was his superb, candid, and sensitive *CBS Reports* on homosexuals—long before that topic came out of the closet in the mass media.

Quickly, he became a key member of the CBS News staff of correspondents, ultimately becoming one of the two original anchors on *60 Minutes*. Can anyone imagine *60 Minutes* without Mike? I can't, and I bet producer Don Hewitt can't either. But I sure imagined it when *60 Minutes* was just beginning. The original plan was for Harry Reasoner to be the sole anchor, and I thought Harry was enough. I wrote Don a memo—I wish I had shredded it. "Who needed Mike?" I wrote. Don knew what he was doing; I didn't. Mike and Harry it was.

After *60 Minutes* finally became a hit and the most profitable program series of any kind in broadcast history, Mike, at regular intervals, gently suggested that I give him a raise. A contract was a contract, I huffed; no raise. It wasn't until after I retired that my more generous and fair successor finally paid Mike more nearly what he was worth. I was a stingy boss who wasn't kind to him. It is a measure of what an extraordinary guy he is that long after I had any power to do anything for him, he has remained a wonderfully warm, thoughtful, and loyal friend.

Despite Mike's appearance in his investigative pieces as a ruthless bulldog of a reporter, in fact Mike is a kind, witty man. He has also done some lovely and admiring profiles for *60 Minutes*. How different viewers' perceptions of a correspondent may be from his real persona is illustrated by the fact that much of the mail I received about Mike accused him of being a liberal anti-Reaganite. In fact, since Mike's early days in Chicago, he had long been a friend of Nancy Reagan's mother, and of Nancy. In 1968, Mike was even offered a job as press secretary for President Richard Nixon. Mike declined—he wanted to continue as a journalist at CBS.

But Mike's on-air persona precipitated some hostile mail. In March 1968, a Philadelphia viewer wrote of her deep distaste for Mike, who she felt was hostile to President Nixon. She asked that we inform Mike that since he had never been president of the United States or a successful lawyer, it was unbecoming of him "to wear a belittling, patronizing, condescending smirk when speaking to Richard Nixon. Also [tell Wallace] to stop taunting him [Nixon] with that 'loser's image.' . . . Please send Mike Wallace to Saigon."

In my answer, I neglected to ask the writer why it was all right to smirk condescendingly and patronizingly if one were either the president of the United States or a successful lawyer, but otherwise I addressed myself to her letter:

> I am afraid that you are reading more into the face that Mike Wallace was born and grew up with than is there. Really, and I've seen his face a good deal over the past years, it looks the same when he's talking to me or any of his other friends as it looks when he's talking to Mr. Nixon. My wife says it's a nice face, and so does Mr. Wallace's wife.
>
> Mr. Wallace is certainly not "taunting" Mr. Nixon with the "loser's image" label. It is a perfectly legitimate question for a reporter to ask Mr. Nixon about, because Mr. Nixon and his advisers have long recognized, and frankly stated, that this image is most troublesome to him and his campaign is designed to overcome it. No reporter worth his salt in interviewing Mr. Nixon about his strategy could fail to ask him about this problem.[6]
>
> I hardly think it is appropriate for you to sign your letter "Kindest Thoughts" less than an inch below a recommendation that I send Mike "to Saigon where Kronkite's (sic) Cameraman and Soundman were wounded." I don't think that's very funny . . . P.S. I did send Mike Wallace to Vietnam. He was there for several months and he came back safely. Sorry.

In March 1975, Wallace did a *60 Minutes* piece reporting on the status of Jews in Syria. He said that while official discrimination still existed, some of the discriminatory laws had been repealed and the situation of Jews in Syria was better than it had been. This outraged some Jewish groups, and a complaint was filed with the National News Council. A Houston, Texas, viewer took issue with the report; his letter included a strong personal attack. "Then the thought came, 'Good God, the Arabs have bought into CBS and even its president and Mike

---

[6]Nixon had lost to Kennedy in the 1960 presidential campaign and, two years later, he lost to Jerry Brown in the California gubernatorial campaign. After he lost to Brown, he held an impromptu press conference at which he told the reporters that they would not have Nixon to kick around anymore.

Wallace have to kowtow.' The Arabs must be very happy with CBS. I certainly am not."

I replied: "I am sorry . . . but when I get a letter half of which is devoted to such an excessive and contemptible paragraph, my own human feelings preclude my giving you a substantive answer."

Some time later, Mike returned to Syria to have a second look, talking to some of the people in Syria whom the critics of the original piece had complained he had not interviewed. *60 Minutes* then broadcast a second Wallace report, which confirmed the accuracy of the first report.

• • •

Morley Safer, one of the great Vietnam reporters and a fine writer and urbane stylist, became an anchor of *60 Minutes* when he returned to the United States after the war. In August 1972, he interviewed Betty Ford, the president's wife, on *60 Minutes*. During the interview he asked a hypothetical question about Mrs. Ford's daughter—raising an issue to which Mrs. Ford had, a short time before, addressed herself in *McCall's* magazine.

A number of viewers were offended. An angry Irvington, New Jersey, viewer who objected to the question had written to Morley, to which, understandably, Morley had not replied. She then wrote me (referring to him as "Morris Safer"), "I asked him if his wife had premarital sex or if he's knowledgeable about illicit sex practices of C.B.S. personnel. I get the impression you media people don't answer questions—just ask them."

I wrote back:

I have your . . . postcard:
1. We have no Morris Safer. His name is Morley Safer.
2. Your characterization of him as a "smirking skunk" tells me more about you than I think you care to have me know.
3. Mr. Safer "conned poor Betty Ford" into nothing. She urged him to ask any questions on any subject and the particular question which so displeased you is one which she had already been asked and to which she replied in a recent *McCall's* magazine interview.
4. Your questions which you wrote to Mr. Safer about his wife's "premarital sex" or "illicit sex practices of CBS" personnel is irrelevant. I would also point out that the question Mr. Safer put to Mrs. Ford, unlike yours to Mr. Safer, was purely hypothetical. He did not ask, and he wouldn't dream of asking, whether Mrs. Ford's daughter had engaged in an affair before marriage. He only asked what Mrs. Ford's attitude would be, if any such thing might happen—a question which concerns many parents today.

• • •

Hughes Rudd was not a stereotypical anchor. With a gravelly voice and a lived-in look, he was a superb reporter with a mischievous eye and pen, and an irreverent mind. He had served with distinction as our Moscow correspondent. In 1973, he was then assigned to anchor the *CBS Morning News*.[7]

In the mid-1970s, Charles Kuralt made a speech at a meeting of the Society of Professional Journalists [SPJ] criticizing the emphasis at many local stations on physical attractiveness rather than journalistic ability in the choice of local anchors. In response, the wire editor of the *Chronicle Telegram* wrote a letter to *Quill*, the magazine published by the SPJ:

> Thank God, somebody like Charles Kuralt finally said what I feel about all those pretty TV newsmen . . .
> I don't feel like "hearing it from a friend." I want to hear the news from somebody who knows what the news is—and how to tell it . . .
> Do the TV news execs ever realize how much of the population is beyond the teen-age years, and how few may really relate to the pretty boys and girls who look like candidates in an All-America pageant?
> Why don't they give us somebody slightly fat and forty, with a pimple, and wrinkles around the eyes from smiling? And a frown from hard work? The real McCoy always sells better than the plastic imitation, in case they hadn't noticed.
> I don't expect to see a newscaster who looks like my kind of journalist (at least in the near future), but it sure is fun to dream.

When I read the letter in *Quill*, I wrote:

> So you want an anchorman who is "slightly fat and forty, with a pimple, and wrinkles around the eyes from smiling . . . and a frown from hard work." So you don't expect to see a newscaster who looks like my kind of journalist (at least in the near future), but it sure is fun to dream. . . .
> Wake yourself up from dreaming any morning, Monday-Friday, 7–8 A.M., New York time, and watch Hughes Rudd and the *CBS Morning News*. There's no pimple, but he's your and my kind of journalist. Why dream when you can have the real thing?

---

[7]*Editors' note:* Hughes Rudd anchored the *Morning News* until October 1977 with several different coanchors—Sally Quinn, Bruce Morton, and Lesley Stahl (Edward Bliss Jr., *Now the News: The Story of Broadcast Journalism* [New York: Columbia University Press, 1991], p. 276).

I do not know whether the editor accepted my suggestion. If he did, unhappily there were too few of him. The circulation of the *CBS Morning News* with Hughes Rudd, like its predecessors and like its successors to this day, was so small that changes had to be made and we felt it necessary to replace him.[8] I was heartbroken: The editor's confidence that "the real McCoy always sells" did not prove out.

---

[8]To a New York City viewer who complained about the change and charged that we were slaves to the ratings, I wrote: "It's heartbreaking that it has met with so little response that I feel it necessary to try a somewhat new tack. You are unfair in saying that we are 'slaves to the ratings.' We are nothing of the kind. But like all news media, we cannot survive forever when our circulation is so low that it becomes a waste of time, effort, and resources. [It] has had a good run, and we have tried everything within reason. . . . I assure you that the basic approach and spirit of the *Morning News* will be left intact . . . Had there been more of you, we wouldn't have this unhappy problem."

Part Six

Stepping Aside: Beyond CBS

CBS Memorandum
To: Vice President, Radio News
From: Richard Salant
Re: Clichés
Date: December 22, 1977

Here comes Salant again. If I heard today's 2:00 P.M. hourly correctly—and please God I didn't—yesterday's "overwhelming lack of support" can move over to be joined on the bench by "thorny deadlock." Sounds like a bird or a new breed of rose or just plain foolish writing. Is anybody (a) writing this; (b) editing it; or (c) monitoring it when it's on the air?

"Something," as my mother used to say when we turned on the faucets and no water came out, "must be done."

28

Pushed Out

I am appalled at what is happening at, and to, CBS and CBS News. The tragedy is that the people in charge are so alien to the special demands and responsibilities of a broadcast businessman (as distinguished from a widget businessman) that they don't recognize what is happening. . . . Granted that the business has vastly changed—the decline in network shares, the new competition, the takeover threats, and Wall Street fiddling—but you don't shape your responses by deciding that street-walking is the way to go. Or am I just one of those old timers who mistakenly think that our time—yours, Frank Stanton's, and mine—was the Golden Age just because we were there then, and aren't now? It's all very depressing.

—Letter to Charles Crutchfield (former manager, CBS affiliate),
Charlotte, North Carolina, November 6, 1985

CBS HAD A RIGID MANDATORY retirement policy—sixty-five years old and out. The only exception had been for Bill Paley, who found it impossible to step aside in favor of Frank Stanton as chief executive officer. Paley stayed on at CBS until he was over eighty.

My sixty-fifth birthday was on April 14, 1979, so April 30 was my retirement date. It would mean the end of twenty-seven years at CBS and sixteen years as head of CBS News. I dreaded retirement. I enjoyed my job and my associates in the News Division—and I was scared to death of having no job to go to each day. I was also reluctant to see all my ties with CBS broken.

At a lunch at Black Rock with John Backe, then president of CBS Inc., and Gene Jankowski, president of the CBS Broadcast Group, I suggested the possibility that CBS might retain me as a consultant after my retirement. Backe quickly agreed and told Jankowski and me to work it out. But I am not sure that Jankowski was enthusiastic about the idea; he seemed to feel uneasy with me. I belonged to an older, unrealistic generation, and besides, I had been around so long, running Paley's and Stanton's pet division, I had been difficult to manage. Gene, I suspect, instinctively knew that we News Division elitists were not in awe of him.[1] Eternally cheerful, he was shrewd in an open way but he had no great interest in news or intellectual depth that was visible to us in our meetings.

During a time when, after many years of ratings leadership, the CBS Television Network's prime-time ratings were being temporarily overtaken by ABC, Gene, who had come up through the sales ranks, used to hold what we called locker-room pep rallies—meetings in a small Black Rock auditorium attended by the officers in the broadcast divisions. All of us from CBS News who attended delighted in forming pools to guess the number of times that Gene would, as he led his pep rallies, exhort us by saying, "If you don't have the steak, sell the sizzle." The winner was the one who predicted the highest number.

This was not quite the spirit or language to which the irreverent News Division people were accustomed. Our worlds were rather different, and I am sure that Gene was aware of our skepticism—or cynicism. This, it seemed to me, was the reason for the languid pace of our negotiations.

Gene turned the matter over to a CBS lawyer who was a good friend and was sympathetic to me. But without guidance concerning what might be acceptable to Gene, we were breaking new ground, since consultation contracts for retirees were rare. I called the lawyer from time to time to ask him when he would have a draft proposal. He, properly, threw the ball back in my court, pointing out that he had no guidance from Gene.

Finally, I suggested a fairly modest retainer of $40,000 a year, along with secretarial help and a small office. The response—with the months passing by and April 1979 looming closer—was that the retainer was all right, but no office, and no secretarial help. I checked on what a secretary—even part-time—a phone, and a small office would cost me: It totaled more than the proffered retainer.

We were on dead center. I was not persistent enough; Gene had other things on his plate. The consultancy never came to be.

---

[1] A CBS News Division friend of many years, who was given to writing me occasional memos as funny and as short as mine usually were endless and solemn, reflected most succinctly and devastatingly a not-uncommon attitude of CBS News people toward Jankowski when he wrote in 1978: "I like my boss a lot better than I like yours." To which I had replied: "Well, I'm damned—with the faintest praise I ever heard."

I have in the years following my retirement from CBS come to regret that my relations with Jankowski were not warmer. I tended to blame him for the failure of the consultancy, when it was at least equally my failure to pursue the matter more vigorously. And I believe that he thought I was disloyal in negotiating with NBC, in the final days, without keeping him informed. (I did not consult with him on that because I did not want to bargain one network against the other.) But Jankowski was a good and conscientious person, and my former associates who were still at CBS News told me that he was a warm supporter of CBS News, who recognized its importance and autonomy. Given the changes at the top of CBS and the passing of the Paley-Stanton era, Jankowski was a good boss.

Meanwhile, during my last year, CBS management had to turn its attention to choosing my successor. I was reluctant to play an active role in this process. First, I did not believe that I should perpetuate myself by playing a major role in the selection process. Second, the two logical candidates were Bill Leonard, my former deputy in documentaries, and Bill Small, my hard news deputy.

They were twin towers of strength, indispensable to me. I had relied heavily on them; and both were good and dear friends. I did not want to choose between them. Either one would have made a superb News Division president. When asked, I confined myself, as objectively and fairly as I knew how, to talking about the management strengths and weaknesses of each of the two men.

The decision was made in late June of 1978—ten months before my retirement. On the evening before my family and I were scheduled to go on vacation to Nantucket, Gene Jankowski, who lived in a neighboring Connecticut suburb, called me at home and told me he was driving over to see me. When he arrived, he told me that Bill Leonard had been chosen as my successor. Leonard was then living and working in Washington, D.C., as CBS's Washington corporate vice president. To provide a smooth transition, Gene told me, Leonard was being appointed executive vice president of CBS News, effective immediately. There never had been an executive vice president of News. I was not a believer in one-over-one management relationships, which tended to duplicate the decisionmaking process and isolate the president.[2]

---

[2]*Editors' note:* Frances Salant recalls that Jankowski arrived in a white Volkswagen convertible with the top down. He was dressed all in white—white shirt, white slacks, white shoes—"much as an angel of death." She said her husband had no inkling ahead of time what Jankowski was going to tell him.

I was puzzled and unhappy that Jankowski had waited to make the announcement the evening before I was going on my long-planned summer vacation. (He had been aware of my plans for many months.) Despite my refusal to play a role in picking my successor, I felt that I ought to be around for the announcement to the News Division personnel. And I certainly thought I ought to be around for Bill Leonard's first month as my executive vice president.

Gene said that it was unnecessary for me to postpone my vacation plans. But I insisted—and stayed the next day to be at the Broadcast Center meeting where Jankowski officially announced that Bill Leonard had been appointed to succeed me the following April and would serve as executive vice president in the meantime. Then, since the meeting had forced me to miss the ferry from Woods Hole to Nantucket (reservations for cars are hard to come by), CBS flew me up to Nantucket in the company plane. I was comforted because it was only the end of June, and I had another ten months to go as head of the division.

It quickly turned out, however, that that was not quite the way it would be—there had been another change that I had not been told about. Les Brown, then the *New York Times* reporter covering the broadcasting beat, called to ask me to clarify Bill's role prior to my actual retirement: Would the people in the News Division continue to report to me, or would they report to Bill?

I thought that was a silly question since Jankowski had said nothing to me about any change in organizational arrangements. I told Brown that, of course, the table of organization would be just the same, and for the remainder of my term, Bill and I would work together, but there were to be no changes in reporting relationships.

Les Brown, accordingly, reported in his story the following day that the news organization would continue to report to me. Promptly, Gene Mater, a Broadcast Group vice president and assistant to Jankowski, called me and asked me why I had said that to Brown. Because, I replied, my answer to Brown reflected my understanding. No, said Mater, that is not the way it was to be. All my news associates who had reported to me were henceforth to report to Leonard. Nobody was to report to me except Leonard, and he was to keep me informed. I asked Gene Mater why Jankowski had not told me of this change, because I would have objected if he had.

It seemed to me that my boss—or bosses—were in an unseemly hurry to have me go. But even though I felt that I had been moved out of the mainstream, it was more a matter of hurt feelings rather than a drastic change. That it was not worse I owed to Bill Leonard—my old and treasured associate, who was also a sensitive and diplomatic friend. He was considerate and thoughtful, and he did keep me apprised. I had become a fifth wheel, but Bill managed to make me feel as though I was, at least, sharing the driving duties.

• • •

With just a few months to go before retirement and still no progress in respect of a CBS News consultancy, I became more and more panic-stricken at the prospect of having nothing to do after April 30. I enjoyed my job too much to relish the prospect of being idle. A few of my friends had retired and insisted they were having a wonderful time. David Klinger told me that he had a very full day: He could now read the *New York Times* carefully from beginning to end—and that took until lunchtime. In the afternoon, he took lessons in baking cakes and cookies.

I was dubious, but Klinger had begun to look younger and healthier than ever. And when he proved to be among the most stimulating conversationalists about current affairs—and science, the home, sports, and whatever else was covered in the *Times*'s special sections—and on top of that, he dropped in from time to time to leave cookies and cakes—I began to believe that retirement could be enjoyable. Just not for me.

Early in 1979, Jane Pfeiffer, the new chairman of NBC, telephoned me. Jane told me that she was trying to learn the business of broadcasting, especially news, and she wondered whether I would stop by for breakfast at the Pfeiffer home in Greenwich, Connecticut. She said she wanted to pick my brain.

I had met Jane Pfeiffer some years before, when she was a vice president at IBM. Later, as a consultant to RCA (then NBC's parent company), she had been instrumental in recruiting Fred Silverman to the presidency of NBC. When Fred was made NBC president, Jane became NBC's chairman.

A few days later, on my way to work in New York City, I did stop by the Pfeiffers. Over English muffins and coffee, Jane, who never wasted time and went to the heart of things, asked me whether I would like to come to NBC. Since I was not eager to retire, I was interested. But I told her that I wanted to know more about what she—and Fred Silverman—had in mind. I also told her that in no circumstances would I consider going to work for NBC until after April 30, the date of my retirement. She said she would be in touch with me.

Meanwhile, shortly after my conversation with Jane, Gene Jankowski, after months of inaction, got in touch with me on the matter of the consultancy arrangement. He indicated that CBS was ready to talk seriously and that the problem of providing me with an office and a secretary, in addition to a retainer, could be worked out. I was asked to specify just what I wanted, and then we could conclude an agreement.

In the course of many contractual negotiations with correspondents and producers at CBS News, I had acquired a distaste—unreasonable, but genuine—for agents who tried to force better terms for their clients with hints, or more than hints, of the generous terms which had been offered by a competing news organization. Having been scarred by that tactic, I did not want to use it on my own behalf. So I told Jankowski that too much time had passed and, at least for the time being (there was no certainty that NBC and I would come to an agreement), I did not want to discuss the consultancy any further.

I do not know what moved Jankowski to renew negotiations and offer to take care of the terms which had troubled me. I could have saved myself a lot of trouble had I been more flexible and less suspicious of word having reached him that Pfeiffer and I had talked.

In February, Jane called and asked me to drop in again. We talked. NBC was offering me the vice chairmanship. The NBC News Division would report to me and I was to be responsible for NBC's long-range planning. They offered me a three-year contract (I never had a contract at CBS) and a generous salary.

I gave Jane my list of dreams. I told her that I had always felt that there had not been an orderly process in scheduling news broadcasts at CBS and that I had always wanted to be a part of that decisionmaking process; she affirmed that would come with the vice chairmanship. Then I told her that the dream dearest to my heart—what I thought network television news and the viewers needed most—was the expansion of the half-hour evening news to a full hour. And finally, I told her that I wanted a more regular, and more desirable, schedule for documentaries.

Jane assured me that all of these things could be worked out. She, too, wanted a regular documentary schedule. She, too, thought that an hour evening news was important; and so, she said, did Fred Silverman. She suggested that we plan to begin the hour news the following fall—in 1979. I told her it would probably take a little longer to work out because of FCC regulations and the reluctance of affiliates. I also told Jane that if I should come over to NBC, it seemed to me that there would have to be some reorganization of NBC News and some replenishment of its reporting and producing staff. Since I, as head of CBS News, had intimate knowledge of the contractual arrangements with CBS News personnel, I felt it would be improper for me to play any role in efforts which might be made at NBC News to recruit CBS

News people. Jane agreed. (Later, when NBC News did raid CBS News and hire away Roger Mudd and Marvin and Bernie Kalb, I had nothing whatever to do with those actions.)

After our discussion, we shook hands in agreement. I then had a brief meeting with Fred Silverman, and he also expressed delight. Fred and I shook hands, and the agreement to become NBC's vice chairman, effective May 1, 1979, was set.

It all looked unbelievably wonderful to me—except for the awful fact that, after all these years at CBS, I would be working for NBC. But I was so excited at the prospect of not having to retire after all, and of getting, at long last, an hour of network evening news and a decent documentary schedule—and of being in on the program decisionmaking process—that I managed, somehow, to put way back in my mind the thought of the wrenching transition I would have to make from my home at CBS News—to NBC.

I had kept Frank Stanton, still a consultant at CBS, abreast of all these developments. He knew how badly I wanted to remain active and how discouraged I had been that there seemed to be no progress in respect of a CBS consultancy. So he encouraged my interest in going to NBC under the terms that had been offered.

Just as soon as NBC and I made our agreement, I called Paley from a roadside telephone booth and asked to see him. His office said that he was at home in his New York City apartment and that he would be leaving momentarily for a holiday in Nassau. When I explained that it was urgent—I did not want Paley to hear about my defection from any other source—his office said that I could see him briefly at his apartment, before he left for the airport.

I immediately drove to Paley's. When I told him that I was going to NBC, he seemed stunned. He asked me why I was doing that now— why I had not waited a couple of years until I had to retire. I explained to him that my retirement was only a couple of months, not a couple of years, away.

Then, it seemed he was anxious for me to leave. He told me he wanted to consult with his associates. As he walked me to the door of his apartment, he put his arm on my shoulder and said, "Dick, this is as though your son came to you during the Civil War and told you he was joining the Confederate Army." I bit my tongue and thought, but did *not* reply, that it would not be so bad if the father was a Southerner.

In honor of my retirement from CBS, Paley had arranged a small farewell lunch for me in his dining room at Black Rock for March 28, 1979. He had invited my closest associates. But when the announcement had been made that I was joining NBC effective May 1, Paley called and told me that it would be inappropriate to go forward with the lunch and asked me to write him a memorandum requesting that the lunch be canceled. I told him that that would not be true; I was not the one who wanted the cancellation. In fact, I would very much like the lunch to proceed as planned. Paley said it would be embarrassing. He was insistent.

So I wrote him a memorandum stating that "at your request" I am asking that the lunch which he had planned be canceled. It was. Unfortunately, word did not reach David Klinger, who came in from his home on Long Island, or Eric Sevareid, who came up from Washington. Both appeared at Paley's dining room to learn that there would be no luncheon.

A few days later, a small package arrived in the interoffice mail. It was a handsome gold watch from Tiffany and Company. On the back was inscribed: "To R. S. Salant, In Appreciation, From His CBS Colleagues, 3-28-79"—the date on which the luncheon would have been held. The CBS vice president of corporate affairs later told me that he was very proud to have personally composed that inscription.

There was, however, a farewell party which did move me tremendously. It was a party given by my associates at the CBS News Division in a studio at Broadcast Center. It was a sad and lovely occasion for me. While I suppose a few of my colleagues thought I was something of a traitor for not leaving quietly and retiring from the broadcast business, others seemed to have taken some delight that I had gone to NBC and beaten the system—in this case the retirement system. In my farewell remarks to my colleagues, I said:

These are pretty unusual circumstances. I know I have very mixed emotions, and I expect some of you do, too. . . .

This decision has been difficult and painful. I leave CBS with great sadness. I go to NBC with great anticipation.

My twenty-seven years at CBS, and particularly my sixteen years at CBS News, have been an enormous joy. I leave CBS because of mandatory retirement, and I leave it with nothing but affection, gratitude, and loyalty. It's been great.

I look forward to my new and challenging role at NBC because it gives me the treasured opportunity to continue to work full-time in the field which I have enjoyed so much. NBC has given me the chance to work toward the realization of some of the hopes and dreams I have for broadcasting and broadcast journalism.

In these circumstances, I was unable to go gently into the night. There is still too much I want to do.

I shall always be deeply in debt to CBS and to all my associates, past, and present. I am grateful to Fred Silverman and Jane Pfeiffer for giving me, at what would otherwise have been the end of a career, this new and exciting opportunity.

Let me add a few thoughts.

Under Bill Leonard's leadership, CND's future is brighter and more secure than ever. To Bill, and to all of you who have carried me so long and so well, my deepest gratitude and my total affection. I shall miss all of you—damn, how much I'll miss you. Being associated with you has been a great, satisfying, and happy experience.

I expect that some of you—few I hope—will look at my decision as pulling a Pete Rose or a Lee Iacocca—or even a Benedict Arnold. But . . . I'm not leaving because Henry Ford didn't like me. And Benedict Arnold didn't have to leave because of mandatory retirement.

No, really. . . . I'm who I am—wanting to keep on working at the kind of thing I know best, and love—and can't give up. You all have made it so enjoyable. You've spoiled me so that I can't face up to mowing a lawn, or doing occasional chores, or getting into a new line of work. And so I hope that you all look upon this step which I'm taking with tolerance and understanding.

To all of you—my friends, I hope: Good-bye—and good luck.

When the News Division party was over and my wife and I went back to 1E8, my old office, to get our coats, I found that all the furniture had already been moved into the hallway so that the office could be redecorated for my successor as promptly as possible. My career at CBS, which had begun through a series of happy coincidences in July 1952, had come to an end.

•　　•　　•

There was some interest and some press comment concerning the fact that I had been the subject of mandatory retirement. I was asked for my views; I was invited to participate on panels discussing the issue. I declined because I was ambivalent. By hindsight, since my years with CBS were such happy ones and my four years with NBC and my one year with the National News Council, on balance, were less than smashing successes, I look on mandatory retirement with personal distaste. I assume that without mandatory retirement I could have stayed at CBS News a while longer—though perhaps that is an unjustified assumption. I may have been just a step away from being fired again, as I had been in 1964. But if I had been able to stay with CBS, I would have avoided five rather difficult and frustrating years.

However, mandatory retirement is an effective way to avoid what management advisers call "blockage at the top." Like it or not, most people are fueled by ambition of one kind or another; most work hard and loyally because they want to get ahead. If incumbents stay in their jobs until death do them part, those below them are barred from moving up. They are forced either to look for another company or to root for their boss's incapacitation. Clearly, such blockage is a major cause of intercompany shifting, and a company loses very good men and women for that reason.

But beyond retaining good people which blockage at the top makes difficult, there is, I believe, an even more important factor involving the continued good health of an enterprise: the new ideas which come with new blood and fresh minds. This is a hard one to admit for those of us who are along in years and who have been forced to retire. We like to think—I catch myself thinking too often, that after our departure, everything went downhill. That is good for our souls and for our self-esteem. In my own experience, it is common to hear people who have served in various capacities, at various levels, talk passionately about the good old golden days and deplore the present-day deterioration of policies, standards, performance, and ways of doing business.

Sometimes it is true, but sometimes it is not. Certainly, I tend to focus on things that are done today that I would not have done or permitted in my day. For example, overemphasizing pictures, which I believe is counterproductive and gets in the way of the message. But my successors, I am sure, have found CBS News policies which they want to change.

And that's the point of mandatory retirement. No incumbent has a monopoly on wisdom or on ideas. A fresh look, fresh questions—those are the lifeblood of any journalistic organization. The alternative is hardening of the arteries, which can be just as fatal to business and news organizations as it is to people. If I sometimes cringe when I watch certain things, it is not important. What is important is that there is ferment resulting from new management, new ways of doing things, new questioning of old ways.

And so, although I might wish that it had not happened to me, as a general principle, mandatory retirement is sound both from a management and an individual point of view. As in all things, a price has to be paid; but on balance, it is worth it.

29

Four More Years— at NBC

Anyone who relies on television as his or her sole source of news is a civic illiterate.

—New Canaan Library Annual Meeting, 1992

WHEN I ARRIVED AT MY NEW OFFICE on the sixth floor of 30 Rockefeller Plaza—NBC's corporate headquarters—I was dazzled by the arrangements. I had a large, handsome office and across a small hall there was a charming and convenient meeting room all my very own. Jane Pfeiffer graciously dropped by to greet me and bring a vase of flowers.

It was May Day 1979. If that date did not give me pause that NBC and I were not suited for each other, the first meeting I attended a day or two later with Ed Griffiths, RCA's chairman and CEO, the RCA corporate staff, and NBC officers should have been a warning. As soon as I reached for the pencil and pad at my place at the table, I was struck by the fact that the pencil's point was broken. I reached for another—a half-length one with a very blunt point. At all CBS meetings, whether high-level ones in the boardroom or lesser meetings elsewhere, the pencils were always new—and sharp.

I knew these were only symbols. NBC's or RCA's success did not hinge on whether its pencils were chewed up, their points blunt. But I was brought up under Frank Stanton, and he recognized that details are symbolic of important underlying attitudes. They symbolize the character of an organization; they reflect the degree to which it cares. A meeting between the top officers of two great companies like RCA and NBC where nobody sees to it that the pencils are sharp, or even usable, is a meeting of corporate leaders who may be careless and in-different about other, more important matters as well.

At that first meeting, Ed Griffiths put on a performance which I was told was typical. He was angry and severe: Costs and personnel had to be cut. He stated flatly that NBC could do just as good a job at signifi-cantly lower costs; he would not, he said, accept arguments to the contrary. It was a rough one-way meeting, with Griffiths's RCA subor-dinates nodding in agreement and the NBC officers silent.

Ed Griffiths was a classic bottom-line man, and those were not the best of times for RCA, whose profits were down. They were even worse times for NBC, which was struggling with its ratings and prof-its. Fred Silverman had not achieved the miraculous turnaround at NBC which RCA unrealistically demanded.

At the meeting's conclusion, Griffiths, whom I had met only once very briefly before I joined NBC, asked me how I liked the meeting. I replied, "I think I'll apply for early retirement." I smiled when I said it, but I knew I was in trouble when Griffiths did not smile back.

The pointless pencils, the downsizing, and the rigid and humorless RCA chief executive officer reminded me that CBS and NBC were dif-ferent places and very different in character and philosophy, going back to their origins with Paley and Sarnoff. That should not have come as a surprise to me, but it did.

•   •   •

Since Jane and Fred had hired me after my years in news, and since NBC News was to report to me, my first priority was to learn as much about the NBC News Division as I could. While at CBS, I had the im-pression that NBC News had become lethargic, peopled by too many 9-to-5 types. In general, it seemed the people in NBC news did not put in the extra effort necessary to turn out distinguished broadcasts.

This puzzled me, as I had enormous respect for NBC's three leading correspondents—John Chancellor, David Brinkley, and Tom Brokaw. Chancellor was a dedicated, thoughtful journalist, scornful of show-business tricks. Most important of all for what ailed NBC News at that time, John was never satisfied with less than the best.

So too with David Brinkley. He remained the wry observer, the mas-ter of broadcast writing. Also, there was Tom Brokaw, whose excellent journalistic experience warred with his boyish good looks. Chancellor, Brinkley, and Brokaw were a strong trio around which a great news or-ganization could be built. And then there were my old and respected as-sociates from CBS News—John Hart, Garrick Utley, Tom Pettit, Doug Kiker, Lloyd Dobbins, Judy Woodruff, Bryan Ross, and Chris Wallace.

But what I faced in trying to diagnose NBC News's problems con-trasted sharply with what I had faced at CBS News. First, after all my years at CBS, I knew the organization and most of the people in it. At NBC, however, I was an alien from another news organization.

A second major difference was my role at NBC News and my different place in the management organization. At CBS News, I was part of the news staff; I could get the feel of it just by walking around and chatting and watching. But at NBC, I was not part of NBC News; I was part of senior corporate management. If I was to remain consistent with my principle of separation between news and corporate management, I could not spend hours wandering around the fifth floor and the news studios, leaning over shoulders.

A third difference lay in the contrast between the management style of my new boss, Fred Silverman, on the one hand, and my old bosses, Frank Stanton and Bill Paley, on the other. Paley and Stanton were alert to structural and organizational weaknesses. (Paley's favorite opening question to me when I had news staff luncheons with him was "How's morale?") But Silverman personalized. Any problem had to be somebody's fault, and the solution was as obvious as it was simple: Identify and fire the culprit; firing and replacement were Fred's quick fix.

After some months of observing and talking to those whom I knew and respected—months during which Fred, and Jane, too, asked me from time to time when they would see results—I reluctantly concluded that able as he was, Les Crystal, the president of NBC News, was not the right person to head the News at that time. The drive and spark essential to a news organization were lacking. A few people among news management were divisive—there was a good deal of backbiting and there were fiefdoms. Some correspondents and editors were just going through the motions.

Excellent news division heads had preceded Les Crystal—the brilliant and imaginative journalist Reuven Frank, a true journalistic philosopher; and the intelligent and articulate veteran of print and broadcast journalism, Dick Wald. Yet something seemed to be missing. For over a decade, like the rest of NBC, NBC News at that time was gradually losing ground both to ABC and CBS News. NBC News, since its glory days of Huntley-Brinkley and Bob Kintner,[1] had not come together.

---

[1]Bob Kintner, a former successful newspaper columnist, and NBC's president in the late 1950s till the mid-1960s, certainly put his own stamp on NBC: It was he, with his journalistic background and interest, who finally transformed NBC News from a stepchild who had to be tolerated to a dedicated, gusty, successful news organization, which, for more than half a decade, became the dominant network news organization. Kintner recognized that to attract the attention of the critics and persuade them that NBC was seriously in the business of news, he had to adopt dramatic, easily identifiable policies—hence the famous, and to competitors like me, frustrating and infuriating, policy for which Kintner became known: "CBS plus thirty"—that is, whenever NBC and CBS were both covering live the same news event, NBC would stay on the air thirty minutes longer than CBS.

NBC News needed something different. It needed a demanding, and insistent, perfectionist—somebody who could get angry and kick the pants of the lazy ones, the burnouts, the shruggers, the nondeliverers, and if that brought no response, let them go. It needed someone who could spot good new blood and bring it in. It needed a motivator, a tough boss, an impatient leader who wanted not love, but performance.

Les, kind, soft-spoken, mild, was none of the above. The nice guy finished last. I had to tell Les that we were looking for a replacement as president of NBC News.

I recommended that Bill Small be appointed as head of NBC News. He had served with great distinction as the chief of CBS's Washington Bureau and, after that, as my senior vice president in charge of hard news. Small was tough and exacting. He did not suffer laziness, carelessness, or fools gladly. He had a fine eye for new talent. And tough as he was, he inspired great loyalty among those who worked directly for him. He was recognized by his peers as a journalist and a leader.

Small had long wanted to head a network news division. When CBS appointed Bill Leonard, instead of him, as my successor to head CBS News, he was angry and disappointed. Small agreed to be president of NBC News after extended negotiations.[2] He set out to breathe new life into the organization with new approaches, new management hires, new correspondents and producers, and some changes in assignments. He emphasized the importance of aggressiveness—and NBC News did become more aggressive. To the delight of some, but to the dismay of others at NBC News, Bill shook things up.

Professionally, Small is a private person. He is insistent on playing his own way. He rarely came to me except when he needed help—help obtaining airtime on the network, or in dealing with corporate personnel, or in other situations in which he felt that he had exhausted the possibilities on his own.[3] That made for some considerable frustration on my part. After sixteen years of running (at least nominally) a news division, I had a new role, and now I had to keep my cotton-pickin' fingers off and leave it up to Bill. Bill saw to it that I did.

---

[2]Bill was a hard bargainer about compensation for himself and about the terms and conditions of his employment. I had learned that when I returned to CBS News in February 1966. One of my first ports of call was the Washington Bureau, which Bill headed; I wanted to say hello to the bureau. I arrived at the hotel late in the evening very tired. To my surprise, Small was in the lobby waiting for me. He insisted on coming up to my room to talk to me. His purpose was to put in a pitch for a raise, which he told me Fred Friendly had promised him . . . and had not delivered.

After some months, I became so frustrated that I wrote an angry memorandum to him suggesting we have regular meetings so that I could be kept abreast of News Division matters—and maybe even contribute some useful suggestions. But Bill disliked meetings, and since meetings at NBC often came to no conclusions, meetings were not a fruitful way of life.

• • •

Apart from my theoretical responsibility for NBC News as NBC vice chairman, I also had a responsibility for NBC as a whole. That led me into a quixotic attempt to define, or redefine, its character. The attempt ultimately led to a document entitled "NBC and You." One of the first things which struck me after a short time at NBC was that NBC was made up of individuals each doing his or her own thing. It was an aggregation of feudalities. They attended meetings and reported on their own areas, but then they shut their ears off for others' reports and went their own way. Like much of NBC News, NBC itself didn't seem to have either common purpose or common character.

It is sophomoric and sentimental to talk of a team in organizations as large and diverse as NBC and CBS. But what had very palpably existed at CBS, especially in the early days when I joined it—the real sense of being a part of a family—was absent at NBC. Soon after I arrived, I decided to try to bring the people at NBC together, by giving them some sense of being a part of an organization with a defined common purpose. With the approval—somewhat bemused as well as amused, I suspect—of Fred Silverman and Jane Pfeiffer, I set out to create a document which would define what the network was, who its constituents were, and what NBC's mission should be.

In 1980, after some months of talking to whoever would give me a few minutes, I composed a small pamphlet called "NBC and You." It was a little more than six pages of text—beautifully printed on the finest of paper. It was addressed to "All National Broadcasting Company Employees" and signed by Jane Pfeiffer and Fred Silverman. It noted that while all American businesses have a social responsibility,

---

[3]An example of Bill's independence came on the night of the 1980 presidential election: Although I had forbidden calling states on the basis of exit polls rather than on the basis of actual vote results in each state, it was apparent that Bill had abandoned my CBS policy and was making calls on the basis of exit polls. He had done so without talking to me. I still believe it is a dangerous policy.

a broadcasting organization has a particularly large social responsibility—with its immense reach to serve the entire public.

The purpose of the pamphlet was to outline that responsibility. Because NBC's "product" was programs which are available to and judged by the public every minute of every day, it proclaimed, "We are what we do." It stated hopefully that "all of us can come to recognize that there is a common identity underlying all our activities . . . which represents something unique, distinctive, innovative, and spirited."

My brainchild was stillborn. It was distributed to all NBC employees; some of them may have read it. I later gave a copy to Thornton Bradshaw when he became chairman of RCA (replacing Ed Griffiths). I gave a copy to Grant Tinker when he became chairman of NBC (replacing Fred Silverman). But I doubt that a year or two after "NBC and You" was issued, there was more than a handful of NBC people who even recalled that it existed.

I am uncertain what lesson is to be drawn from the failure of this chore I undertook at NBC. It might well be that organizations of 6,000 people cannot be infused with a spirit, a sense of community, a sense of pride, or even an understanding of what, beyond ratings and profits, the business is all about—at least not by carefully crafted words printed on expensive paper. An organization takes its character from its history, from what, in fact, it does and how it does it. That depends on the tone which its chief officers set—and they set that tone by what they do, not what somebody else writes down for them.

Looking at NBC with perspective from the passage of years, it appears to me now that Grant Tinker proved I had the cart before the horse. I now believe that the pride, the cohesion, the striving for excellence, the tone which I was seeking by the use of words, Tinker realized by leadership and performance. My basic error, looking back on the exercise, was that I foolishly believed an organization could be turned around by words—that one could talk it into a new character. I was naive.

•   •   •

While senior management at CBS was patient up to a point, Fred Silverman had no patience whatever. Two Silverman traits—his personalizing and his impatience—gave me little time to deliver what Silverman expected me to deliver. And what he expected me to deliver, I quickly realized, was to restore NBC News to its former Huntley-Brinkley-Kintner days of glory—overnight.

I realized that Fred had agreed to hire me for what he regarded as my name in the news business. Jane and I were to serve as "the class" to Fred's street-fighter approach. Jane and I were the respectables; Fred was the activist. And once Silverman hired someone to solve a particular problem, that was that—the new person was Lochinvar, who rode out of the West (West 57th Street) and immediately solved NBC's News Division problems.

I was unable to deliver; NBC's problems were not solved while I was there. News divisions cannot be turned around overnight. What Fred failed to realize was that whatever success and reputation I had acquired at CBS were due to two factors absent at NBC. First, turning around a news organization is a long, slow process, as I learned the hard way at CBS News. (Remember, it was not until 1968, seven years after I first became president of CBS News, that the *CBS Evening News* regained its number one ratings.) And second, CBS was a tremendously strong organization, with pride, tradition, and cohesion. CBS News was strong enough to make me look good.

Fairly quickly, NBC came to the realization that I was not of great use to it, and I came to the realization that NBC was not a place where I could find a way to be particularly comfortable or useful. There was the necessary business of getting NBC into the zone of reasonable profits and out of what the press usually referred to as its "dismal third" in the ratings. That had to be Fred Silverman's—and his colleagues'—first order of business, if only because RCA and its head, Ed Griffiths, were most insistent about it.

• • •

At the same time as my life at NBC became more complicated and uncomfortable, internal problems surfaced between Fred Silverman and Jane Pfeiffer. They were an odd couple with different standards, backgrounds, and ways of doing business with their associates. Fred was the ultimate hands-on programming pragmatist—volatile, impatient, blunt, with a short fuse. (When an elevator failed to arrive promptly, he shouted and kicked at the elevator door.) He was not diplomatic with his subordinates, whom he cowed rather than persuaded.

Jane was as gentle as Fred was explosive. An expert in managing people, Jane was an idealist with a vision of the quality and high standards she thought broadcasting could achieve. But she was unsophisticated in the ways of broadcasting and broadcast executives. Both Fred and Jane always professed complete mutual admiration and an entirely harmonious and close working relationship. I found it astonishing; but they put on a superb act, and I willingly suspended my disbelief.

However, neither Fred nor Jane ever won the support or loyalty of the NBC old guard, and by the summer of 1980, the harmony and the possibility for coherent, progressive change started to unravel. Ed Griffiths, who had brought Jane Pfeiffer into NBC originally, soured on Jane for a variety of reasons apparently related to positions she took as a member of the RCA board of directors. Jane's position was made even more tenuous by the pockets of hostility toward her within NBC itself. Many of the old-time holdovers resented her and what they regarded as her naïveté and her alleged lack of understanding of the broadcasting business.

Fred Silverman himself was under attack at the time: The miracle he had been expected to perform did not occur. The network's ratings remained dismal. Fred's position was not strong, and when Griffiths became disenchanted with Jane, Fred decided, at the least, not to fight it. Jane's contract was not renewed; a settlement was arranged, and I was left as a vice chairman with no chairman.

Once Jane left, Silverman transferred to me the divisions which had reported to her: press information, audience research, personnel and labor relations, and the Law Department. I knew very little about these divisions and, more important, except for law, I had little idea either of how they operated or the quality of their personnel. I did the only thing I could do: I left them alone while I tried to learn about them. I knew that most of these areas needed strengthening, both in developing new concepts and approaches and in personnel. But I had much to learn before I could make any major changes.

In any event, it became apparent before many months had passed that my functions in respect of these new areas of responsibility should be put on hold. Early in 1981, Thorton Bradshaw (from Atlantic Richfield) replaced Ed Griffiths as chairman and CEO of RCA.

During the interim period before Bradshaw officially became RCA's chairman, he invited me to have lunch with him. (This was Frank Stanton's suggestion. He was Bradshaw's friend and a member of the Atlantic Richfield board.) As I tried to describe for Bradshaw some of NBC's difficulties—its factionalism, its lack of vision and cohesion—I told him that I believed that his major function—the major function of any chief executive officer—was to define the goals, set the tone for the organization, and motivate, rather than drive, all his associates to do their best.

At the lunch, Bradshaw also sought my views about Silverman. I declined, telling him that I thought it was improper for me to evaluate the man for whom I worked. Bradshaw did not press me, but I came away from our meeting with the clear impression that he had already decided to replace Silverman. And I was right. As soon as Bradshaw took office at RCA, Fred resigned. Bradshaw persuaded Grant Tinker, who was then a highly regarded independent Hollywood producer of network entertainment programs and before that, an NBC executive, to take over as NBC's chairman and CEO.

It was a brilliant choice. The miracle worker Silverman had been looking for to fix NBC was the man who replaced him. Within two years—and after I left NBC—NBC rose from last to first in the ratings and was transformed from a money-losing to a profitable operation. Tinker did it by quiet management, by patience, by setting a tone, and aiming for (and, more than most, achieving) quality.

In July 1981, a month after Tinker took office at NBC, I was on vacation at Martha's Vineyard. Driving back to our house after a day's sail with Walter Cronkite, I heard on the radio that Tinker had appointed Bob Mulholland as NBC president and chief operating officer. (Tinker later told me that he had tried to reach me by phone to tell me of the Mulholland appointment; but because I was on Cronkite's boat, I was unreachable.) When I heard of Mulholland's promotion, I knew I was in trouble and that whatever my functions were at NBC they would now be still further restricted.

After I returned from the Vineyard in early August, *Variety*, the weekly show-business trade journal, reported that Irwin Segelstein, a former CBS executive who had come to NBC several years earlier, was to replace me as NBC vice chairman. I went in to see Tinker to find out whether the *Variety* report was accurate. It was.

Always quiet, straightforward, and a gentleman, Tinker seemed to be uncomfortable. Although he told me he thought that Mulholland and Segelstein would make a good combination as his chief associates, I suspected that it was Bob Mulholland's idea to promote Segelstein and that Tinker had reluctantly acceded. I pointed out that my contract still had a year to run—until April 1982. It provided that if my office and functions were changed during the life of the contract, the contract was automatically terminated at my option, with full pay until its expiration in a year.

Tinker said he needed my continued advice and asked me to stay on as a consultant. After some quiet and cordial discussion, during which both Bradshaw and Tinker assured me that they wanted my continued counsel and advice, I finally agreed to stay on as NBC senior adviser. My contract, otherwise without change, was extended for an additional year, to April 1983. All my responsibilities, both those I had originally and those which had been added after Silverman's departure, were transferred to Irwin Segelstein. News was transferred to Bob Mulholland.

• • •

A measure of how far away I had come from my original responsibility for NBC News, and a measure as well of the internal politics of NBC, became evident when Bill Small was fired without my knowing it, in 1982, after less than three years as president of NBC News. I learned of it one morning when I was in my office, talking with a visitor. Unannounced, Small walked in and insisted that I come out into the hall to talk to him. He told me that he had just been fired by Bob Mulholland. Had I known in advance, I would have opposed it.

True, Small was sometimes blunt and undiplomatic. True, he played his cards close to his vest, and he tended to consult superior officers only when he wanted something from the corporation. And true above all, he was a thorough professional who knew the craft to which he had devoted his life. Small demanded the same dedicated devotion to the craft of news as he gave to it.

In his few years at NBC, Bill made progress in rebuilding NBC News, but inevitably, when a tough-driving editor embarks on reinvigorating a sluggish and discordant news organization, he steps on toes and makes enemies. As a result, an anti-Small group formed within NBC News. It would have been unimportant and ineffective had it not gravitated around Bob Mulholland, who, because of his long experience within NBC News, regarded news as his special turf.

Many in NBC News had been Mulholland's former associates, and a number of those were people whom Small was bypassing. Mulholland, as a result, became a magnet for those who were anti-Small. The internal politics of the situation was further compounded by a group of people within NBC News as well as within NBC itself who resented what they regarded as a CBS invasion and an attempt to make NBC over into a CBS clone. This group felt that any changes which the ex-CBS people sought to make were a reflection on them and the way they had done things.

Bill Small was dismissed before he had a real chance. He later told me that Tinker had expressed regret to him that he had accepted Mulholland's advice to fire him. The virulence of the anti-Small resentment among the old guard of NBC News was reflected by the fact that Richard Valeriani, one of the senior correspondents in the NBC Washington Bureau whom Small did not especially admire either for industry or competence, gave a well-attended party celebrating Bill's being fired. I would have fired Valeriani on the spot for lack of professionalism.

• • •

In April 1983, my contract as an independent adviser to NBC expired. There was no discussion of its extension, and no desire to prolong the relationship on either side. During my last two years—when I was "senior adviser"—I had even less to do than during the first two years as vice chairman. Although Grant put me in charge of NBC's almost successful effort to expand its network evening news to an hour, that too finally failed.

I spent my final year at NBC gazing out my windows at Radio City Music Hall across the street. In the spring of 1983, with my contract about to expire, Tinker graciously asked me whether I would like a farewell party. I declined. He said that he expected that I would say no, and that he understood.

My career in broadcasting ended on April 30, 1983. During my four years at NBC, I was unable to accomplish any of the purposes which led me to accept Jane Pfeiffer's offer in the first place: to participate in the program decisionmaking process so that I could help determine how much time would be devoted to news—and when; to expand the network news to an hour; and to add prime-time documentaries and news specials to the NBC schedule. Although before I came to NBC, Jane Pfeiffer had enthusiastically assured me that each would happen, neither Jane nor Fred, for reasons beyond their control, could make any of these happen.

I wanted to go quietly, and I did, sure that nobody but the driver of my car, the receptionist on the sixth floor of 30 Rockefeller Plaza, and the clerk who made out my biweekly checks would notice that I was no longer with NBC. I was right: I discovered a couple of months after I had left that mail addressed to me at NBC had been returned to the sender stamped "Addressee Unknown."

30

National
News Council

*It [the National News Council] was a noble experiment. And I
have to believe that what is sound, what is good, and what is
right will ultimately prevail; just as I believe that the concept of
a news council must prevail. Not because a handful of outside
do-gooders impose the concept on the press, but because the
press itself will come to realize the vital importance of a news
council as a safeguard of, not a threat to, the press's freedom.*

—*University of California Commencement,*
Berkeley, May 5, 1984

IN 1983, AT THE END OF MY FOUR YEARS with NBC, still afraid
to retire, I moved over to be president and chief executive officer of
the National News Council. The council had been born in 1973; it
died March 31, 1984, just a year after I took over. Its burial service was
described by an unsympathetic friend of mine as a requiem for a light-
weight. But it was much more than that.

I was involved in the news council idea from the beginning, but at
first I was not in favor of it. In September 1969, my deputy, Bill Small,
suggested that some sort of outside press council be established, either
for CBS News alone or for all the networks. He thought the council
could be made up of distinguished journalists to consider public complaints of unfairness or inaccuracy.

I replied negatively to him by memo on September 26, 1969:

As for your press council concept, my hang-up is simply that as soon as
we or anybody else establishes a single body for oversight, no matter how

private the auspices, there is the brooding danger that its judgments will one way or another become government judgments. And as long as we are licensed, that is an exceedingly mischievous thing. This is precisely what happened with the NAB [National Association of Broadcasters] code, which, in effect, the FCC has adopted and [it] has applied licensing sanctions to help enforcement of the code. The moment we can find some way to disentangle news from licensing, I believe I would vote enthusiastically to support some kind of press council.

A year later, the Twentieth Century Fund established a task force to consider whether there ought to be a National News Council. I was a member of that task force which, in 1971, unanimously recommended in favor of it. The chairman of the FCC at the time had informally assured us that the FCC would not take into account any council findings adverse to a broadcaster.

The council came into being with the Twentieth Century Fund task force stating the case for a council this way:

Disaffection with existing institutions, prevalent in every sector of society, has spread to the media of public information—newspapers and magazines, radio and television. Their accuracy, fairness, and responsibility have come under challenge. The media have found their credibility questioned, their freedom threatened, by public officials whose own credibility depends on the very media they attack and by citizens whose own freedom depends on the very institutions they threaten.

Such a statement could have been written with even greater applicability today. I was enthusiastic about the concept of the council. And CBS News was one of the few news organizations, and the only network, actively to support the council and to commit itself to noting in its broadcasts any council conclusions adverse to CBS News.

Initially, the News Council was "to receive, to examine, and to report on complaints concerning the accuracy and fairness of news reporting in the United States, as well as to initiate studies and report on issues involving the freedom of the press." After it came into being, the council added a third important function: to study recurring issues of journalistic policies, practices, and ethics. Finally, the News Council provided a safety valve for public resentment and an unresponsive press by investigating complaints, thereby stimulating the press into thinking through its problems and then choosing its own solutions.

The council was entirely private. It had no sanctions other than the persuasiveness of its own decisions and reports. And in contrast to press councils in all other nations, it had to stand or fall on its own. It was not a government agency. There could be no mailed fist of government intervention if the velvet glove of self-regulation by a council failed. Clearly, that is because our unique First Amendment precludes the unacceptable "or else" of government regulation.

I believed that the council had but a single, vital purpose—to preserve press freedom. All its activities were intended to contribute to that end. We recognized that by its free-press guaranty, the Constitution had singled out the press as the only component of our free competitive enterprise system that was assured government would stay off its back—with no strings attached.

To my great personal disappointment, the News Council didn't work out—at least this time around. There was very little support for the council, with notable exceptions like the Louisville papers, Gannett, as well as CBS News. Too much of the press was indifferent at best, hostile, at worst. The president of the American Society of Newspaper Editors said that the council was a bunch of busybodies with nothing better to do. Rupert Murdoch, from his tower across the Atlantic, and the *New York Times*'s Punch Sulzberger and Abe Rosenthal,[1] from theirs, all agreed that news councils were an abomination which threatened their independence and freedom. At least news councils can claim credit for making some strange bedfellows.

I don't contend that all of this hostility was not genuinely felt. The first and most vital line of defense for the press must be each news organization itself. I don't believe there should be a monolithic prescription of what's good and what's bad, what's right and what's wrong. I contend only that the council could help protect and improve the press—along with self-criticism, and a more systematic examination of the press by professional journalists, in reviews and in columns and in news articles specializing on the important news beat.

The council did *not* want to be a single voice. It *did* want to be a voice which would be heeded and pondered by the press—not to scold, not to prescribe inflexible rules, not to punish; but to contribute to that linchpin of democracy: freedom of the press.

I made one last effort to reorganize the council and to persuade major news organizations to support the council by reporting its deci-

---

[1]A. O. Sulzberger, in a memorandum to the news and editing staffs of the *Times* and the News Service, wrote, "We have decided not to participate in the work of the Council. This means that we will not be a party to Council investigations. We will not furnish information or explanations to the Council. In our coverage, we will treat the Council as we treat any other organization: we will report their activities when they are newsworthy." (From Patrick Brogan, *Spiked: The Short Life and Death of the National News Council*. A Twentieth Century Fund Paper [New York: Priority Press Publications, 1985], p. 117).

sions. Newspaper editors and network executives listened politely, briefly, but rejected my pleas. We could stand, indeed we welcomed, criticism. We could not stand, we could not survive, being crumpled and tossed into the wastebasket, unread, along with all the public relations handouts. The general press blackout of the council's decisions and the lack of press support resulted in the public's ignorance of its existence. This forced me to conclude the council was serving no useful purposes.

And so the council folded. At the final meeting of the News Council, March 22, 1984, when we were debating the painful step of shutting up shop, one of the council members urged that we hang on a few years longer. It was her experience that the new generation of journalists wanted a council and felt it was useful to them. One of the more ancient and bruised council members—me—replied that once these young and friendly reporters grew older and became editors and publishers, they would sing a different tune and join in the choirs of the current nay-saying decisionmakers of the press. Perhaps that other member of the council was right, and I was wrong, and someday a new news council will serve the press and its vital freedom, and hence, society. I hope that a less self-satisfied, or more concerned, or more far-seeing, more conscientious, and wiser press will someday see the value of a news council—and bring it back into being.

With the end of the National News Council in April 1984, at the age of seventy, at last I retired. In hindsight, looking at the frustrations and failures I faced after I left CBS News, I retired five years too late. I had interesting experiences and I learned new things, but there were too few satisfactions, too few contributions from me, to mark the extra five years.

What it comes down to is that by April 1984, it had become clear to me that I should have retired earlier. It's more satisfying to quit while you are ahead. There are, it turns out, two tricks to career paths: The first is to find one; the second is to know when to get off because you have come to the end.

Editors' Epilogue

RICHARD SALANT FINALLY RETIRED in April 1984. Although it was "five years too late" in his view, that did not stop him from continuing to be an advocate for better broadcast journalism. In the last eight years of his life, in addition to writing his memoirs, he spoke out frequently as a knowledgeable media critic, giving dozens of speeches about the public service responsibilities of broadcasters.

"He lived on speeches," Frances Salant remembered, and copies of his remarks from this period stack nearly a foot high. Among them were topics such as:

- "Ethics and Broadcasting: Profits Versus Social Responsibility," for the Center of Communications in 1987
- "Television Network News: Its Future, If Any," for the Benton Lecture at the University of Chicago in 1988
- "Network News—Getting Better? Getting Worse?" at Columbia University in 1990

Salant's themes included a litany of what was wrong with the broadcast news business. He decried the disappearance of serious issue documentaries and prime-time instant news specials, which he believed had been replaced by entertainment and trivia. He disliked the times when network television acted like British tabloids in broadcasting unsubstantiated reports about the alleged affairs of Presidents Bush and Clinton. It was his oft-repeated admonition that "the network evening news shouldn't compete with the reading material at the [supermarket] checkout counter."

He was harshly critical of corporate owners who saw broadcasting as a mere business, usually a very profitable one, but not one with the social responsibility he believed was fundamental. He said in one speech that in all his years at CBS, public service journalism was something CBS believed it owed "to the public and to its own conscience."

As an example, he cited his experience with the *CBS Morning News*:

> All through my tenure we struggled with the *CBS Morning News*—whose ratings were so bad that Nielsen didn't even register them, and our only advertiser was something called Silly Putty, whose address was [the] local post office. Paley and Stanton kept on telling me that they didn't care what the ratings were—just keep [the morning broadcast] serious, professional hard news, no matter what *Today* or *Good Morning America* did.

• • •

Salant gave his last speech on February 16, 1993.[1] He spoke that day before the Senior Men's Club of Fairfield, Connecticut. About thirty-five club members gathered at noon on this particular Tuesday at the Fairfield Country Club to chat with friends over lunch and listen to their neighbor, the former network news executive.

Salant's overall theme, one that continued to concern him, was the blurring of the line between news and entertainment. Salant took the three major broadcast networks to task for their recent reenactments of the then celebrated case of Amy Fisher, the teenager who shot the wife of her lover, a car mechanic. "The docudrama device totally confuses fact with fiction. I don't like them; they are heavy on the drama and light on docu; you can't tell where fact ends and fiction begins, especially where real names are used."

All of the networks, Salant said, along with the tabloid TV shows, the syndicated talk shows, and local news broadcasts, are committing the same cardinal sin. These shows "were not on the air for their news value or genuine dramatic values but for ratings. . . . And the ratings showed this pandering and exploitation to be enormously successful. I don't want to think about what this says about the broadcasters and the viewers."

However popular and profitable such programs were, Salant said, he couldn't help worrying about the effect of mixing news and entertainment on the credibility of television news. He wondered, at the end of his remarks, if television viewers were beginning to be confused between real news and dramatizations. He was concerned, for example, that the jury which heard the case against members of the Los Angeles police force had rendered a not-guilty verdict because they somehow discounted the reality of the videotape showing the brutal beating of Rodney King.

---

[1]CBS distributed a transcript of Salant's remarks in a pamphlet called "The Last Word."

And so in my darkest moments, I have sadly asked myself: Could it be that the Rodney King verdict was a warning about television news's credibility? I don't know. I do know that it is a serious enough question that the people responsible for television news—the people all the way up to the top—ought to stop and think and set a tone and set standards that insist on their news divisions' and their entertainment divisions' drawing clear lines between entertainment and news, between reality and dramatization, between fact and fiction, between genuine news judgments and corporate self-aggrandizement.

After his formal remarks, Salant began to take questions from club members. Cameron Clark, club program chairman and the man who had introduced him, asked Salant one of the first questions. They were facing each other, Clark said later. "Our eyes were locked." Then, Clark said, "the glitter in his eyes just went blank, and he dropped to the floor." An ambulance rushed Salant to the Clark City Hospital but he died almost instantly from heart failure.

• • •

Salant's immediate family and his extended CBS family gathered the following Monday morning, February 22, 1993, for a memorial service in an auditorium of the Museum of Television and Radio in New York City.

A pianist playing a ragtime tune greeted guests. "You didn't expect a string trio for Dick Salant, did you?" was the way Frances Salant opened the assembly. She noted that her husband had never wanted a memorial service. "He told me that many times, then one day he added, 'because no one would come.' Thank you for coming." They were there to mourn the sudden loss of a gutsy news executive, friend, and leader of broadcast journalism. But a sense of nostalgia was also present for a lost era, a Golden Age at CBS News which many felt was ebbing away, along with the men who had created and sustained it.

Mike Wallace served as master of ceremonies. "I'm afraid that these memorial meetings are starting to come too close together. First there was Charlie Collingwood back in 1985, then Doug [Edwards], and Bud [Burton Benjamin] four years ago. Then Harry [Reasoner] in 1991, Eric [Sevareid] last year, and now our friend Dick. Our class has begun to dwindle."

The service was full of remembrances celebrating Salant's life. Amid the stories and tributes, there were a few chuckles, for example, when Wallace described Salant as a "tightwad" when it came to salaries at a time when CBS had plenty of money.

The one common memory everyone shared, Wallace said, was "that this New Deal lawyer–turned–company counsel–turned–journalist, though he always resisted calling himself that, was a man of real courage, a man of uncommon integrity, a man of deep loyalty to those of us who knew him down the years."

Dan Rather said Salant believed in ethics and integrity and led others into believing in them:

> This included being a frontline fighter for the First Amendment. It included fighting for the right to engage in fiercely independent news coverage, independent from entertainment values, independent from the corporation, independent from government. It also included being a leader in opening up opportunities for women and minorities in journalism at a time when it cost Dick something to do that.

Bill Leonard, who had been Salant's deputy and his successor as CBS News president, remembered, "The happiest times of my working life were the years that I spent hand in hand with Gordon Manning trying to help Dick Salant run CBS News."

Leonard said Salant believed the job of keeping the nation informed as fully, as fairly, and as honestly as possible was an important calling and that CBS News is what made CBS a great company:

> The strength of that belief gave him the courage to stand firm against considerable buffeting, considerable buffeting from within that company, sometimes even including its chairman [William Paley]. It gave him the strength to stand up against the attacks of the American establishment, including, as you know, two presidents [Nixon and Johnson]. And so, the little man who started out not as one of us came to stand for the best in all of us.
>
> Now he's gone. It's my fervent hope that the future of broadcast news will see a man of comparable strengths and vision and courage to do as much for some future news organization, but I doubt it. Life holds only one Dick Salant, and CBS news was blessed to have had him as its leader.

Frank Stanton said, "In the early days of CBS it was Ed Klauber [from the *New York Times*], more than any other man, who gave standards of integrity and responsibility to American radio news. But when the definitive history of television at CBS is written, it will be Dick Salant who gave CBS News its code of behavior and made it work for the benefit of the American people."

For Walter Cronkite, Salant "had a clearer picture of what we were about in [television broadcast] journalism . . . than any of the rest of us or perhaps all of us combined." It was incredible, Cronkite said. "He understood our role in democracy. He understood that we could only serve that role if we had unalloyed freedom of government and management interference."

Andy Rooney was succinct in his praise. "We all knew Dick was determined that CBS News would give people what they ought to know and not what they wanted to hear, but we may have forgotten that he did not try to make CBS News popular and, with this philosophy, made it the most popular."

Reminding people how well Salant wrote, Rooney cited a number of Salant's speeches he had at home. "I often look at them, and there are phrases in them that ring in my ears. 'Journalism,' he said in one of them, 'is a business enterprise, but it is also a moral enterprise.' That could be his epitaph."

Speaking last, Salant's stepson Peter Goldmark Jr.[2] gave one of the most eloquent eulogies among many in that articulate assembly. Goldmark explained why he thought Dick Salant was a great man:

> The fragile balance on which our democracy rests depends like no other in the world on the interplay of press and government. And in that fragile balance at moments of uncertainty or peril, in the crossfire of conflicting imperatives of powerful interests, [there are] a few closely drawn issues, a few agonizing decisions about where to draw the line and what the line means—these things tell enormously in the history of the country. At the intersection of those two forces—the free press and public power—this man lived his professional life. At this high-intensity, pressure-filled intersection which has destroyed others of less mettle, Dick made countless decisions, appointments, and choices in a career of deep involvement with the news which spanned four decades. At that intersection from which so many have returned defeated or compromised, he more than once staked his honor and more than most prevailed in the fight for what he believed.
>
> He believed the news should be free—free of restraint, not responsibility. He fought for a news that was fair—not popular, but fair. And he stood for a news that was fearless—not to be intimidated, not to be compromised, but to be respected and trusted beyond doubt. That was his passion. He engaged that passion and exercised his skills, as you have heard today, very, very well. To have applied those talents well and with honor at that intersection in American history is to be a great man.

[2]At the time, Goldmark was head of the Rockefeller Foundation. He is now publisher of the *International Herald Tribune* in Paris.

Chronology

April 14, 1914	Born, New York City; only son of Louis and Florence Salant
1931	Graduated, Phillips Exeter Academy, NH, cum laude. Editor, the *Exonian* and *Paean*
1935	Graduated, Harvard College, English, magna cum laude
1938	Graduated, Harvard Law School, cum laude. Board of Editors, *Harvard Law Review*
1938–1941	Attorney, National Labor Relations Board, Washington, DC
June 14, 1941	Married Rosalind Robb; four children
1941–1943	Attorney, Solicitor General's Office, Justice Department
1943–1946	Active duty, U.S. Naval Reserve, ensign; lieutenant commander
1946–1952	Associate/partner, Rosenman Goldmark Colin and Kaye, New York City, CBS was a client; began work with Frank Stanton; represented CBS in RCA-NBC color TV battle
1952–1961	Joined CBS, Inc., vice president, corporate officer; assistant to Stanton; left the law ("best move I ever made")
August 1955	Divorced
December 31, 1955	Married Frances Trainer; one child
1961	President, CBS News, first time; CBS Board of Directors; $20-million budget; 469-member news staff
1962	Walter Cronkite replaces Douglas Edwards as anchor
1963	*CBS Evening News* expanded to thirty minutes
1964	Fred Friendly takes over as president of CBS News; Salant returns as assistant to Stanton

1966	Friendly resigns; Salant reappointed CBS News president
1967	The CBS News with Walter Cronkite finally passes Huntley-Brinkley ratings
1968	60 Minutes begins with Producer Don Hewitt
1971	"The Selling of the Pentagon" airs; CBS under attack
1973	Frank Stanton forced to retire by mandatory retirement
1976	60 Minutes becomes big hit at 7:00 P.M. EST Sundays
April 30, 1979	Salant forced to retire from CBS at age sixty-five; replaced by his deputy, Bill Leonard; CBS News budget is $90 million, 1,000 staff
1979	Salant receives numerous awards for sixteen years of leadership at CBS News, including the George Foster Peabody Award, George Polk Award, DuPont–Columbia University Silver Baton, Society of Professional Journalists Award, Radio and Television News Directors Award, and International Radio and Television Society Gold Medal
May 1, 1979	Salant joins NBC as vice chairman; brings Bill Small from CBS to run NBC News
March 1981	Dan Rather replaces Cronkite as Evening News anchor
November 1981	Gordon Van Sauter becomes president of CBS News, replacing Bill Leonard; Sauter revolution seeks more "emotional moments," less hard news analysis; old guard criticized as "yesterday" people
1983	Salant leaves NBC, becomes president of the National News Council
1984	Because of lack of press support, National News Council is terminated; Salant retires, begins to write his memoirs
1985	Lawrence Tisch begins to buy CBS stock, joins the CBS board, and gains control of CBS in 1986
1987	CBS News budget is $300 million. Tisch makes cuts reducing the budget by $30 million and

the staff by 100. Altogether, between 1985 and 1987, CBS cuts a total of 359 news staff members

February 16, 1993   Salant dies of heart failure, speaking to the Fairfield, Connecticut, Senior Men's Club

Index